RETHINKING
SCHOOL
FINANCE

Allan R. Odden
Editor

RETHINKING SCHOOL FINANCE

AN AGENDA FOR THE 1990s

Jossey-Bass Publishers · San Francisco

For sales outside the United States, contact Maxwell Macmillan International Publishing Group, 866 Third Avenue, New York, New York 10022.

Manufactured in the United States of America.

 The paper used in this book is acid-free and meets the State of California requirements for recycled paper (50 percent recycled waste, including 10 percent postconsumer waste), which are the strictest guidelines for recycled paper currently in use in the United States.

Library of Congress Cataloging in Publication Data

Rethinking school finance : an agenda for the 1990s / Allan R. Odden, editor.
    p. cm. — (The Jossey-Bass education series)
    Includes bibliographical references and index.
    ISBN 1-55542-451-1
    1. Education — United States — Finance. 2. Education and state —
United States. I. Odden, Allan. II. Series.
LB2825.R445 1992
379.1'22'0973 — dc20   92-11512
                                     CIP

FIRST EDITION
HB Printing   10 9 8 7 6 5 4 3 2 1   *Code 9254*

The Jossey-Bass
Education
Series

Contents

Preface

In the late 1980s, state supreme courts overturned school finance structures in Kentucky, New Jersey, and Texas. Additionally, there were active or planned cases disputing education finance in nearly half the states. At the dawn of the 1990s, school finance reform was once again high on state education policy agendas. Almost simultaneously, a set of ambitious education goals was adopted by President Bush and the fifty state governors. Because of the breadth and depth of the education reforms needed to accomplish these goals, school finance reforms in the 1990s are likely to be quite different from those of the 1970s and 1980s. The purpose of this book is to lay the groundwork for rethinking school finance in the context of these new directions in education policy.

A consensus on the education reform strategies that will accomplish the nation's bold education goals seems to have emerged:

- Set clear student learning outcome goals.
- Determine high-quality curriculum standards.
- Create an assessment or monitoring system calibrated to world-class criteria that indicates the degree to which outcome objectives are being accomplished.
- Manage implementation at the site, allowing teachers to have major influence and power over implementation.
- Have a sharp-edged accountability system with real rewards and real sanctions.
- Provide school choice, at least within the public sector.

These proposed reforms give rise to several school finance issues:

- Linkage between the basic school finance structure, education goals, and the costs of effective schoolwide strategies
- Site-based budgeting
- Teacher compensation
- Accountability systems that include school-based performance incentives
- Funding of school choice

Further, since the ambitious education goals set by the president and the governors are meant to apply to all students in each state, the issue of state disparities in fiscal capacity, education spending, and student achievement emerges. Finally, the topic of school-linked noneducation services has gained increasing attention because the nature of the student body is changing; there are increasing numbers of poor, limited-English-proficient, immigrant children — many from broken families — who need extra family and social services supports.

Together, these issues represent a school finance agenda dramatically different from the traditional concern with fiscal disparities across school districts within states. The purpose of this book is to begin the analytical discussion of the finance issues embedded in these new topics.

Intended Audience

This book should be useful to policy makers and their staffs, scholars of school finance, and local education leaders. Most chapters not only discuss the various finance dimensions of these new issues but also describe programs that various states and local districts have adopted to address them. Each chapter presents new information and analysis in language understandable by the informed policy maker and practitioner and useful to the policy researcher. In addition, most chapters end with suggestions for policy action on the topic. Thus, the information provided can be used by policy makers to design and enact new policies, by education leaders to tailor local responses, and by analysts to raise new questions and probe uncharted dimensions of public school finance.

Organization of the Book

In Chapter One, Allan R. Odden provides an overview of the new issues addressed by subsequent chapters in the book. This chapter also locates school finance of the 1990s in the context of the evolving education reform agenda.

In Chapter Two, Allan R. Odden and Sharon Conley address the issue of whether teacher pay can be linked to education productivity, a long-sought but never attained goal. Drawing on research in the private sector, where a revolution in work organization and compensation has been occurring, they propose an entire new structure for teacher compensation, from recruitment through fringe benefits. The heart of their argument is that teacher compensation should shift from paying on the basis of indirect indicators of expertise—education and experience—to paying on direct measures of knowledge and skills. Knowledge- and skills-based pay is increasingly being used in emerging high-involvement managed organizations, all of which have characteristics similar to schools. The notion of basing pay on knowledge and skills is buttressed by proposals to make beginning teacher licensure dependent on demonstrating competence in both content (knowledge) and pedagogical expertise (skills). Experienced teachers would be board certified by demonstrating advanced competence in the same areas. Thus, paying teachers for knowledge and skills (rather than education and expertise) would make these factors the basis for licensure, compensation, and advanced recognition.

If ambitious education goals are to be attained by all students, schoolwide programs that work need to be implemented at all education levels. The logical questions are, what types of school programs are needed and what do they cost? David D. Marsh and Jennifer M. Sevilla address this issue in Chapter Three by costing out both developmental and operating costs for the restructured middle schools proposed by the

Carnegie Task Force in its 1989 report, *Turning Points*. Interestingly, Marsh and Sevilla find that such dramatically new middle schools do not cost that much more to operate if current funds are reallocated but do require a onetime developmental cost of an extra 25 percent.

Taking school-based reform seriously, several states and big-city school districts have initiated a variety of school-based management policies. Priscilla Wohlstetter and Thomas Marshall Buffett summarize and assess these approaches in Chapter Four. They find that school-based management of the 1990s has made significant progress in decentralizing budget and personnel authority to individual schools. They also observe that while the rationale for school-based management is improved student performance, the accountability strategies for linking these new management approaches with outcomes are quite weak. They cite differences in state and local versions of decentralized management and report that school leaders have difficulties responding to conflicting signals. Wohlstetter and Buffett conclude with a set of policy design suggestions to improve school-based management programs.

A variety of incentives were enacted by state education policy makers in the 1980s and the early 1990s. In Chapter Five, Lawrence O. Picus reminds us that intergovernmental aid theory can be used to analyze how various incentives can be created and what their likely effects will be on school district spending patterns. Further, Picus shows how incentives can be built into the general school aid formula rather than designed and operated as a stand-alone categorical program. Picus reviews several state approaches to incentive funding and discusses the pros and cons of each. He also argues that, when properly designed, incentives can have more powerful effects on local behavior than mandates. He ends his chapter with a set of design questions each state must address in creating school-based incentives.

Policy makers, analysts, and education leaders want indicators of education system outcomes, as well as other indicators that can be used to suggest why outcomes are improving or declining. In Chapter Six, James W. Guthrie begins a conversation on school finance indicators and questions whether a global indicator, such as the Dow Jones Index, can be developed for state school finance systems. He proposes that the concepts of liberty, equality, and efficiency can be used to construct such a global indicator, provides examples of how such an indicator would work for a state, and discusses what types of data would be needed to create it. The idea of a global school finance indicator is both intriguing and controversial. This chapter concludes with arguments for and against developing and using such an indicator.

The question of school choice is rapidly entering the education policy arena. A decade ago, choice—in the form of vouchers—was a dead issue. In the mid 1980s, however, the notion of choice (restricted to public schools) began to gain increasing policy support, and by the close of the decade over a dozen states had enacted versions of public school choice. Allan R. Odden and Nancy Kotowski in Chapter Seven review the key dimensions of these programs, particularly their finance features, and discuss the finance issues related to designing state public school choice programs. They conclude that the easiest way to produce the appropriate revenue flows is simply to count the student in the district attended for the purposes of both general and categorical aid calculations. Such an approach, simple to incorporate into state policy, is quite different from what many states have done. Odden and Kotowski also propose a new form of supplemental fundraising that is school-based and linked to state (or national) income tax structures, similar to district-based guaranteed tax base systems.

Since the student performance objectives embodied in the nation's ambitious education goals apply to all students in the United States, Allan R. Odden and Lori Kim in Chapter Eight assess and analyze disparities across the states in fiscal capacity, tax effort, education need, education spending, and student achievement. They document substantial disparities and show that spending-per-pupil differences are almost totally explained by variations in fiscal capacity, tax effort, education need, and price differences. They also show that differences in student achievement between the top- and bottom-scoring states are linked to variations in curriculum, teacher expertise, and education spending. Odden and Kim argue that a federal role is necessary to ameliorate these differences and provide a variety of options for an ambitious new federal role in education financing.

One of the most promising developments in education policy is the realization that education can be considered under the broader umbrella of children policy. The primary rationale for such an approach is that an increasing number of children need a variety of health, family, psychological, and social service supports in order to come to school ready to learn every day. Because the social service delivery system is so fragmented and uncoordinated, the notion of "one-stop shopping" is gaining prominence. Under one-stop shopping, a variety of social services would be made available at single locations at or near schools. In Chapter Nine, Michael W. Kirst discusses how such a new approach to providing social services could be financed. He shows how the bulk of the funding for school-linked services is provided by the federal government and suggests how the revenue streams of the current disjointed service delivery system could be diverted to these one-stop shopping locations. This approach would substantially increase the level of social services provided while not further eroding education budgets.

Finally, in Chapter Ten, Allan R. Odden argues why many of the above issues and the strong school-based aspect of the 1990s reform agenda could support a shift from a district- to a school-based funding structure over the course of this decade. Such a shift accommodates devolving budget authority under school-based budgeting, aligns with most incentive structures (which are school, rather than district or individual, based), is consistent with public school choice programs, could be addressed by both state and federal school finance policy, and also fits with school-linked social services. While such a dramatic shift may seem politically impossible, Great Britain has adopted such a program. Great Britain allocates 85 percent of all education general aid and categorical program funds directly to each school, which has sole authority over how to spend them (subject only to a total spending constraint). A full shift to a school-based funding structure in the United States might not occur in all states for all programs over the 1990s, but the intensity of the school-based component of the overall reform strategy combined with school-based budgeting and school-based incentive funding might produce a finance structure by the close of the decade that has substantially more school-based financial mechanisms than presently exist.

The exciting and encouraging conclusion of these chapters is that school finance is unlikely to remain focused on the interdistrict fiscal disparities with which it has dealt for the past seventy-five years. States are designing a wide variety of new school finance mechanisms, and the pace of innovation is likely to increase. *Rethinking School Finance* hopes to help the rethinking of school finance in the 1990s. As other analysts turn their attention to these issues and new ideas are used to craft novel school finance mechanisms that support education reform, the linkages between school finance and education programs will be strengthened, resulting in improved student achievement and increased education productivity—the goals of current policy interest in education.

Los Angeles, California   Allan R. Odden
June 1992

To James A. Kelly,
friend and colleague,
who introduced me to school finance
and taught me to search for the new issues
while also attending to the traditional

The Authors

Allan R. Odden is professor of education at the University of Southern California, director of the University of Southern California Center for Research in Education Finance, co-director of the Finance Center of the Consortium for Policy Research in Education (CPRE), and a co-director of Policy Analysis for California Education (PACE).

Thomas Marshall Buffett recently received his M.A. degree in public policy from the School of Public Administration at the University of Southern California.

Sharon Conley is associate professor of educational administration in the College of Education at the University of Arizona.

James W. Guthrie is professor of education at the University of California, Berkeley, a former president of the Berkeley School Board, and a co-director of Policy Analysis for California Education (PACE).

Lori Kim is a graduate student in the policy and organization doctoral program in the School of Education at the University of Southern California.

Michael W. Kirst is professor of education at Stanford University, a research fellow with the Consortium for Policy Research in

Education (CPRE), and a co-director of Policy Analysis for California Education (PACE).

Nancy Kotowski is a graduate student in the policy and organization doctoral program in the School of Education at the University of Southern California.

David D. Marsh is professor of education at the University of Southern California and the southern California coordinator of the Coalition of Essential Schools.

Lawrence O. Picus is assistant professor of education at the University of Southern California, associate director of the University of Southern California Center for Research in Education Finance, and a research fellow at the Finance Center of the Consortium for Policy Research in Education (CPRE).

Jennifer M. Sevilla is a graduate student in the policy and organization doctoral program in the School of Education at the University of Southern California.

Priscilla Wohlstetter is assistant professor of educational politics and policy at the University of Southern California and a research fellow at the Finance Center of the Consortium for Policy Research in Education (CPRE).

RETHINKING SCHOOL FINANCE

1

School Finance and Education Reform: An Overview

Allan R. Odden

After taking a back seat to education program reform during the 1980s, school finance has returned as a critical issue. Increased state funding during the 1980s, ambitious national education goals, and a barrage of new court cases overturning state school finance structures have prominently placed education finance on state and federal education policy agendas. This chapter discusses the changing contours of school finance through the 1970s and 1980s and outlines the key school finance issues for the 1990s. Specifically, the chapter links new directions in school finance with new directions in education policy reform (Smith & O'Day, 1991; Business Roundtable, 1991). Subsequent chapters discuss in more depth several issues raised in this overview.

This chapter is divided into three sections. The first reviews school finance issues during the 1970s and 1980s. The next discusses public school funding increases in the decades from 1950 to 1990. Based on historical funding patterns since 1950, this section argues that funding likely will increase substantially during the 1990s. The policy issue may be how to use additional money productively rather than how to obtain additional money.

The last section addresses seven key areas likely to dominate school finance policy in the 1990s. The first area is the linkage between the basic school finance structure and state (or national) education goals. The issue is how the school finance system needs to be reconceptualized in order for state school systems to accomplish the nation's student performance goals (White House, 1990). The second area is the issue of teacher compensation and whether strategies can be crafted that pay teachers for knowledge, skills, and productivity and also support school collegiality and cooperation. The third key area is site-based management and site-based budgeting. With goals being set at the top of the system, implementation is increasingly delegated directly to school sites. The fourth topic reviewed is a stronger accountability system, which includes both site-based awards (such as annual monetary bonuses or regulation waivers for schools meeting student performance goals) and site-based sanctions (such as takeover or dismissal for schools consistently not meeting goals). The fifth issue is school choice, particularly the financing of public school choice and the funding of "charter schools," schools that receive public funds and are accountable to the public, but that are not run by local school districts. The sixth topic is a series of complementary state education policy and finance roles, including state-supported staff development, site-based education improvement grants, and controlled restructuring experiments. Finally, the seventh area encompasses several noneducation and nontraditional education issues such as preschool, extended-day kinderarten, and integrated noneducation children's services.

School Finance in the 1970s and 1980s

School finance inequities derive from the way states finance public elementary and secondary schools. In most states, local property tax dollars are a major source of school revenues. Indeed, early in the twentieth century, property taxes provided nearly all school revenues, with states providing only small amounts and the federal government providing barely any revenues.

Nationally, local revenues still constitute about 44 percent of education revenues; states provide about 50 percent and the federal government 6 percent. Heavy reliance on local property taxes produces fiscal inequities because the property tax base is not distributed equally across school districts. As a result, some districts have a large property tax base per pupil, while others have a small base. At a given tax rate, therefore, districts high in property wealth raise more money per pupil than districts low in property wealth. In many states, wealthy districts can raise ten times more in local revenues than can districts low in property wealth.

While a variety of school finance programs can eliminate these local revenue-raising inequities (Odden & Picus, 1992), typical state programs reduce inequities but do not eliminate them. As a result, revenues (from local and state sources) per pupil vary considerably in most states, with a high correlation between per-pupil revenues and the local per-pupil property tax base. High-revenue–per-pupil districts usually are rich in property wealth per pupil and levy below-average tax rates, while low-revenue–per-pupil districts usually are poor in property wealth per pupil and levy above-average tax rates.

School Finance During the 1970s

These fiscal disparities were the subject of several court cases in the 1970s, beginning with *Serrano* v. *Priest* in California. Using both the equal protection clause of the 14th Amendment to the U.S. Constitution and state constitution education clauses, cases filed in several states argued that it was unconstitutional for local property wealth to be linked with revenues per pupil. These suits proposed district revenues per pupil as a measure of quality of education. While the 1973 U.S. Supreme Court decision in *Rodriguez* v. *San Antonio Independent School District* held that these fiscal disparities did not violate the 14th Amendment to the federal constitution, cases continued in state courts on the basis of both state equal protection and state education clauses. In about a third of the cases between 1971 and 1985, state courts overturned school finance structures; in the other cases, state courts found that school finance systems with similar fiscal disparities did not violate constitutional requirements (Odden & Picus, 1992).

A direct result of a court mandate or the threat of such a mandate led over thirty-five state legislatures to enact fundamental changes in their school finance structures between 1971 and 1985 (Odden, McGuire, & Belsches-Simmons, 1983). These reforms had five major characteristics. First, they revamped the school finance equalization formula, sending more state funds to property-poor, lower-spending districts. Second, they increased the overall state role in funding schools. Third, they increased state funding for special needs student programs — compensatory, special, and bilingual education programs. Fourth, the reforms often increased aid for the extraordinary needs of large urban districts. Fifth, many reforms were accompanied by education tax and spending limitations that restricted local fiscal control over tax rates and curbed annual increases in expenditures per pupil.

While riveting attention on the fiscal inequities that derived from unequal property tax bases, school finance court cases and subsequent school finance policy reforms left a major policy issue unresolved. Was the policy issue variation in the tax base, that is, variation in ability to raise revenues, or differences in spending per pupil? Each implies a different solution.

The remedy for resolving variation in the local tax base is to enact a guaranteed tax base (GTB) program (or district power equalizing program) in which all districts are guaranteed a minimum tax base by the state (Odden & Picus, 1992, chap. 7). Then school tax rates would produce equal revenues per pupil from state and local sources for districts with per-pupil property wealth below or equal to the state guaranteed level. All districts, rich and poor, would raise substantially the same amount of money per pupil if they levied the same tax rate. GTB programs let local districts decide how high a tax rate to levy. Different tax rates produce different expenditures per pupil. Thus, GTB programs allow for spending differences, but differences are related to tax effort, not local property wealth.

If the school finance problem is defined as differences in spending per pupil for whatever reason — differences in tax bases or differences in local preference for education—the remedy is a school finance system that mandates equal spending across all school districts (albeit with appropriate adjustments for different pupil needs and different education prices). California, Florida, Hawaii, and Washington have systems that restrict local spending above a common base per-pupil funding level.

Lack of clarity over the nature of the problem has plagued school finance policy for decades. State policy makers need to decide if their definition of the school finance problem is unequal ability to raise local revenue or unequal expenditures per pupil. The former requires a school finance program that provides equal access to revenues while allowing for differences in local per-pupil spending; the latter requires a program to mandate equal spending.

The strongest school finance trend during the 1970s was the change in sources of school revenues, as shown by Table 1.1. Local revenues dropped from over 50 percent of total revenues in 1970 to 43.4 percent in 1980, while state revenues rose from about 40 to 47 percent. The expanded state role is not surprising since only the state can equalize local education tax bases or school spending across districts.

School Finance During the 1980s

Despite the reform ferment begun in the 1970s, school finance did not change much during the 1980s, particularly with respect

**Table 1.1. Percentage of Revenues by Source for U.S.
K–12 Public Education: 1960–1988.**

Government Level	Year			
	1960	*1970*	*1980*	*1990*
Federal	4.4%	8.0%	9.8%	6.4%
State	39.1	39.9	46.8	48.7
Local and other	56.5	52.1	43.4	44.9

Source: Data from National Center for Education Statistics, 1991; National Education Association, 1991.

to sources of revenues and the typical fiscal inequities. As Table 1.1 shows, sources of education revenues at the end of the 1980s were about the same as at the beginning, although state sources rose a bit (to almost 50 percent) and federal sources dropped slightly.

Further, school finance inequities across the country did not change much from the mid 1970s to the mid 1980s. The disparity in expenditures per pupil rose modestly (with the coefficient of variation increasing from 0.16 to 0.19) and the relationship between revenues and wealth declined a bit (the correlation coefficient dropping from 0.55 to 0.50), but both statistics remained high (Schwartz & Moskowitz, 1988). Another study indicated that expenditure-per-pupil disparities decreased moderately from 1980 to 1987 (Wycoff, in press). Generally, structural fiscal inequities did not change significantly.

School Finance Litigation During the 1980s

The 1980s saw a resurgence of—and new directions for—school finance litigation. While there was not much litigation at the beginning of the decade, by 1990 court cases had been filed or were planned in about twenty-five states. During the 1980s, state supreme courts in Arkansas, Kentucky, Montana, New Jersey, and Texas found school finance systems unconstitutional. Further, the Texas and New Jersey cases represented a second round of litigation, each state having experienced a court suit during the 1970s as well. The school finance case in Kentucky broke new ground by overturning the state's entire education system— its organization, structure, and programs—as well as the school finance system.

Second Decisions. Interestingly, courts were not averse to rendering second decisions. Indeed, even during the 1970s, courts in Connecticut and Washington found systems unconstitutional in second cases. The late 1980s Texas case was noteworthy in two ways. First, the earlier Texas case—*Rodriguez* v. *San Antonio Independent School District*—had reached the U.S. Supreme Court, which upheld the Texas system and thereby eliminated the federal courts as a route for challenging school finance inequities. Second, prior to the 1989 ruling, several new, conservative justices had been elected to the Texas Supreme Court. Yet the court surprised the state—and the country—by unanimously finding the Texas school finance structure unconstitutional. Moreover, about eighteen months later, the court again unanimously overturned the reform enacted by the Texas legislature in mid 1990.

Focus on Spending Disparities. The new legal decisions suggest an emerging focus on spending differences per se rather than on the relationship between spending and wealth. The Texas decision revolved around differences in spending between the bottom fifty and top fifty districts. The Kentucky court required a much higher per-pupil spending base across all districts. And the New Jersey decision required that spending in the bottom districts be equal to that of the top-spending districts. It appears the balance is tipping toward a requirement for equal expenditures per pupil (with legitimate adjustments for pupil need and education price differences) and away from requiring equal access to local property tax bases. Indeed, courts seem to have become more restrictive in the magnitude of fiscal disparities allowed. In both the Kentucky and Texas cases, the vast majority of districts spent close to the state average, and the courts still overturned the finance systems.

New Issues. The New Jersey and Kentucky cases, moreover, raised intriguing new issues. In New Jersey, the court focused its decision on the poorest twenty-eight school districts and found the system unconstitutional only for those districts. Those twenty-eight districts are primarily large urban school systems with low property wealth per pupil and high concentrations of poverty and minority students. The decision required the state to make the per-pupil spending in these districts "substantially equal" to the spending in the highest-wealth suburban districts. A political reading of the New Jersey decision—and the legislative response—suggests substantial movement toward equal spending for all districts.

In Kentucky, the court went far beyond ruling on the school finance system. By holding the entire education system unconstitutional, the Kentucky court may have set a precedent for the direction of school finance litigation—as well as education policy—during the 1990s. The court essentially ruled that disparities in local tax bases and dollar inputs were only part of the problem and required the state to redesign the entire education system—structure, governance, program, and finance.

National Education Goals. The emergence of bold new national education goals has begun to focus the education system on outcomes, on what students know and can do. The national goals include bringing all students to high levels of thinking, problem solving, and communication in basic content areas and having U.S. students rank first in the world in mathematics and science. The policy interest includes the programs and strategies to accomplish these goals (Smith & O'Day, 1991; Business Roundtable, 1991), the costs of such programs and strategies, and the school finance structures required to fund and implement these programs and strategies. It may be difficult for school finance—and school finance litigation—to be limited to the fiscal and dollar input issues of the 1970s and 1980s. School finance policy in the 1990s will have to directly address issues related to student outcomes and the school strategies required to produce those outcomes.

Yet the public and policy makers continue to focus on money. Indeed, when President Bush and the U.S. secretary of education introduced their America 2000 schools proposal (White House, 1991), the proposal was widely criticized as requiring too little money. Although the president and the secretary argued the key issues were ideas, programs, and effective school strategies, others argued the key issue was money.

Public School Funding Changes: 1950–1990

This section reviews public school funding changes in the four decades between 1950 and 1990; the data show that funding has increased continuously. For each of the past four decades, funding per pupil (after adjusting for inflation) has risen by a minimum of one-third and up to two-thirds.

Nevertheless, predictions of education funding increases always seem to be pessimistic. When the 1980s began, Kirst and Garms (1980) wrote that the optimistic fiscal scenario for the 1980s would be a steady fiscal state—enough funds to cover enrollment growth and inflation but no real increases. When *A Nation at Risk* (National Commission on Excellence in Education, 1983) was issued, several individuals (for example, Odden, 1984) suggested that implementing its recommendations would require an extra 20–25 percent in real per-pupil resources—too high a price—and recommended lower-cost strategies for education improvement. When the Carnegie Forum on Education and the Economy issued *A Nation Prepared: Teachers for the 21st Century* (1986) on transforming teachers into a full profession, the recommendations were priced at an additional 26 percent in real per-pupil spending. Although Kelly (1986) wrote that 26 percent was about the level of increased education spending for the previous decade, few were confident that the nation would put that level of new resources into public schools, even during an era of education reform.

While school funding increased substantially by the end of the 1980s (Odden, 1990b), the proposals of neither report were fully implemented. The country, educators, education policy makers, and teachers simply did not believe that the funds for these ambitious reform programs would be provided. If, as is argued in this section, real public school funding continues its historical climb during the 1990s, a hope is that the new funds will be used to support powerful strategies most likely to accomplish the national education goals.

If a poll were taken of superintendents, administrators, teachers, and public education policy makers today, it would likely show that most believe school funding will not increase much during the 1990s and that education will do well to keep its nose above the fiscal waterline, that is, to stay even fiscally. Indeed, as the 1991 recession hit state revenue coffers and education aid was cut along with aid for other functions, the

Table 1.2. Total and Current Expenditures per Pupil: 1950–1990.

Year	Total Expenditures per Pupil[a]		Real Decade Change	Current Expenditures per Pupil		Real Decade Change
	Nominal	Real		Nominal	Real	
1950	$ 260	$1,018	—	$ 210	$1,029	—
1960	471	1,857	82%	375	1,479	44%
1970	955	2,929	58%	816	2,502	69%
1980	2,491	3,716	27%	2,272	3,390	35%
1990	5,276[b]	4,818[b]	30%	4,814[b]	4,396[b]	30%

a Current expenditures plus capital expenditures and debt service.
b Author estimate.
Source: Data from National Center for Education Statistics, 1991.

fiscal scenario for education looked bleak, making the steady fiscal state scenario seem optimistic.

But while perceptions about education funding are (and probably always have been) bleak, the actual numbers paint a different picture. The reality is that Americans have allocated large amounts of new money for schools every decade for nearly half a century! The facts are shown in Table 1.2.

The numbers in Table 1.2 show that both total expenditures (current expenditures plus capital expenditures and debt service) per pupil and current expenditures per pupil have increased by substantial percentage amounts—in real terms—every decade since 1950. During the 1980s, real expenditures per pupil increased 30 percent, despite the pessimistic predictions made at the beginning of the decade. That was enough to fund the recommendations in many reform reports. This large increase occurred even though the country experienced one of its most severe recessions of this century in the early 1980s.

Moreover, the substantial increase in both total and current expenditures per pupil during the 1980s was not an anomaly but simply the continuation of historical patterns. For example, as also shown in Table 1.2, real current expenditures per pupil increased 35 percent in the 1970s, 69 percent in the 1960s, and 44 percent during the 1950s. In other words, in each of the

past four decades educational spending per pupil has risen by at least 30 percent and by more than double that in some decades. That is an impressive pattern of spending growth.

The fact is that during modern times education expenditures have consistently increased by large amounts. Further, this has been true during periods of enrollment growth (the 1950s and 1960s), enrollment decline (the 1970s), and enrollment stability (the 1980s). Moreover, this pattern is true despite the occurrence of recessions, which tended to happen about every seven years before the 1980s.

The implications of these fiscal trends for the 1990s are clear. Unless history completely reverses itself, public school funding per pupil will likely rise again during the 1990s. If the increase just matches the lowest decade increase of the recent past, funding will rise 30 percent. That is a substantial increase. This level of funding increase was hard to contemplate during the cuts caused by the 1991 recession. But while real education revenues also dropped during the recession of 1981–1982, funding increases for the remainder of the decade more than compensated for those losses.

In short, a strong argument can be made that public education funding—in real per-pupil terms—is very likely to increase substantially over the decade of the 1990s. Such increase has been the pattern for each of the past four decades. Assuming that pattern continues in the 1990s, a key question is how to use those funds productively. Put differently, if public school funding rises by almost one-third during the 1990s, the major fiscal policy issue is how to spend those dollars.

In past decades, funding increases have been spent on overall increases in teacher salaries and reductions in class size, but student performance—and thus education productivity—have not improved that much (Odden & Picus, 1992). The education productivity issue for the 1990s is whether an extra one-third in real resources can be deployed to improve student achievement and education productivity by a commensurate amount.

To be more specific, could a 33 percent hike in resources be used to finance the types of overall program strategies that

have been proposed to attain the nation's education goals? The next section addresses these issues.

School Finance for the 1990s

There is an emerging consensus (Business Roundtable, 1991; National Governors' Association, 1990; Peters & Waterman, 1982; White House, 1991) on the macro strategy for accomplishing major school change that produces quantum improvements in student learning and helps accomplish the nation's bold education goals.

- Set clear student learning outcome goals
- Have a high-quality curriculum program
- Implement site-based management, allowing teachers to have major influence and power over implementation
- Have an assessment or monitoring system calibrated to world-class standards that indicates the degree to which objectives are being accomplished
- Have a sharp-edged accountability system with rewards and sanctions

This reform strategy gives rise to the following school finance related issues:

- The linkage between the basic school finance structure and education goals
- Teacher compensation
- Site-based management and site-based budgeting
- Accountability systems linked to student performance goals
- Public school choice
- Complementary state policy roles
- Nontraditional education issues such as preschool, extended-day kindergarten, and noneducation children's services

Linkage of School Finance to Education Goals

The first step in school finance for the 1990s will be to link a school finance structure to substantive education objectives,

more specifically to programs designed to accomplish national student performance goals. State student performance goals will increasingly come to resemble the national goals. While state goals may ultimately differ from national goals, all states are moving to (1) increase the high school graduation rate to 90 percent or higher; (2) have all students demonstrate competence in challenging subject matter of reading, writing, science, mathematics, and history; and (3) substantially improve student proficiency in mathematics and science (National Governors' Association, 1990).

If these goals are taken seriously, states will need to provide a base school finance system that allows all local school districts to meet these performance goals. Since these goals include teaching *all* students how to think, solve problems, and communicate at levels much higher than most districts accomplish today, the cost of the base program is likely to be high. This education agenda is very ambitious; only a few districts have tried to carry out similar plans.

Determining the actual dollar cost of this base program is technically complex. Conceptually, the task is to identify the programs and strategies needed at different education levels and for different types of students to produce these desired levels of student learning and then to cost them out. The education strategies likely would include several programs for special needs students, as well as cross-district price adjustments. The best guess is that the price tag is much higher than what most districts currently spend and much higher than the basic foundation program supported by each state's school finance general aid program, which ranged in 1990 from about $2,000 per student in the lowest-spending states to almost $10,000 in the highest-spending states.

To determine the price tag, programs and strategies need to be identified in detail. Smith and O'Day (1991) begin to outline the overall systemic reforms needed to produce desired levels of student performance. Specific curriculum changes have been described for mathematics (National Council of Teachers of Mathematics, 1989), science (American Association for the Advancement of Science, 1989), social studies (National

Commission on Social Studies in the Schools, 1989), and language arts (California State Department of Education, 1987).
Elementary programs that show great promise include Success
for All Schools (Slavin, Madden, Karweit, Livermon, & Dolan,
1990), Accelerated Schools (Levin, 1988), the School Develop-
ment Program (Comer, 1980), which integrates noneducation
services and parent involvement, and many others (Wilson &
Corcoran, 1987). Middle school reforms have been proposed in
Turning Points (Carnegie Task Force, 1989) and *Caught in the
Middle* (Superintendent's Advisory Task Force on Middle
Schools, 1988). High school programs include the Coalition of
Essential Schools (Sizer, 1990), the National Education Associa-
tion's Mastery Learning Schools, the American Federation of
Teachers' Charter Schools, and others (Wilson & Corcoran,
1988).

The additional costs of these schoolwide secondary programs may not be that great (Chapter Three of this book; Sizer,
1990). While the effectiveness of all of these models has not yet
been documented, research on most is currently in place. Further, implementation costs for all new initiatives could be substantial. Nevertheless, these programs represent the types of
detailed programs that, if implemented, would help accomplish
ambitious new student performance goals.

Thus, the design of school finance formulas in the 1990s
should entail a close working relationship between program
analysts and finance analysts, with program analysts identifying
the strategies that work for producing high levels of student
achievement and finance analysts costing out those strategies,
calculating the most cost-effective strategies and determining
the dollar level for the state's base funding program.

The new system would link education and fiscal systems. It
would be a system driven by education goals and student
achievement, with a finance structure designed to support the
programs and strategies required to meet the goals.

Teacher Compensation

Teacher compensation is likely to be the second major component of the new school finance of the 1990s. Teacher pay was the

focus of several education policy initiatives in the 1980s, including programs to increase beginning teacher salaries and career ladder programs designed to provide a promotional structure within teaching. By the end of the 1980s, thirty states had beginning teacher salary policies and nineteen had statewide minimum teacher salary schedules (Fuhrman & Associates, 1991). Teacher compensation is the largest component of school district budgets, and concern with how to pay teachers to improve education productivity may continue.

Addressing teacher compensation comprehensively requires attention to the following six issues:

- Recruitment into the profession, including recruitment into preservice training through fellowship or loan programs
- Beginning salaries, especially a policy benchmark for beginning teacher salaries
- Base pay, including whether to pay for the job and provide annual increments for education and training or to provide pay increments for teachers' knowledge and skills
- Pay-for-performance that avoids the flaws of individual-based incentive and merit pay programs of the past and draws on successful private-sector practices that reward all individuals in production units and foster teamwork and collegiality
- Benefits
- Pensions

In Chapter Two, Odden and Conley propose a new teacher compensation structure derived from a review of research on compensation strategies that work in the private sector, especially knowledge production organizations, and from research on what has and has not worked in education (Lawler, 1990). Their proposal addresses each of the six items above. While their specific recommendations can be debated, they nevertheless comprehensively discuss the array of issues that policy makers will need to address as teacher compensation continues to be a policy target in the 1990s.

The primary thrust of Odden and Conley's proposed changes is to shift teacher pay from education and experience to knowledge and skills. While education is an indirect indicator of knowledge, and experience is an indirect indicator of skills, the technology is now in place to pay teachers directly for knowledge and skills. In a skill-based pay system, individuals are paid for the number and kind of skills and depth of knowledge they develop and use. Salary increases are provided for a growing repertoire of skills and knowledge rather than just for the execution of a job.

This approach is well suited to professional settings because it emphasizes the continuous upgrading of professional skills and knowledge; it has been shown to be effective in knowledge industries (Lawler, 1990). Paying the person, that is, paying for what individuals know and can do, helps the organization actively manage the knowledge and skill acquisition process by motivating and then rewarding individuals for learning specific knowledge and skills.

Interestingly, Odden and Conley in Chapter Two show how a redesigned teacher compensation system could undergird an education system that is goals-oriented, produces high levels of student achievement in higher-level thinking and problem-solving skills, fosters teacher involvement in professional decision making, spurs development of norms of collegiality and continuous improvement, stimulates teachers' ongoing development of professional knowledge and skills, improves teachers' total compensation—including paying the most skilled and effective teachers more—enhances the ability of education to recruit and retain more able individuals in teaching, and supports the continued professionalization of teaching. Further, Odden and Conley identify eight very specific recommendations for changes in school finance structures to support such a new way to compensate teachers and help improve education productivity.

Site-Based Management

The third component of school finance in the 1990s will be site-based management. Nearly all the strategies required to meet these ambitious education goals recommend increased implementation autonomy for schools—the service delivery units in the education system. With outcome goals set at the top of the system—at the national, state, and district levels—schools need to be given responsibility for accomplishing those goals. This focused-at-the-top and loose-at-the-bottom approach follows from techniques that have been successful in the private sector (Peters & Waterman, 1982), from research on effective schools (Purkey & Smith, 1983; Hawley & Rosenholtz, 1984; Wilson & Corcoran, 1987, 1988; Deal & Peterson, 1990), and from principal-agent theory in economics that has been used to probe microapproaches to productivity (Moe, 1984; Eisenhardt, 1989).

Taking site decentralization seriously in fiscal terms requires site-based budgeting. Unlike current approaches to budgeting, in which districts make nearly all decisions on how dollars will be allocated and spent (Guthrie, 1988), site-based budgeting allocates substantial portions of school district revenues in a lump sum to schools, and professionals at the school level make decisions on how to use those funds (Hentschke, 1986, 1988).

While there are numerous issues that need to be addressed in designing workable approaches to site-based budgeting, state school finance policy could take the lead in developing approaches. For example, Kentucky has required all school districts to implement site-based management strategies by the mid 1980s. State policy could be even more ambitious. States could stipulate that a fixed percentage of base funding be allocated directly to schools as a lump sum. States could require districts to allocate a fixed percentage—or all—of instructional expenditures to schools. In other words, states could become very aggressive players in stimulating serious site-based management by forcing dollars to flow directly to schools. In Chapter Four, Wohlstetter and Buffett show that district and state approaches to site-based management in the early 1990s entail considerable devolution of fiscal decision making to schools, contrary to past site-based management initiatives (Malen & Ogawa, 1988).

Of course, such policies raise the issue of which functions

districts should provide and which functions schools should provide. Should operation, maintenance, and substitute teachers be run and funded centrally or decentralized to schools? Hentschke (1988) argues that cost efficiencies would result from decentralizing these functions to schools. Further, should districts decide on school staffing patterns or should schools receive the dollars and devise staffing patterns themselves? Who should provide transportation? While answers to these questions could vary across states and districts, states nevertheless could drive more discretionary funds to the school site by simply requiring direct allocation of some portion of the base funding to flow directly to schools.

These issues move beyond functional allocation to the governance issue of the role of school boards. Local school boards were not centrally involved in designing the 1980s education excellence programs (Usdan & Danzberger, 1986). Further, there have been recent proposals to eliminate local district school boards (Finn, 1991). On the other hand, Chicago decided to diminish the role of the district board but to create mini school boards at each school. Teacher professionalism proposals, moreover, suggest that teachers should run and manage schools, a suggestion that fits with professionalism (Sykes, 1991) but runs counter to the traditional lay control of American schools (McDonnell, 1991). The point is simply that school-based management, including school-based–lump-sum budgeting, may not be just another aspect of the new school finance of the 1990s; if taken quite seriously, it also raises issues related to traditional lay control of schools.

Accountability: Real Incentives and Sanctions

The fourth component of school finance in the 1990s is a sharp-edged accountability system, with real incentives and sanctions driven by school outcomes. The general idea is to reward schools that succeed in accomplishing student performance objectives and to sanction schools that consistently do not. The use of real rewards and sanctions would be a significant departure for education generally, as well as for school finance structures.

There is growing interest in new approaches to accountability that include rewards and sanctions (Business Roundtable, 1991).

While there are many aspects that need to be addressed in designing a comprehensive accountability system (Brown, 1990), one issue specifically related to school finance is whether the system should focus on dollar inputs, the practice in the past, or provide dollar incentives for producing student outcomes, a practice increasingly being adopted by states (Richards & Shujaa, 1990). About a dozen states either have or are developing programs that provide monetary awards to schools for meeting certain student performance goals (see Chapter Five of this book).

The South Carolina program, for example, provides about $30 per pupil to schools that meet certain outcome objectives. Student performance is the leading objective, but others, such as student and teacher attendance, are also included. Research shows, moreover, that such incentives did not flow disproportionately to wealthy districts but were concentrated among schools most in need of improvements (Richards & Sheu, 1991). Kentucky's proposed school-based incentive program will provide staff bonuses up to 40 percent of annual salaries to schools that meet outcome goals.

Nearly all new incentive programs are *school* — not individual teacher — based. Thus, they avoid the pitfalls of plans that seek to reward individual performance. School-based incentive plans foster cooperation and collegiality within school staffs to accomplish schoolwide student performance objectives. Similar plans have been quite effective in the private sector in improving organizational productivity (Blinder, 1990), including private-sector–knowledge-producing organizations (Lawler, 1990). School-based performance incentives could also become important elements of a dramatically revised teacher compensation structure (see Chapter Two).

Most traditional school finance structures focus on dollar and process accountability. For example, most pupil-weighted school finance programs require that a certain percentage of the extra dollars provided be spent on appropriate services for the weighted students. Further, many states require that a minimum

percentage of the general fund be spent on instruction or stipulate a maximum percentage that can be spent on administration. Few of these requirements have real teeth, and none are
related to outcomes.

More recent proposals have suggested a horse trade, as
the governors characterized it (National Governors' Association,
1986). Schools would be given greater flexibility in spending
funds if they accomplished certain outcomes. Specifically, the
governors proposed regulation flexibility — and even waivers —
for schools that produced targeted improvements in student
achievement. In 1990–91, South Carolina began to implement
precisely such a program, reducing regulations for schools that
had met targeted outcome goals. The issue of regulation flexibility is not completely straightforward (Fuhrman & Elmore, 1991)
and requires careful attention to design in order to forge approaches that produce the desired impacts.

A full-fledged accountability system requires not only
rewards for accomplishing goals but also sanctions for not
doing so. States have begun to implement several variations of
sanctions, but these rarely have a finance dimension. It would be
shortsighted to remove dollars from schools and districts not
achieving student outcomes, but it would be equally shortsighted to do nothing. The sanctions currently used entail a
phased-in takeover of consistently underperforming schools (or
school districts). The first step usually entails provision of technical assistance, including planning, staff development, curriculum change, and so on. In several states, the final step can be a
state takeover of a district, as happened when New Jersey took
over the Jersey City School District. In Kentucky, end-of-the-
process sanctions for consistently nonperforming schools include teacher dismissal, loss of tenure, and even loss of teaching
(and hopefully administrative) credentials.

These new directions in education accountability — fiscal
incentives and real sanctions — are controversial. Further, designing incentives and sanctions that work, that is, that have the
desired effects, entails complex decisions on several theoretical
issues (see Chapter Five; Fuhrman & Elmore, 1991). Nevertheless, rewards — in the form of school-based fiscal incentives and

regulatory flexibility—and sanctions—in the form of school takeover or staff dismissal—seem to be part of the overall school finance and education policy agenda for the 1990s.

Choice

A fifth component of school finance in the 1990s is likely to be school choice. Originally proposed, and rejected, as vouchers or tuition tax credits during the 1970s, choice emerged in the latter half of the 1980s as a new education reform, supported by political leaders on both sides of the aisle (National Governors' Association, 1986). While the governors supported only public school choice, both public and private school choice were placed on the agenda in 1990 by two scholars, Chubb and Moe (1990), and in 1991 by President Bush in his America 2000 schools proposal (White House, 1991). Indeed, by February of 1991, private as well as public school choice proposals were appearing at an accelerating rate (Olson, 1991).

This chapter cannot review all the various issues related to school choice proposals; there are numerous places where those issues have been analyzed (Nathan, 1989; Elmore, 1990; Boyd & Walberg, 1990; Clune & Witte, 1990). One important issue, however, is the linkage of choice with site-based management and teacher professional control of schools. Many argue that if new discretion is given to site professionals to implement strategies they craft to accomplish student performance goals, then parents need to be given a choice to select schools on the basis of their preference for education philosophy or the learning styles of their children. The point here is not to support choice proposals but to note that choice could well be linked to other key dimensions of school finance policies for the 1990s.

Only one state has attempted to implement a private school choice proposal, and that program affected only one school district. Wisconsin enacted a program that allowed a fixed number of low-income and minority students to use a voucher to attend any school—including private schools—in Milwaukee. That program has been declared unconstitutional, but the 1991 legislature likely will modify the procedural issues that made it unconstitutional. The Wisconsin Supreme Court did not categorically rule out the idea of public funds supporting student attendance at private schools; it noted specific procedural problems with the legislative enactment process that caused it to be unconstitutional.

Ten states had enacted versions of public school choice by 1990 (see Chapter Seven). There are several school finance aspects of public school choice programs. While only state aid followed choice students in the earliest programs, recently states have begun to count the child as a pupil in the distrct attended for the purposes of calculating state general and categorical aid. The effect of this simple stipulation is that total base funding is shifted from the resident to the attending district. Odden and Kotowski (Chapter Seven) conclude this is the most equitable and simple way to structure revenue shifts for students who move to an out-of-resident-district school in an interdistrict, public school choice program.

The most problematic aspect of the financing of public school choice programs concerns district decisions to spend above the base funding level. Parents of students who do not live within the district attended can neither vote for or against local property tax referendums to increase taxes nor pay more taxes if such a vote passes. Odden and Kotowski (Chapter Seven) argue that this is a structural problem caused by a *district*-based funding structure that has become overlayed with a *school*-based attendance structure. To remedy this structural bind, they suggest that districts be prohibited from spending above the base and that this fiscal option be given to schools.

Odden and Kotowski propose a mechanism that allows schools to spend above the base. The mechanism is linked to a state's income tax and would function in a manner similar to current guaranteed tax base programs that are used in many states for district financing. Except for base funding, states have not addressed this finance problem associated with interdistrict open enrollment programs.

Finally, there is growing interest in charter schools, that is, public schools that receive public funds and are accountable to the public, but not necessarily to a local school district. Charter schools could be operated by groups of professional teachers who decide to create a school on their own and according to their vision. Charter schools could be one type of America 2000 schools proposed by President Bush. Minnesota became the first state to implement the charter school concept by enacting a charter school bill during the 1991 legislative session.

Complementary State Policy Roles

In addition to the specific policies outlined above, there are several complementary state policies needed to implement the systemic reform necessary to accomplish the 1990s education goals. Each of these complementary policies, moreover, has finance dimensions. Five complementary policies are discussed here.

Curriculum Frameworks and Staff Development. The first policy is development of ambitious state curriculum frameworks. These frameworks not only outline the school curriculum but delineate learning outcomes for children; they are indispensable in an outcomes-driven education system. Reference was made earlier to new, thinking-oriented curriculum frameworks that have been developed by several professional organizations.

The finance dimension of these new curriculum directions is connected to implementation. While emerging research suggests that teachers, schools, and districts are responding positively to these initiatives (Marsh & Odden, 1991; Armstrong, Davis, Gallagher, & Odden, 1988), research also shows that a thinking-oriented curriculum requires substantial change in classroom practice that will take years to accomplish (Cohen & Peterson, 1990).

A critical ingredient to successful implementation over time will be consistent and high-quality professional staff development (Porter, Archibald, & Tyree, 1991). Few states and school districts have invested sufficient funds in staff development, and such funds often are the first to be cut in times of fiscal stress, such as the 1991 recession. Thus, just at a time when large investments in professional staff development are needed to implement a new, thinking-oriented curriculum in mathematics, science, language arts, and social studies, staff development funds are being cut at both state and local levels.

States need to consider seriously the need to develop and fund effective staff development programs; if they do not, it is highly unlikely that the new curriculum frameworks will be implemented in classrooms and thus unlikely that students will learn to think, problem solve, and communicate (Fullan, 1991; Porter et al., 1991). While states could develop a series of staff development categorical programs and while some programs can be powerful agents in stimulating bottom-up professional networks (Marsh & Odden, 1991; McLaughlin, 1991), a more straightforward approach is to use the general aid formula and simply stipulate that 1 percent must be used for professional staff development. In California, that would amount to about $35 per child; in New Jersey, that would be $95 per child. Neither amount is excessive. While there could be disagreements about whether the funds should be retained at the district or lump-sum budgeted to the school site, such a requirement could permanently build staff development into the ongoing activities of districts and schools. Further, such small sums of dollars could support the most critical programs for changing classroom practice in directions that have students exposed to a thinking-oriented curriculum.

Student Assessment. A second complementary state policy would be to develop new and comprehensive student assessment structures. Such structures would need to avoid the emphasis on basic skills and fragmented testing that has characterized local and state student assessment in the past (Resnick & Resnick, 1990). Indeed, new student assessments will need to be driven by the curriculum framework; the emphasis will need to be placed on actual student performance, that is, on tasks and activities that students complete, and student performance will need to be matched against proficiency standards that are calibrated to world-class standards.

Such systems will probably not use matrix random sampling techniques to produce data on what students know and can do at school, district, and state levels. New state assessments will include individual assessments for each student at specified grade levels (California State Department of Education, 1991). Further, there is rapidly increasing discussion of national student examinations that could be given at key grade levels (O'Neill, 1991).

Performance assessments are powerful instruments in identifying what students know and can do. If calibrated to world-class standards, they would help drive a thinking-skills curriculum and give more comprehensive information on student performance. While no new integrated state assessment system has been designed or costed out, costs could be more than ten times what is now spent on state student-testing programs. In short, while the policy interest in performance testing of all students is high, such new approaches will require substantial funding.

Instructional Materials Development. Developing new instructional materials, including microchip-based technologies, is another critical ingredient in implementing a thinking-skills curriculum as a strategy to meet national and state education goals. At one level, this strategy entails using extant dollars for better instructional materials. But it will be several years before textbook publishers produce sufficient numbers of new instructional materials that could be used to implement the new curriculum frameworks (Porter et al., 1991). If states continue to adopt bold new curriculum frameworks and pressure publishers to revise their materials to reflect new emphases on thinking and problem solving for all children, commercially available instructional materials could improve incrementally over time.

States might also want to stimulate development of more sophisticated microcomputer-based technologies. Perlman (1989) argues that such technologies are critical for increasing education productivity and student achievement during the 1990s. States such as Iowa and Kentucky have begun to finance development of both satellite technologies to beam courses into isolated areas and a fiber-optic structure to which schools could connect and then have access to data bases, simulations, and interactive instructional materials from around the world.

Developing new instructional materials — whether using public money or providing incentives for private-sector response — that can be used to implement a thinking-skills curriculum is another important state policy focus for the 1990s.

Front-Loaded–Site-Based Education Improvement Grants. Very few schools have substantial amounts of discretionary dollars. While site-based budgeting might provide increasing amounts of such dollars, states could front load the process by creating a site-based education improvement program that would provide between $50 and $100 per pupil for each school site to plan and implement an education improvement program. California has had such a program for several years (Marsh & Bowman, 1989), and it has been relatively effective.

Kentucky has also taken this approach. While it is phasing in a site-based management program over several years, it has created in the short term an education improvement program that provides schools with discretionary funds to plan strategies for accomplishing Kentucky's ambitious new goals. If, moreover, a state subsequently implemented a lump-sum–site-based budgeting program, the school improvement dollars could be rolled into the amount budgeted to each school.

Controlled Restructuring Experiments. Implementing a thinking-skills curriculum that is effective in teaching all students to think and problem solve may entail dramatic school restructuring, that is, how schools are organized, staffed, and managed (Elmore & Associates, 1990). At the present time, the designs of effective restructured schools are not known. Restructured schools that work will have to be created. This creation process will likely produce several successes as well as several failures.

States could spur the learning curve for designing and implementing effective restructured schools by providing both developmental funds for schools to create and implement different restructured schools and assessment funds for analysts to document the process and the impact of different designs. The purpose would be less evaluation and more intelligence gathering to share knowledge about what works and what does not.

States could easily identify a pot of dollars that could approximate $30 per child in the state and allocate from that sum a total of $250 per student for development actions in 10 percent of all schools and $50 per student in those schools for formative assessments of the developmental and implementation process. Such a strategy would be relatively low-cost but potentially highly productive by consciously stimulating local attempts to design new school strategies that work in teaching thinking and problem-solving skills to all students and to immediately share both successful strategies and strategies that do not work.

Complementary Programmatic Strategies

The last component of school finance in the 1990s concerns financing several nonschool or nontraditional school programs. These programs address the goal of having all students come to school ready to learn. Several programs could be included in this category; all have price tags, but nearly all have been shown by research to have both short- and long-term payoffs.

Preschool. Nearly all studies show that early childhood education programs have long-term impacts and, even when future benefits are discounted to present values, significant net benefit-to-cost ratios (Barnett, 1985; Grubb, 1989a). Early childhood education programs for poor children improve student academic performance in the basic skills in elementary through high school, decrease failure rates and below–grade level performance at all grade levels, decrease discipline problems, and improve high school graduation rates. Early childhood education programs can provide long-term returns of four dollars for every one dollar invested (Barnett, 1990).

Extended-Day Kindergarten. Kindergarten was a full-day program until World War II, when teacher shortages cut it to a half day. Research syntheses suggest that students from poverty backgrounds who receive a full-day kindergarten program perform from 0.5 to over 1.0 standard deviation better on basic skill activities in the early elementary grades than those who do not (Puleo, 1988; Slavin, Karweit, & Madden, 1989). Both expanded early childhood education and extended-day kindergarten cost more money. Yet they give students from poverty backgrounds a substantial boost in successfully learning the basic skills in early elementary grades.

Child Care for Working Parents. As women increasingly enter the workforce in full-time jobs, there is a growing need to provide child care for students both before and after traditional school hours (Grubb, 1989b). While there is only scant research on the educational achievement effects of variations in level and quality of child-care services, the fact remains that increasing numbers of children are not under the supervision of an adult after school ends. Whether from public or private sources, child-care services will consume expanding percentages of the nation's personal income in the future unless the work behavior of women and men changes dramatically.

Integrated Children's Services. A child's ability to experience success in school depends to a substantial degree on other nonschool conditions, such as the home environment, physical health, mental health, and so on. Further, students at-risk usually are at-risk along several dimensions. Yet a growing body of research shows that the structure of delivering noneducation services to children — including health, family, psychological, parole, medical, preschool, and child- and day-care services — is fragmented and increasingly ineffective (Kirst, 1989). Integrated children's services is a policy proposal being recommended across the country. The idea is to have all — or at least a great variety of — children's noneducation services provided at one location. The school is a prime candidate because nearly all children spend large portions of each day at a school. Schools then could employ case brokers who would work with individual students and broker needed services from the various service providers. The Carnegie Task Force report (1989) on middle schools, for example, proposed having a health coordinator at each school.

The New Beginnings project in the San Diego public schools is one of the most recent attempts to provide school-based integrated services for children (Cohen, 1991). California's new governor, Pete Wilson, proposed a similar program for all California schools in his 1992 budget. Integrating social and education services in one location, with schools being a prime locale in most states, is very likely to add a new dimension to school finance during the 1990s. The key issue is how to create such programs without further financially burdening schools; the policy trick is to direct the flow of resources for children's noneducation services (primarily from the federal government) to some central locality, such as the school (see Chapter Nine).

Poverty and Health Programs. While the governors and the president did not raise the issue of reducing poverty as a means of having more children come to school ready to learn, the growing number of children in poverty (Pallas, Natriello, & McDill, 1989), the increasingly sophisticated understanding of policies that would dramatically reduce poverty, especially the number of children in poverty (Ellwood, 1987), and the continued linkage of low student performance with poverty suggest that reducing children's poverty, a laudable objective in itself, would also help accomplish the education goals of the country and the states during the 1990s. Further, programs such as the Women, Infant, and Children's Program that provide prenatal care for pregnant mothers are highly cost-effective in producing healthy children and reducing the incidence of learning disabilities. In short, reducing poverty and expanding effective health and nutrition programs that enhance a child's family environment and result in healthy children are noneducation and preschool programs that will help schools accomplish their tasks once children begin formal schooling.

Expanded Definitions of School Finance Equity

These changes in the school finance menu for the 1990s require that the traditional definition of school finance equity stated in terms of dollar inputs at the district level must be dramatically transformed. While the Berne and Stiefel (1984) framework helped bring conceptual, intellectual, and technical clarity to school finance equity discussions during the 1970s and 1980s, that framework now needs expanding (Odden & Picus, 1992).

First, school finance equity analysis needs to link indicators of school finance equity to the developing work in educational indicators more generally (Odden, 1990a; Shavelson, McDonnell, & Oakes, 1989; Smith, 1988; Council of Chief State School Officers, 1990). There is renewed interest in improving national data bases in school finance (Forgione, 1990), enhancing interstate measures of the status of state school finance systems, and including finance and other related data in broader attempts to provide indicators of the current and changing status of the U.S. and state education systems. These events place the earlier attempts to define and measure school finance equity into a broader policy context in which finance indicators are part of a set of more comprehensive educational indicators (Oakes, 1986).

Second, school finance equity frameworks need to move beyond expenditures and revenues as indicators of education resources and look at the curriculum and instructional education resources into which dollars are transformed. Indeed, while fiscal inequities have dominated school finance for decades, dollars are used by school districts to purchase education resources. Further, the curriculum and teaching to which students are exposed are key determinants of what students learn (McKnight et al., 1987; Schwille et al., 1982; Bryk, Lee, & Smith, 1990). Since a key goal of the education system is student learning, knowledge of the equity of the distribution of the key resources most directly linked to student learning—curriculum and instruction—ought to be an integral part of a comprehensive school finance equity framework (Porter, 1991).

Third, both school finance and curriculum and instruction data need to be developed on a *school* basis, not just at the district level as is common practice today. Indeed, the major thrust of education policy in the 1990s will be directed at the school site. Site-based budgeting, site-based performance incentives, site-based management, and site-based data on student performance all require that detailed fiscal and resource information be available on a school-by-school basis. Expenditures by function and program and curriculum, and instruction resources actually provided are key school-based data needed to implement both new education policy initiatives as well as to analyze the functioning of the system, including school productivity.

Summary and Conclusions: School Finance for the 1990s

It is clear that school finance in the 1990s will be a much more complicated enterprise than it has been in the past. At several levels, school finance and education programs and strategies will become more inextricably linked. The school finance focus will shift to the school level and will require more school-level data than are currently available at the district level in most states today. Finally, school finance and education productivity will become linked to a broader range of nontraditional education programs as well as several noneducation programs.

While funds will be tight during the first few years of the 1990s because of the recession, strong historical trends for the past forty years suggest that dollars per pupil after adjusting for inflation are likely to continue to rise during the 1990s. School leaders and state policy makers need to begin planning now for how to use these new funds in productive ways. In the year 2000, it will be too late to say that more could have been done if we had known so much new money would enter the public education system.

The following appear to be the major new school finance emphases for the 1990s as the country and most states seek to bring all students to high levels of thinking and problem solving in the key content areas:

1. Link the base school finance structure (the foundation expenditure in school finance terms) to the programs and strategies needed to bring all students to acceptable levels of thinking and problem solving in mathematics, science, social science,

and language. This will likely entail large increases in education revenues. The assumption is that education revenues, at least nationally, will rise by one-third during the 1990s, which is equal to the minimum amount they have risen in real terms every decade since 1950.

2. Investigate various ways to change the way teachers are compensated in order to recruit and retain more able individuals in the teaching profession, foster teacher collegiality, and help make schools more productive. Consider raising beginning teacher salaries to some benchmark target, such as the average beginning salary for all college graduates; switch from paying teachers for education and experience to paying teachers for skills and knowledge; provide annual bonuses to staffs in schools that meet student improvement targets; provide flexible benefit packages; and change pensions from state-funded–defined-benefit structures to district-funded–defined-contribution programs.

3. Provide for site-based management, including site-based budgeting. The state could stipulate that a certain percentage of the foundation expenditure — even all of it — be lump-sum budgeted directly to schools.

4. Develop a real accountability system with rewards for schools achieving improvements in student performance and sanctions for those that do not. Rewards could be small amounts like the $30 per pupil that is provided in South Carolina, large amounts like the 40 percent teacher salary bonus that will be offered in Kentucky, or regulation waivers. Sanctions could include school takeover or a professional dismissal strategy for schools that consistently fail to produce student achievement.

5. Study and consider implementing some type of school choice mechanisms, such as interdistrict, public school choice programs, and charter schools. For such programs, prohibit districts from spending above the base program.

6. At the state level, invest funds in developing new, thinking-oriented curriculum frameworks in mathematics, science, social science, and language arts; staff development that could be funded using 1 percent of the state foundation program; new student assessment structures that include student performance as the basis of assessment; front-loaded–site-based education improvement grants of between $50 and $100 per child to be used by schools to plan and implement locally designed education improvement programs; and a series of controlled restructuring experiments for the purposes of developing restructured schools that work and developing information on how restructured schools can be designed and implemented.

7. Support investments in nonschool or nontraditional school programs such as preschool, full-day kindergarten, child care, and coordinated children's noneducational services provided at the school site.

School finance cannot afford to stay dormant in the 1990s as it did in the 1980s (Barro, 1987). There are too many new school finance issues that states need to address. The key issue is how to invest and reallocate resources to bring all students up to adequate performance levels. To resolve this issue, school finance in the 1990s must push beyond fiscal inequities and determine connections among student outcomes, education programs, and education funding. School finance ducked those issues in the past; the issues cannot be dodged in the future.

References

American Association for the Advancement of Science. (1989). *Science for all Americans* (Project 2061 Report). Washington, DC: Author.

Armstrong, J., Davis, A., Gallagher, J., & Odden, A. R. (1988). *The impact of state policies on improving science curriculum*. Denver, CO: Education Commission of the States.

Barnett, S. W. (1985). Benefit-cost analysis of the Perry Preschool Program and its policy implications. *Educational Evaluation and Policy Analysis, 7*, 333–342.

Barnett, S. W. (1990). Developing preschool education policy: An economic perspective. *Education Policy, 4*, 245–265.

Barro, S. (1987). *School finance equity: Research in the 1980s and the current state of the art.* Washington, DC: Decision Resources Corporation.

Berne, R., & Stiefel, L. (1984). *The measurement of equity in school finance: Conceptual, methodological, and empirical decisions.* Baltimore, MD: Johns Hopkins University Press.

Blinder, A. (1990). *Paying for productivity.* Washington, DC: Brookings Institution.

Boyd, W. L., & Walberg, H. J. (1990). *Choice in education: Potential and problems.* Berkeley, CA: McCutchan.

Brown, P. (1990). *Accountability in public education.* San Francisco: Far West Regional Education Laboratory.

Bryk, A., Lee, V., & Smith, J. (1990). High school organization and its effects on teachers and students: An interpretive summary of the research. In W. H. Clune & J. F. Witte (Eds.), *Choice and control in American education* (Vols. 1–2) (pp. 135–226). Philadelphia: Falmer.

Business Roundtable. (1991). *Essential elements of a successful education system.* Washington, DC: Author.

California State Department of Education. (1987). *Language arts curriculum framework.* Sacramento, CA: Author.

California State Department of Education. (1991). *A proposed plan for a new integrated assessment program for California schools.* Sacramento, CA: Author.

Carnegie Forum on Education and the Economy. (1986). *A nation prepared: Teachers for the 21st century.* Washington, DC: Author.

Carnegie Task Force. (1989). *Turning points: Preparing American youth for the 21st century.* New York: Carnegie Corporation.

Chubb, J., & Moe, T. (1990). *Politics, markets and America's schools.* Washington, DC: Brookings Institution.

Clune, W. H., & Witte, J. F. (Eds.). (1990). *Choice and control in American education* (Vols. 1–2). Philadelphia: Falmer.

Cohen, D. K., & Peterson, P. (Eds.). (1990). *Education Evaluation and Policy Analysis, 12*(3).

Cohen, D. L. (1991, January 23). San Diego agencies join to ensure "new beginning" for families. *Education Week*, p. 1.

Comer, J. (1980). *School power.* New York: Free Press.

Council of Chief State School Officers. (1990). *State education indicators: 1990.* Washington, DC.: Author.

Deal, T. E., & Peterson, K. D. (1990). *The principal's role in shaping school culture.* Washington, DC: U.S. Government Printing Office.

Eisenhardt, K. (1989). Agency theory: An assessment and review. *Academy of Management Review, 14*, 57–74.

Ellwood, D. (1987). *Family poverty in America.* New York: Basic Books.

Elmore, R. (1990). *Working models of choice in public education.* New Brunswick, NJ: Rutgers University, Consortium for Policy Research in Education.

Elmore, R., & Associates. (1990). *Restructuring schools: The next generation of educational reform.* San Francisco: Jossey-Bass.

Finn, C. E., Jr. (1991, January 23). Reinventing local control. *Education Week*, p. 40.

Forgione, P. (1990). *A guide to improving the national education data system: An agenda.* Washington, DC: National Center for Education Statistics.

Fuhrman, S., & Associates. (1991). *Final report: Center for Policy Research in Education.* New Brunswick, NJ: Rutgers University, Consortium for Policy Research in Education.

Fuhrman, S., & Elmore, R. (1991). *Takeover and deregulation: Working models of new state and local regulatory relationships.* New Brunswick, NJ: Rutgers University, Consortium for Policy Research in Education.

Fullan, M. G. (with S. M. Stiegelbauer). (1991). *The new meaning of educational change* (2nd ed.). New York: Teachers College Press.

Grubb, W. N. (1989a). Young children face the state: Issues and options for early childhood programs. *American Journal of Education, 97*, 358–397.

Grubb, W. N. (1989b). Child care and early childhood programs.

In M. W. Kirst (Ed.), *Conditions of children in California* (pp. 63–95). Berkeley: University of California, School of Education.

Guthrie, J. W. (1988). *Understanding school budgets*. Washington, DC: U.S. Department of Education.

Hawley, W., & Rosenholtz, S. (Eds.). (1984). Good schools: What research says about improving student achievement [Special issue]. *Peabody Journal of Education, 61*(4).

Hentschke, G. C. (1986). *School business administration: A comparative perspective*. Berkeley, CA: McCutchan.

Hentschke, G. C. (1988). Budgetary theory and reality: A microview. In D. H. Monk & J. Underwood (Eds.), *Microlevel school finance: Issues and implications for policy* (pp. 311–336). New York: Ballinger.

Kelly, J. A. (1986). *Financing education reform*. New York: Carnegie Corporation.

Kirst, M. W. (Ed.). (1989). *Conditions of children in California*. Berkeley: University of California, School of Education.

Kirst, M. W., & Garms, W. I. (1980). The political environment of school finance policy in the 1980s. In J. W. Guthrie (Ed.), *School finance policies and practices* (pp. 47–75). New York: Ballinger.

Lawler, E. E., III. (1990). *Strategic pay: Aligning organizational strategies and pay systems*. San Francisco: Jossey-Bass.

Levin, H. (1988). *Accelerated schools for at-risk students*. New Brunswick, NJ: Rutgers University, Consortium for Policy Research in Education.

Malen, B., & Ogawa, R. T. (1988). Professional-patron influence on site-based governance councils: A confounding case study. *Educational Evaluation and Policy Analysis, 10*, 251–270.

Marsh, D., & Bowman, G. (1989). State initiated top-down versus bottom-up reform. *Education Policy, 3*, 195–216.

Marsh, D., & Odden, A. R. (1991). Implementation of the California mathematics and science curriculum frameworks. In A. R. Odden (Ed.), *Education policy implementation* (pp. 219–239). Albany: State University of New York Press.

McDonnell, L. (1991). Ideas and values in implementation analysis: The case of teacher policy. In A. R. Odden (Ed.), *Education policy implementation* (pp. 241–258). Albany: State University of New York Press.

McKnight, C. C., Crosswhite, F. J., Dossey, J. A., Kifer, E., Swafford, J. O., Travers, K. J., & Cooney, T. J. (1987). *The underachieving curriculum: Assessing U.S. mathematics from an international perspective.* Champaign, IL: Stipes.

McLaughlin, M. W. (1991). The Rand change agent study: Ten years later. In A. R. Odden (Ed.), *Education policy implementation* (pp. 143–156). Albany: State University of New York Press.

Moe, T. M. (1984). The new economics of organization. *American Journal of Political Science, 28,* 739–777.

Nathan, J. (1989). *Public schools by choice: Expanding opportunities for parents, students and teachers.* Minneapolis, MN: Institute for Learning and Teaching.

National Center for Education Statistics. (1991). *Digest of education statistics: 1990.* Washington, DC: U.S. Department of Education.

National Commission on Excellence in Education. (1983). *A nation at risk: Imperative for reform.* Washington, DC: U.S. Department of Education.

National Commission on Social Studies in the Schools. (1989). *Charting a course: Social studies in the 21st century.* Reston, VA: Author.

National Council of Teachers of Mathematics. (1989). *Curriculum and evaluation standards for school mathematics.* Reston, VA: Author.

National Education Association. (1991). *Estimates of school statistics, 1990–1991.* Washington, DC: Author.

National Governors' Association. (1986). *Time for results.* Washington, DC: Author.

National Governors' Association. (1990). *Educating America: State strategies for achieving the national educational goals.* Washington, DC: Author.

Oakes, J. (1986). *Educational indicators: A guide for policymakers.* Santa Monica, CA: RAND Corporation.

Odden, A. R. (1984). *Education Finance in the States: 1984.* Denver, CO: Education Commission of the States.

Odden, A. R. (1990a). Educational indicators in the United States: The need for analysis. *Educational Researcher, 19,* 24–29.

Odden, A. R. (1990b). School funding changes in the 1980s. *Educational Policy, 4,* 33–47.

Odden, A. R., McGuire, C. K., & Belsches-Simmons, G. (1983). *School finance reform in the states: 1983.* Denver, CO: Education Commission of the States.

Odden, A. R., & Picus, L. O. (1992). *School finance: A policy perspective.* New York: McGraw-Hill.

Olson, L. (1991, February 20). Proposals for private-school choice reviving at all levels of government. *Education Week,* p. 1.

O'Neill, J. (1991). Drive for national standards picking up steam. *Educational Leadership, 48*(5), 4–9.

Pallas, A., Natriello, G., & McDill, E. (1989). The changing nature of the disadvantaged population: Current dimensions and future trends. *Educational Researcher, 18*(5), 16–222.

Perlman, L. (1989). *Closing education's technology gap* (Briefing Paper No. 111). Indianapolis, IN: Hudson Institute.

Peters, T., & Waterman, R. (1982). *In search of excellence.* New York: HarperCollins.

Porter, A. C. (1991). Creating a system of school process indicators. *Educational Evaluation and Policy Analysis, 13,* 13–30.

Porter, A. C., Archibald, D. A., & Tyree, A. K., Jr. (1991). Reforming the curriculum: Will empowerment policies replace control? In S. Fuhrman & B. Malen (Eds.), *The politics of curriculum and testing* (pp. 11–36). Philadelphia: Falmer.

Puleo, V. T. (1988). A review and critique of research on full-day kindergarten. *Elementary School Journal, 88,* 425–439.

Purkey, S., & Smith, M. (1983). Effective schools: A synthesis. *Elementary School Journal, 83,* 427–452.

Resnick, L. B., & Resnick, D. P. (1990). Assessing the thinking curriculum: New tools for education reform. In B. R. Gifford & M. C. O'Conner (Eds.), *Future assessments: Changing views of aptitude, achievement and instruction.* Boston: Kluwer.

Richards, C., & Sheu, T. M. (1991). *The South Carolina school incentive reward program: A policy analysis.* New Brunswick, NJ:

Rutgers University, Consortium for Policy Research in Education.

Richards, C., & Shujaa, M. (1990). State-sponsored school performance incentive plans: A policy review. *Educational Considerations, 17*(2), 42–56.

Schwartz, M., & Moskowitz, J. (1988). *Fiscal equity in the United States*. Washington, DC: Decision Resources Corporation.

Schwille, J., Porter, A., Belli, G., Floden, R., Freeman, D., Knappen, L., Kuhs, T., & Schmidt, W. (1982). Teachers as policy brokers in the content of elementary school mathematics. In L. Shulman & G. Sykes (Eds.), *Handbook of teaching and policy* (pp. 370–391). New York: Longman.

Shavelson, R., McDonnell, L., & Oakes, J. (1989). *Indicators for monitoring mathematics and science education*. Santa Monica, CA: RAND Corporation.

Sizer, T. (1990). Educational policy and the essential school. *Horace, 6*(2), 1–3.

Slavin, R., Karweit, N., & Madden, N. (1989). *Effective programs for students at risk*. Needham Heights, MA: Allyn & Bacon.

Slavin, R., Madden, N., Karweit, N., Livermon, B., & Dolan, L. (1990). Success for all: First-year outcomes of a comprehensive plan for reforming urban education. *American Educational Research Journal, 27,* 255–278.

Smith, M. S. (1988). Educational indicators. *Phi Delta Kappan, 69,* 487–491.

Smith, M. S., & O'Day, J. (1991). Systemic school reform. In S. Fuhrman & B. Malen (Eds.), *The politics of curriculum and testing* (pp. 233–267). Philadelphia: Falmer.

Superintendent's Advisory Task Force on Middle Schools. (1988). *Caught in the middle*. Sacramento: California State Department of Education.

Sykes, G. (1991). In defense of teacher professionalism as a policy choice. *Educational Policy, 5,* 137–149.

Usdan, M. D., & Danzberger, J. P. (1986). *School boards: Strengthening grass roots leadership*. Washington, DC: Institute for Educational Leadership.

White House, The. (1990). *National goals for education*. Washington, DC: Author.

White House, The. (1991). *America 2000: An education strategy*. Washington, DC: Author.

Wilson, B., & Corcoran, T. (1987). *Places where children succeed: A profile of outstanding elementary schools*. Philadelphia: Research for Better Schools.

Wilson, B., & Corcoran, T. (1988). *Successful secondary schools*. Philadelphia: Falmer.

Wycoff, J. (in press). The intrastate equality of public elementary and secondary education resources in the U.S., 1980–87. *Economics of Education Review*.

2

Restructuring Teacher Compensation Systems

Allan R. Odden
Sharon Conley

The concept of paying teachers for productivity moved high onto the education policy agenda during the 1980s. Initially states tried versions of merit and incentive pay, schemes that had failed before (Murnane & Cohen, 1986); such approaches failed again in the 1980s. The demise of the Florida merit pay program was the most visible example. Then states enacted career ladder programs designed to promote the best teachers into broader leadership roles within schools and school systems. The Tennessee career ladder program was the most well-known example of this approach. These systems, too, experienced difficulties. Many argued that by the end of the decade these programs, originally proclaimed the second wave of reform, had barely produced ripples (Firestone, Fuhrman, & Kirst, 1989). Finally, the 1980s saw more general proposals to transform teaching into a full profession, but the compensation structure for this new world was never described clearly (Carnegie Forum on Education and the Economy, 1986). States continue to focus policy attention on teacher pay. As of February 1991, at least

Note: The authors thank Yvonne Caro, Joann Hurley, and Ralph Levinson for their comments and suggestions.

twenty-two states had developed or were developing some type of alternative teacher compensation system (see Table 2.1).

Several factors explain this attention to teachers and teacher compensation. First, teachers were recognized as key to the implementation of the nation's hopes for a dramatically improved education system (Darling-Hammond, 1984). Second, there existed a sincere belief that the "best" teachers ought to be rewarded more; merit pay, career ladders, and professional status were seen as potential routes to this end (National Commission on Excellence in Education, 1983). Third, education was one of the major components of the service sector of the national economy, and productivity improvements in all services — including education — were needed to spur economic growth (Johnston, 1987). Fourth, accomplishment of the president's and governors' national education goals — teaching all students how to think, problem solve, and communicate — required more productive use of funds. Thus restructuring teacher compensation to foster teacher collegiality and accomplish national education goals seemed a proposition worth exploring.

This chapter examines the following question: can teacher compensation be restructured to foster both teacher collegiality and the development of the professional expertise necessary to accomplish the national education goals? If so, how? This chapter does not address all teacher policy issues, such as preservice education, alternative certification, or length of school year. Neither does it discuss the politics of implementing the proposed ideas.

We draw upon extensive research in the private sector as well as research on school attempts to align compensation systems with organizational goals, that is, to pay for productivity. Private-sector research findings and proposals to pay for productivity in the private sector are derived primarily from Lawler (1990). In *Strategic Pay*, Lawler, one of the country's foremost authorities on compensation structure design as it relates to individual and group motivation and organizational productivity, synthesizes decades of research on the key issues of effective

Table 2.1. Alternative Teacher Compensation Plans.

State	Pilots with State Funding of Assistance	Full Implementation of State Program	State Program Under Development
	Teacher Incentive Plan		
Colorado	x		
Connecticut			x[a]
Iowa		x	
Massachusetts		x[a]	
Missouri		x	
New Jersey		x[a]	
New York		x	
South Carolina		x	
	Career Ladder or Other Career Compensation Plan		
Arizona	x		
Indiana	x[a]		
Kentucky	Completed in 1987		
Louisiana	x		
Missouri		x	
North Carolina	x		
Ohio	x		
Oregon	x		
Pennsylvania	x[a]		
Tennessee		x	
Texas		x	
Utah		x	
	Mentor Teacher		
California		x	
Vermont			x
Washington		x	

Note: States with local initiatives: Arizona, California, Colorado, Connecticut, Indiana, Iowa, Kentucky, Louisiana, Massachusetts, Missouri, New Jersey, New York, North Carolina, North Dakota, Ohio, Oregon, Pennsylvania, South Carolina, South Dakota, Tennessee, Texas, Utah, Vermont, Wisconsin.

[a] Compensation plan includes a mentor teacher component.

Source: Adapted from Southern Regional Education Board. *Career Ladder Clearinghouse.* Atlanta, GA: Southern Regional Education Board, January 1990, with permission.

compensation systems that both motivate and reward individuals and help foster attainment of organizational goals.

This chapter is organized as follows. The first section
summarizes the country's new education goals and research
conclusions on how teacher knowledge and skills, school organization and culture, and education management relate to accomplishing those objectives. We then identify a set of principles that a redesigned teacher compensation structure would
need to meet.

The second section addresses teacher recruitment into
teacher training programs and into the profession, with a focus
on the role of beginning salary. The third section addresses pay
for teachers, the largest portion of teacher compensation. The
issue discussed is whether teachers should be paid for the *job* of
being a teacher or for the *knowledge and skills* needed to be
successful in the job. Then, the fourth section reviews pay for
productivity, discussing the feasibility of including a gainsharing and school-based productivity component in teacher compensation structures. The fifth section briefly assesses two issues
related to total compensation: fringe benefits and pensions. The
final section summarizes the recommendations and discusses
implications for state school finance policy.

Teacher Effectiveness and Principles
for Redesigning Teacher Compensation

Designing a compensation system is more than simply determining how to pay individuals. It is an activity that must (1) identify the organization's primary goals, (2) create a structure that
supports strategies needed to accomplish the goals, and (3) use a
management approach that fits the organizational structure
(Lawler, 1990). For education, these considerations raise several
issues, including basic education goals, definition of the teaching job, school organization, and school culture and norms.

In terms of education goals, the key issue is the basic
orientation of the system: Is the focus on inputs and processes
(which has been the focus of the past) or on outcomes, that is,
student achievement (which many argue should be the focus of

the future)? This is a key issue for future education management as well as teacher compensation policies. In the past (and to a substantial degree in most school systems today), the organizational emphasis has been on fairness, due process, and equity for all. These are laudable emphases. A compensation structure that rewards all individuals equally, as does the education and experience single-salary schedule, fits quite well with this model.

Today, however, there is an emerging consensus that education should focus more on outcomes. Indeed, national education goals have been stated in terms of outcomes, focusing on what students should know and be able to do at various grade levels and upon secondary school graduation (White House, 1990). The emphasis is on producing students who can think, solve problems, and communicate across all content areas and rank first in the world in mathematics and science. Further, the most effective schools have an outcomes focus (Deal & Peterson, 1990; Hawley & Rosenholtz, 1984; Purkey & Smith, 1983; Rosenholtz, 1985a; Wilson & Corcoran, 1987, 1988) as do the most effective school leaders (Manassee, 1985; Murphy, 1989; Sergiovanni, 1990). The current salary schedule, it is argued, is not linked to goals and does not have either a knowledge and skills or a student outcomes orientation.

A redesigned compensation system could help foster an outcome orientation based on student achievement. This statement may seem to advocate evaluating and compensating teachers based on output (student achievement) rather than knowledge and abilities (skills). On the contrary, we advocate evaluating and paying primarily on the basis of knowledge and skill development, since we assume that it is the most highly skilled and knowledgeable teachers who are most capable of maximizing student learning.

In terms of defining the teaching job, there is also a divergence beween past definitions and evolving understandings. Traditionally, a teacher was prepared for a job — preservice training that ended with a teacher license or certificate — and then given a teaching job with full responsibilities. Individuals were hired into teaching jobs that were quite well defined. Pay was linked to the job; pay increased with experience on the job and additional education and training. There were no promotional opportunities within teaching. Promotion entailed leaving teaching and moving to another type of job, usually in administration but sometimes support positions in curriculum and staff development. Large pay increases were thus linked to job changes.

There is a growing understanding, however, that teachers' knowledge and skills are the key ingredients of teacher effectiveness. There is consensus that effective teaching of higher-level thinking and problem-solving skills is an intellectually demanding task that is better performed by bright individuals with a liberal arts education that includes deep understanding of the subject matter to be taught (Holmes Group, 1986; Lampert & Clark, 1990; Smith & O'Day, 1988). Teachers need to know very well the subject matter they teach, how students learn that subject matter, and how that subject matter is effectively taught to different kinds of students at different ages. There also is a rapidly developing knowledge base of effective teaching, both of basic as well as higher-level thinking skills (Porter & Brophy, 1988; Smith & O'Day, 1988; Walberg, 1990; Wittrock, 1986).

Further, while there is some evidence that more experienced teachers have more knowledge and skills than less experienced teachers (Carter, Cushing, Sabers, Brown, & Berliner, 1988; Lampert & Clark, 1990; Richardson, 1991), education and experience are indirect measures of knowledge and skills. In addition, after three to five years of experience, the relationship between knowledge and skills is not well documented (Murnane, 1983). At the same time, the most effective teachers, and teachers who view themselves as professionals, consider continuous development of professional expertise a primary focus (Little, 1982; McLaughlin & Yee, 1988; Rosenholtz, 1989).

In addition, an understanding is slowly emerging that while teachers can acquire some of their knowledge and skills in preservice training, they need to continue this knowledge and skill development once they begin teaching (Hawley, 1985; Rosenholtz, 1985b, 1989). Moreover, the most effective teachers highly value professional development—the continuous learning of knowledge and skills that help them be more effective in the classroom; many teachers may value opportunities for professional development as highly as or even more highly than opportunities for increased pay (McLaughlin & Yee, 1988; Rosenholtz, 1985b). Further—and contrary to popular perception—teachers support evaluation systems that focus on knowledge and skill development (McLaughlin & Pfeifer, 1988; Rosenholtz, 1985a; Wise & Darling-Hammond, 1985). The current compensation structure at best only indirectly supports these more effective and professional views of teaching. A new compensation structure could more directly emphasize and reward the continuous development of professional knowledge and skills.

In terms of organizational structure, schools generally reflect hierarchical bureaucracies with a command and control structure that flows from the superintendent to the principal to the teachers. But the most effective schools are characterized by high levels of teacher involvement in professional decision making, intense collaboration among teachers and between teachers and administrators, and discretion allocated to service providers, that is, the teachers. An education and experience salary structure that links pay and pay increases to particular jobs (for example, teacher, principal) is appropriate for a large, bureaucratically organized system but not for a system that wants to foster continuous development of professional skills through teacher collegial interaction and involvement in schoolwide management and decision making (Lawler, 1986).

Further, in terms of culture, the norms and values of traditional schools must give way to those of more effective schools if the bold national education student outcome goals are to be accomplished. Traditional values foster norms of teacher isolation and autonomy, as well as organizational stability (Johnson, 1990). But schools that are effective in producing student achievement and increasing the professional skills and knowledge of teachers are characterized by norms of collegiality, continuous improvement, professional experimentation, and teacher involvement in professional decision making (Goodlad, 1983; Lieberman, 1988; Little, 1982, 1987, 1990; McLaughlin & Yee, 1988; Rosenholtz, 1989; Johnson, 1984,

1990). In other words, strategies that stimulate professional interaction and cooperation among teachers are vastly more effective in helping to expand their professional repertoire, especially in comparison to strategies, such as traditional incentive and merit pay, that have teachers competing against one another (Conley & Bacharach, 1990; Rosenholtz & Smylie, 1984). For example, dissension among teachers and friction between teachers and administrators were the chief reasons why districts historically abandoned merit pay plans (Johnson, 1984, 1990).

Indeed, even economists have concluded that in knowledge-production industries in the private sector (similar to schools in the public sector) nearly all forms of cooperative worker involvement plans improve organizational productivity (Blinder, 1990). Consequently, a new compensation structure should reinforce development of organizational norms that focus on the continuous improvement of teachers' professional skills, student learning, and collegiality.

In summary, if a new teacher compensation structure is to reinforce core beliefs related to school effectiveness, it must

- Be linked to student outcomes
- Focus on providing teachers with knowledge and skills necessary for student learning
- Support continuous development of professional expertise, that is, the knowledge and skills needed to teach all students to think, solve problems, and communicate
- Incorporate high-involvement management techniques, including teacher participation in professional decision making
- Create norms of continuous improvement, collegiality, and teacher involvement in schoolwide issues

While the current compensation structure for teachers, which bases pay on increased education and experience, does not contravene these findings, at best it only indirectly fosters them (Bacharach, Lipsky, & Shedd, 1983, 1984). Support for the current type of teacher pay architecture has been justified largely because most strategies to change teacher compensation have included some form of individual merit or incentive pay strategies that foster teacher competition rather than collegiality (Bacharach et al., 1983; Murnane, 1981; Murnane & Cohen, 1986). In other words, most proposed strategies to pay teachers for productivity have been designed in ways that contravene research findings on how teachers and schools are effective and thus stimulate a defense of the current education and experience teacher salary schedule. The greatest strength of the present system is thus what it does not do; it does not encourage teachers to withhold information from each other or keep problems from coming to the attention of superiors (Bacharach, 1983). However, it also does not, in and of itself, promote greater teacher interaction or information exchange between teachers and administrators.

The more complex question is whether a teacher compensation structure can be designed that reinforces research findings on teacher and school effectiveness, including fostering collegiality and sharing knowledge about teaching effectiveness. If such a structure could be designed, it would enhance collegiality among teachers and between teachers and administrators and reward teachers for developing the skills likely to produce the largest improvements in students' abilities. The remainder of this chapter identifies how a new compensation architecture for paying teachers might accomplish these objectives.

Teacher Recruitment

In the early 1980s, research began to show that there was an emerging problem in the quantity and quality of individuals entering and remaining in the teaching profession (Darling-Hammond, 1984; Schlechty & Vance, 1983). Reminiscent of the 1960s, states began to enact incentives to recruit teachers into preservice preparation programs. Loan forgiveness programs were the most popular. Indeed, in 1990 a major bill was introduced in the Congress to stimulate enrollment in teacher training; its largest component was a loan forgiveness program.

In addition, states began to raise entry-level teacher salaries to make teaching look more attractive as a career option for college graduates. Nearly all states across the country debated the need to raise beginning teacher salaries, and many states enacted policies to increase entry-level pay.

Few of these policy debates, however, probed the efficacy of loan forgiveness programs as a recruitment tool; even fewer discussed an appropriate policy target for beginning teacher pay. While responding to the need to develop incentives to recruit more able individuals into teaching, these policy initiatives were not designed very effectively.

Recruitment into Preservice Training Programs

Four general strategies may serve as incentives for able individuals to enter a teacher training program and thus the teaching profession: (1) loan forgiveness programs, (2) fellowships with service payback requirements, (3) targeted work-study programs, and (4) beginning pay. This section discusses the first three strategies, and the next section analyzes beginning pay.

Loan Forgiveness Programs. Arfin (1986) reviewed the efficacy of the first three of these strategies in education, the health professions, and the military and concluded that they have very different impacts. Loan forgiveness programs, while the most popular in education, tend to be the least effective. Loan forgiveness programs are similar economically to a salary bonus when a prospective teacher begins to work. The prospective teacher must pay all college costs and sign all loan notes. The up-front commitment is quite high. Loan forgiveness begins only when the teacher leaves preservice training and begins teaching. Most programs, moreover, offer to forgive loans only at the rate of 10–15 percent annually. If the total amount of student loans is, for example, $20,000 (a reasonable amount for a college graduate), the loan forgiveness amounts to only $2,000–$3,000 a year.

Economically, the benefit is a tax-free salary supplement that must be used to repay the loan. It is not a large benefit, and it comes at the end rather than the beginning of the process. The risk is totally assumed by the prospective teacher. Indeed, the loan forgiveness program in Connecticut, begun in the mid 1980s, showed the nature of this risk. The first graduates met a declining job market. Not only could they not find teaching jobs in Connecticut after graduation but they also had to begin paying back their loans! In short, loan forgiveness programs are not very effective recruitment incentives.

Despite their modest impact, loan forgiveness programs are an acceptable mechanism for providing differential teacher pay. Florida's program, for example, provides extra pay to reduce loans for high-priority content areas. Further, salary supplements are used to reduce loans incurred not only for attending Florida universities but for attending any college or university in the country.

Fellowships with Service Payback Programs. Fellowship programs with service payback requirements function just the opposite of loan forgiveness programs and have been very successful in both the health professions and the military (for example, ROTC). First, these programs tend to be merit- and not need-based, that is, they are only offered to bright and able individuals. Second, the government incurs the full cost of college (or even graduate training). Often, a small stipend is included in the fellowship. These large, up-front awards are provided even to individuals who attend more costly private colleges and universities. Third, recipients are required to serve in the profession for a number of years (usually three to five). Fourth, the programs also require more than a one-to-one payback if the individual decides not to enter the profession; indeed, most health services programs require a three-to-one dollar payback for not providing the agreed-upon services. Arfin (1986) found that individuals respond to these large, initial economic incentives and that such programs have been quite effective in recruiting able individuals into the military and health professions, especially in rural areas.

For education, Arfin (1986) suggested that states (or the federal government) could provide such fellowships for 10 percent of the new teachers needed each year, making the awards available only to the top 25 percent of eligible students. Based on results from recruitment into the health and military professions, he suggested that such a program would be highly effective in attracting many of the best and brightest into education.

Work-Study Programs. A third strategy is sponsored employment or targeted work-study. Arfin (1986) showed that work-based student aid has been effective, especially for low-income students if the work does not exceed sixteen hours per week. He suggested that work-study regulations could be modified by stipulating that the work be performed in local districts as a teacher aide. This strategy would especially help low-income students pay for their college education and gain experience in education by working in paraprofessional teaching roles.

In short, the most effective incentives for recruiting individuals into teacher training and thus into beginning teaching roles are:

- Fellowship programs for able individuals with a three-to-five-year teaching requirement after training. States or the federal government would pay the college costs. Individuals who did not complete the teaching requirement would be required to pay back college costs at least on a dollar-for-dollar basis.
- Targeted work-study. Individuals eligible for work-study and enrolled in a teaching program would be given work-study opportunities in various paraprofessional roles in schools.
- Loan forgiveness programs (a distant third option). The effectiveness of these programs would be enhanced if the level of loan forgiven were substantially increased, for example, to above $5,000 a year.

Recruitment into Teaching: Beginning Salaries

Beginning teacher salaries are also powerful in recruiting individuals into the profession. Beginning teacher salaries make a difference. Ferris and Winkler (1986), Jacobson (1988a),

Hanushek (1989), and Richards (1988) found significant teacher response to the economic incentives of higher beginning salaries. Ferris and Winkler (1986) confirmed, on the recruitment side, that a 10 percent increase in teacher salaries produced a 21 percent increase in female and a 36 percent increase in male entrants into teaching; on the retention side, a 10 percent increase in salaries produced a 6 percent decrease in female and a 24 percent decrease in male attrition rates. Jacobson (1988a) found during a ten-year period in New York that districts that increased their relative beginning salaries were able to recruit more able teachers (that is, with greater education and experience) into their districts. Finally, Bruno (1981) found that salary bonuses for teaching in racially isolated urban schools were particularly effective for young and inexperienced teachers.

In short, beginning teacher salaries can affect both the quantity and quality of individuals entering the teaching profession. The higher the salaries, the greater the number of able individuals encouraged to become teachers. Thus, state policies to raise beginning teacher salaries seem to be on the mark.

The substantive policy issue, however, is the benchmark for beginning teacher salaries. At the minimum, we suggest that beginning teacher salaries should be set at the average beginning teacher salary for individuals with a liberal arts degree. Nearly all teacher reform reports (Carnegie Forum on Education and the Economy, 1986; Holmes Group, 1986) and scholars researching teacher professionalism issues (Wise & Darling-Hammond, 1987) recommend that teachers have a liberal arts education in addition to professional training. Teachers need to be broadly trained as well as deeply trained in the content they will teach (Smith & O'Day, 1988); a liberal arts education provides substantial breadth and depth in subject matter coverage.

A liberal arts degree is appropriate as a minimum, moreover, because the major education reform issues are at the elementary level, where advanced specialized knowledge is less critical. Indeed, many reform proposals call for interdisciplinary approaches, for example, mathematics/science, history/language arts, and writing across the curriculum (Carnegie Task Force, 1989). Further, teaching mathematics and science in elementary and middle schools requires less knowledge of advanced mathematical analysis or advanced physics; what is needed is a deep understanding of mathematical and scientific principles, how students learn those principles, and how teaching can aid students in learning those principles. In short, the preferred profile of a prospective teacher is someone broadly trained in the liberal arts with a deep understanding of either mathematical or scientific principles or the humanities.

The overall recruitment pool for teachers, however, includes all college graduates with bachelor's degrees. Consequently, the policy target for beginning teacher salaries arguably could be the average salary for occupations requiring comparable levels of education and training. But in order to recruit technically prepared individuals into teaching—those who major in mathematics, science, or computer science—or to recruit liberal arts graduates who could pursue more lucrative graduate professional degrees, the beginning salary target should be higher. If the target were the average beginning salary of all college graduates, the teaching profession would be even more competitive at the recruitment stage.

Table 2.2 indicates the anticipated average beginning salaries by job categories for 1990. The data show that, nationwide, average beginning teacher salaries were above beginning salaries for liberal arts graduates but below beginning salaries for most other college graduates. Nationwide, then, the minimum beginning teacher salary target—equality with beginning salaries for liberal arts graduates—is being met. But the target level needs to be increased if education is to be competitive in recruiting all individuals who graduate from college.

Of course, teachers are not recruited nationally; they generally operate in state and local labor markets. Table 2.3 presents data on average beginning teacher salaries by state and compares these figures to the average salaries of liberal arts graduates. Column 1 provides an index of the cost-of-living differences across the states. It is normed at 1.00 at the national average cost of living. These indices are used to adjust each state's average beginning teacher salary (column 2) to a nationwide comparable figure (column 3). This nationwide compara-

Table 2.2. Expected Average Beginning Salaries by Job Categories: 1990.

Bachelor's Degree	Beginning Salary
Chemical engineering	$33,380
Mechanical engineering	32,256
Electrical engineering	32,107
Computer science	31,389
Industrial engineering	30,557
Physics	28,777
Civil engineering	27,707
Nursing	27,358
Accounting	27,051
Chemistry	25,938
Mathematics	24,968
Financial administration	24,359
Marketing/sales	24,100
Geology	24,080
Agriculture	22,802
General business administration	21,845
Social science	21,310
Personnel administration	21,033
Telecommunications	20,880
Communications	20,735
Education	**20,650**
Hotel/restaurant management	20,553
Liberal arts	**20,244**
Advertising	19,662
Retailing	18,909
Natural resources	18,840
Journalism	18,255
Human ecology/home economics	18,157

Source: Data from "Dimensions," 1990.

ble figure is then compared to the national average beginning salary for a liberal arts major (column 4) Ratios at or above 1.00 indicate that the state's average beginning teacher salary exceeds that of a liberal arts major; ratios below 1.00 indicate that the state's average beginning teacher salary is lower than that of a liberal arts major.

The results are striking. Twenty-five states already meet or exceed the minimum beginning teacher salary target. Indeed, the states that meet or exceed this policy target enroll 70 percent of the nation's public school children. Seven of the eight largest

Table 2.3. Beginning Teacher Salaries by State and Comparisons
to Beginning Liberal Arts Degree (B.A.) Salaries.

State	(1) Cost-of- Living Index	(2) 1989–90 Average Beginning Salary	(3) 1989–90 Adjusted Beginning Salary	(4) Ratio of (3) to Average Beginning Liberal Arts (B.A.) Salary
Alabama	.914	$19,364	$21,186	1.05
Alaska	1.300	29,763	22,895	1.13
Arizona	.978	21,100	21,575	1.07
Arkansas	.884	16,673	18,861	0.93
California	1.074	22,780	21,210	1.05
Colorado	.980	19,234	19,627	0.97
Connecticut	1.273	23,783	18,683	0.92
Delaware	1.062	20,123	18,948	0.94
D.C.	1.284	22,983	17,900	0.88
Florida	.962	21,586	22,439	1.11
Georgia	.918	18,892	20,580	1.02
Hawaii	1.270	23,281	18,410	0.91
Idaho	.918	16,214	17,662	0.87
Illinois	.968	19,667	20,317	1.00
Indiana	.921	19,847	21,549	1.06
Iowa	.915	19,145	20,923	1.03
Kansas	.911	19,348	21,238	1.05
Kentucky	.891	17,530	19,675	0.97
Louisiana	.913	15,544	17,025	0.84
Maine	.899	16,599	18,464	0.91
Maryland	1.115	22,172	19,885	0.98
Massachusetts	1.205	20,295	16,842	0.83
Michigan	.937	21,575	23,026	1.14
Minnesota	.932	21,157	22,701	1.12
Mississippi	.891	18,750	21,044	1.04
Missouri	.916	19,851	21,671	1.07
Montana	.913	17,750	19,441	0.96
Nebraska	.921	17,690	19,207	0.95
Nevada	.954	20,000	20,964	1.04
New Hampshire	1.059	19,126	18,060	0.89
New Jersey	1.293	22,500	17,401	0.86
New Mexico	.923	18,795	20,363	1.00
New York	1.160	25,000	21,552	1.06
North Carolina	.912	19,140	20,987	1.04
North Dakota	.895	15,882	17,745	0.88
Ohio	.947	17,721	18,713	0.92
Oklahoma	.898	16,900	18,820	0.93
Oregon	.944	19,418	20,570	1.02
Pennsylvania	1.039	21,350	20,549	1.02
Rhode Island	1.105	19,635	17,769	0.88

Table 2.3. Beginning Teacher Salaries by State and Comparisons
to Beginning Liberal Arts Degree (B.A.) Salaries, Cont'd.

State	(1) Cost-of-Living Index	(2) 1989–90 Average Beginning Salary	(3) 1989–90 Adjusted Beginning Salary	(4) Ratio of (3) to Average Beginning Liberal Arts (B.A.) Salary
South Carolina	.901	19,039	21,131	1.04
South Dakota	.891	15,820	17,755	0.88
Tennessee	.903	19,800	21,927	1.08
Texas	.912	20,000	21,930	1.08
Utah	.902	16,040	17,783	0.88
Vermont	.960	17,970	18,719	0.92
Virginia	.967	21,217	21,941	1.08
Washington	.976	18,965	19,431	0.96
West Virginia	.896	15,778	17,609	0.87
Wisconsin	.931	20,000	21,482	1.06
Wyoming	.917	19,200	20,938	1.03

Source: Data from American Federation of Teachers, 1990, and authors' calculations.

states — California, Florida, Illinois, Michigan, New York, Pennsylvania, and Texas — which enroll 43 percent of the nation's students, have an index at or higher than 1.00, essentially meeting the minimum policy target. In short, the minimum beginning teacher salary targets have already been met in states that enroll the majority of students.

But few states have set a policy target for beginning teacher pay. Indeed, the policy conversation is still that teacher pay, including beginning teacher pay, is too low. The data in Table 2.3 indicate that if the policy target for beginning teacher pay were the beginning salary for liberal arts graduates, most states should consciously begin to shift the teacher compensation discussion to issues beyond beginning pay and to allocate future inflation-adjusted salary increases to those teachers already in the system in order to boost the retentive impact of teacher compensation.

The policy points of this section are the following:

1. States should have a policy target, a benchmark, for beginning teacher salaries; most states do not.
2. The minimum benchmark—the average beginning salary for liberal arts graduates—has been exceeded nationally, but beginning teacher salaries are still below those of all college graduates.

Base Pay for Teachers

This section discusses issues related to base pay, the bulk of compensation teachers or any workers receive. The key issue is whether to pay for the job or to pay for the individual, that is, to pay for knowledge and skills.

Paying for the Job

Most private-sector organizations as well as school systems pay for the job. Organizations identify jobs that need to be performed, for example, teacher, teacher aide, assistant principal, principal, staff developer, curriculum development specialist, science coordinator, assistant superintendent, and superintendent. A job description that specifies in some detail what the person in that job is supposed to do is written for each job. Companies and school systems then have elaborate job evaluation systems that grade or rank jobs, primarily through an internal comparison of the job tasks, and provide a salary range generally linked to some external market. Pay, therefore, is determined by the job and the predetermined salary range for the job.

Educators and individuals in most corporations are familiar with this approach to compensation. Increases in annual pay are generally linked to experience or seniority; the longer one is in the job, the higher is the salary. In education, salary increments are provided for additional education and training, as well. This type of compensation structure produces comparisons of job tasks across organizational subunits within a large organization, provides pay equity across those units, and fosters central control. According to Lawler (1990), such an approach to compensation is appropriate for large organizations in stable environments with one business, such as the old AT&T Corporation.

It is less effective for small organizations in rapidly changing environments and knowledge-production organizations, including elementary schools, secondary schools, colleges, and universities. In fact, Lawler (1990) argues that the rapidly changing nature of the economy makes this approach to compensation appropriate for fewer and fewer organizations. Synthesizing the findings from large numbers of studies addressing organizational needs in a rapidly changing economic environment, Lawler lists several disadvantages of this approach to compensation:

- It promotes bureaucratic and hierarchical approaches to management. It reinforces hierarchy, which is the last thing needed in a knowledge-production organization (see also Von Glinow & Mohrman, 1989).
- It implicitly specifies what not to do and so encourages individuals "to do things right" rather than "to do the right things."
- It de-emphasizes paying people for the skills they have and the jobs they can do; the former is problematic for knowledge-production organizations, and the latter is problematic for organizations with rapidly changing technologies.
- It fosters an internal equity focus rather than an external market or outcomes focus.
- It makes organizational change more difficult because change requires altering and regrading all jobs.
- It fails to encourage continuous skill development, technological specialization (for example, grade leaders, mathematics/science lead teachers, staff development, and so on in education), and horizontal career changes, all of which are important ingredients of successful and productive knowledge industries.
- It makes promotion (out of the classroom and into administration in education) too important because higher pay comes primarily with promotion. Moreover, since the trend

in the private sector is to reduce management layers in organizations, it makes promotion increasingly difficult and available to very few individuals.

These disadvantages are clearly applicable to schools as one particular type of knowledge organization.

Not only have school systems traditionally paid for the job but newer career ladder programs, which became popular in the mid 1980s, also advocate such an approach. Career ladder programs, ushered in by the Carnegie Forum on Education and the Economy (1986) and the Holmes Group (1986), introduced the notion of linking teacher compensation to a differentiated profession. Perhaps the best illustration is the Holmes Group's endorsement of the concept of differentiated staffing as a method to provide a "staged career that would make and reward formal distinctions about responsibilities and degrees of autonomy." Differentiated staffing would "improve the quality, engagement, and commitment of the teaching force" (Sedlak, 1987, p. 7).

The report of the Holmes Group (1986) proposed three levels of teachers: instructors, professional teachers, and career professionals. As a teacher advanced in the system, he or she would decrease the amount of classroom teaching performed and assume responsibility for such new functions as curriculum development, preparation of instructional materials, and conducting research. Career ladder experiments in many states were developed essentially along the lines outlined in the Holmes report.

Career ladder programs were often formulated, at least initially, with the specific intention of developing teachers' professional skills and knowledge. Many career ladders, however, actually created a hierarchical ordering of different job tasks, ranking and paying them according to their supposed level of professional responsibility. Thus, the systems became what Lawler (1990) suggested is clearly inappropriate for knowledge organizations: a pay structure based on a comparison of job tasks. Indeed, teachers were urged to assume new tasks in order to increase their income, for example, develop curriculum, join committees, or mentor beginning teachers. The activities themselves, rather than the teacher's skill development, were rewarded.

In education, the idea of paying teachers for assuming new tasks and responsibilities is not new (Freiberg, 1985). In the 1950s, designers of differentiated staffing plans attempted to circumvent teacher movement out of the classroom (and into administration) by assigning tasks to individual teachers that would restructure their relationships to administration (Bacharach et al., 1983). Differentiated staffing was thus a method of integrating teaching and administrative functions within upper-level positions, for example, "evaluation specialist, curriculum developer and diagnostician of learning difficulties" (Cooper, n.d., p. 50). Current career ladders have been developed along these same basic lines.

However, in paying teachers for new sets of tasks, such systems often perpetuated the situations they were attempting to correct; the most qualified teachers became marginally tied to the classroom, and the greater portion of their time was consumed with administrative work (Bacharach et al., 1983). Career ladders that pay teachers for tasks may increase teacher attrition in the classroom by downgrading the classroom function, by encouraging teachers who want to achieve full salary to assume tasks unrelated to the basic teaching function, and by requiring that significant percentages of time be spent outside of the classroom. In addition, teachers must submit a great deal of paperwork documenting their tasks, making the system administratively cumbersome for teachers and principals alike (Watson, Poda, & Miller, 1987; Tennessee Education Association, 1988).

Moreover, some career ladders demote teachers to a lower level of the system if they fail to perform the tasks designated at that step (Bacharach, Conley, & Shedd, 1986). Such systems restrict administrators from assigning tasks to certain teachers and teachers from assuming tasks in which they may be interested but which are not designated at their level. As Lawler (1990) suggests, the system promotes an inflexible lockstep division of responsibilities.

The research literature on teacher career development provides some additional insights regarding the deficiencies of a system that links pay to the job or to specific tasks, usually those performed outside of the classroom. McLaughlin and Yee (1988) found that one-third of the teachers they interviewed planned to apply for expanded roles at some point in their careers. However, although teachers voiced a desire to assume larger organizational responsibilities, they went on to discuss how those responsibilities were closely grounded in improving their own classroom effectiveness (see also Yee, 1986). A system that moves teachers out of the classroom into quasi-administrative roles or diminishes the status of regular classroom teaching would seem to be inconsistent with these teacher perspectives.

Paying for Knowledge and Skills

Pay-for-knowledge plans compensate employees for the job-related skills and knowledge they have, rather than just for the activities or tasks that they perform (Tosi & Tosi, 1986). Salary increases are awarded in recognition of a growing repertoire of skills and knowledge rather than for performing a job. Paying the person, that is, paying for what individuals know and can do, helps organizations actively manage the knowledge and skill acquisition process by motivating and then rewarding individuals for learning specific knowledge and skills.

This approach differs significantly from paying teachers for tasks. To take an analogy, one would expect that a promotion from associate to partner in a law firm (with a subsequent increase in pay) would not happen simply because certain tasks have been done. The promotion and additional pay would instead be in recognition of growing competence in one's legal practice. Further, since partners charge more per hour, client willingness to pay is due, in part, to receiving a higher level or quality of legal service.

A pay-for-knowledge system is also different from a pay-for-the-job system because it takes into account how the professional develops his or her skills over time. For example,

Schlechty (1989) compared two career ladder plans: a pay-for-performance plan in Tennessee and a career development (pay-for-knowledge) plan in Charlotte-Mecklenberg, North Carolina. The Tennessee plan failed to establish a relationship between career levels and teachers' stages of professional development; instead, career levels designated differences in performance (that is, teachers at the top of the system scored higher on a variety of performance measures than teachers at the bottom). The Charlotte-Mecklenberg plan related career levels to professional development, clarified expectations for the growth and development of (pretenured) teachers, and committed school and district resources to support such development.

In a skill-based pay system, individuals are paid for the number, kind, and depth of knowledge and skills they develop and use. To use such a pay system, organizations must:

- Specify the tasks that need to be performed
- Identify the knowledge and skills needed to perform those tasks
- Devise a set of measures and assessments to determine whether an individual has learned and can use the skills
- Price the skill or specify the pay increment that will be provided for each set of knowledge and skills identified
- Tell all individuals which knowledge and skills the organization would like them to learn and be able to use

The base compensation structure comprises an entry-level wage and pay increments. Pay increments are provided for demonstrated performance of knowledge and skills that are key to accomplishing organizational tasks and meeting organizational goals. New sets of skills can either be horizontal (skills needed to work up and down a production line in manufacturing or skills needed to teach in the primary, upper elementary, or middle school level in education) or skills that lead to specialties that allow for the development of technological ladders. For example, universities and corporate law departments have had technical ladder programs for decades. Schools could, for example, provide for specialties in mathematics/science and humanities/social studies.

Knowledge- and skill-based pay is a rapidly emerging trend in the private sector. While most private-sector research on knowledge-based pay has been conducted in manufacturing settings (Gupta, Schweizer, & Jenkins, 1987), the approach seems well suited to professional settings because it emphasizes the continuous upgrading of professionals' skills and knowledge and has been shown to be effective in knowledge industries (Lawler, 1990). It is used in some degree by 40 percent of large corporations (Lawler, Ledford, & Mohrman, 1989) and used frequently by high-involvement organizations (Lawler, 1986). During the past twenty years, skill-based pay systems have been installed in several high-involvement manufacturing plants (Lawler, 1986), and productivity has usually improved. It has been used in universities for decades. Skill-based pay is strongly recommended for industries involved with rapidly changing technology and for knowledge industries (Lawler, 1990), which include elementary and secondary schools.

There are many advantages to skill-based compensation systems (Lawler, 1990). Such systems are:

- Flexible in using individuals to perform multiple tasks
- Compatible with organizations whose success depends on the knowledge and skills of its workers (increasingly true for all American corporations, as well as for schools)
- Supportive of an external- or an organizational-outcomes focus, as the skills rewarded can be aligned with the tasks needed to accomplish organizational goals
- Supportive of career enhancement within a job category, rather than promotion

Lawler concluded that skill-based pay systems provide several important subsidiary benefits, including:

- Development of a strong tradition for inservice training
- Creation of a norm of personal growth
- Encouragement for employees to try new things

Futrell (1986), then president of the nation's largest teacher union, strongly endorsed the idea of career-development plans that link salary increases to growing teacher expertise, that is, to improving such skills as mastery of subject matter and ability to manage a classroom. Such a system would assess each teacher's growth relative to set standards rather than to the performance of other teachers. Accordingly, standards would be criterion-rather than norm-referenced (see Freiberg, 1985). Thus, knowledge- and skills-based pay systems would also avoid a quota on organizational rewards (Lawler, 1990).

In short, knowledge-based pay for teachers appears to have several advantages. It is compatible with a national goal of assisting teachers to develop the skills and knowledge necessary to maximize student learning, thinking, and problem solving. Since there seems to be a pattern to the way teachers go about acquiring and building on their knowledge and skills (Burden, 1982), organizational rewards could be linked to these developmental stages. Further, knowledge-based pay could help foster norms of collegiality and continuous improvement, which characterize the most effective schools and the type of work environment that teachers prefer (Conley & Cooper, 1991; Johnson, 1984, 1990).

Key Knowledge and Skills Rewarded. While a knowledge-based pay system should be tailored to a district's own needs, the following four categories might be considered generally by districts planning to implement such a structure. The specific pay increment for each knowledge and skill rewarded should be market sensitive, that is, reflective of the supply and demand for the skill.

Content knowledge. Elementary, middle, and high school teachers teach content. Knowing well the content they teach is a prerequisite for being able to help students think and problem solve in the content domains (Smith & O'Day, 1988).

Knowledge of how students learn. While this is different from being able to *use* such knowledge to teach students effectively, it nevertheless is a separate and identifiable area of knowledge.

Knowledge of pedagogy. This is knowledge of instructional

strategies that are effective with different types of students and, for elementary teachers, different content areas. Again, while this is different from being able to use such knowledge to teach students effectively, it is a separate and identifiable knowledge domain.

Effective use of pedagogical skills, including classroom management. This entails assimilation of the first three sets of knowledge into action. While there has been disagreement in the past about how to assess proficiency in use of these skills, there is rapidly advancing knowledge that will make this feasible in the near future. To implement such a developmental approach requires linking a teacher's demonstration of classroom skills with knowledge areas, a major change in performance appraisal (Conley & Bacharach, 1990) and teacher evaluation (McLaughlin & Pfeifer, 1988; Wise & Darling-Hammond, 1985). One notion suggested by Bacharach, Conley, and Shedd (1990) would differentiate each knowledge base into three progressive sets of skills: application, variety/integration, and leadership. Briefly, in terms of pedagogical knowledge, a beginning teacher would first show the ability to apply such knowledge by conducting one type of instructional strategy in the classroom (for example, establishing lesson motivation). The second, more advanced skill for a new teacher would be to demonstrate a variety of ways of applying the instructional strategy and also to integrate the strategy with other classroom objectives. A third, more advanced skill would be to share innovations in instructional strategies with other teachers in the school (leadership).

Indicators of professional skills other than direct classroom observation include the following:

Evidence of board certification. Rewards should accrue for becoming board certified by the National Board for Professional Teaching Standards, the National Association of Social Studies Teachers, or any other professional group that seeks to identify outstanding experienced teachers.

Portfolios/dossiers. As the country changes its student assessment strategies to performance-based systems, teachers increasingly will be required to provide examples of student performance on a variety of tasks. This entails yet an additional arena of complex skills.

Schoolwide leadership skills. These are skills needed to participate effectively in schoolwide education improvement activities. Although mentoring new and experienced teachers and providing coaching and staff development assistance to teachers represent important avenues for teachers' skill growth, a number of other mechanisms exist.

New Evaluation Emphases. It seems obvious that a compensation system that attempts to reward teachers for professional skills and expertise should be accompanied by a new type of teacher assessment and evaluation system to help develop and assess those qualities. Indeed, a compensation system is only as good as the assessment system that supports it. Although an extensive treatment of teacher assessment is beyond the scope of this chapter, it is discussed by one of the authors elsewhere (Bacharach et al., 1990). Two considerations concerning the linkage between a compensation system and its supporting assessment system are critical.

First, when rewards are linked to what teachers know and can do, evaluators are often pressured to generate measures of performance that are (1) broad and general and (2) strictly objective in nature. As a result, teacher assessments begin to reflect the most superficial aspects of performance. Evaluation criteria are needed that reflect the actual nature of teachers' professional skill and expertise.

In examining the actual nature of teacher expertise, numerous researchers suggest that the most capable teachers conduct complex problem solving and decision making in response to varied, unpredictable, and changing classroom circumstances (Buchman, 1987; Carter, 1991; Feiman-Nemser & Buchman, 1985; Gitlin, 1990; Griffin, 1985; Lampert & Clark, 1990). Teachers, for example, constantly engage students in the subject matter and meet the counseling needs of individual students while in the midst of managing a highly interactive classroom. Evaluations that assess teachers' judgment and problem-solving capacities would emphasize the complex and uncertain nature of classroom situations. They would *not* reflect the most easily implemented or assessed aspects of teaching (Wise & Darling-Hammond, 1985).

Second, in a system that links teacher evaluation to compensation, evaluators may conduct short-term or one-shot assessments in order to ensure that evaluations are as uniform as possible. In this context, the formal procedural evaluation receives a great deal of emphasis (Rosenholtz, 1985a). The time period *between* evaluations receives little emphasis; often few, if any, resources are allocated to help teachers correct identified weaknesses and build upon noted strengths. This system not only devotes sparse attention to the acquisition of expertise but brings a heavily bureaucratic and judgmental character to evaluations. This discourages teacher participation in the evaluation process and genuine cooperation between teachers and evaluators. For example, in one school, a teacher would loan his or her difficult students to another teacher on evaluation day. Thus, teachers presented a facade that the classroom was as bureaucratic and predictable as evaluators expected it to be.

A supportive evaluation system for a knowledge-based pay system would place heavy emphasis on the period *in between* summative evaluations by scheduling formative, diagnostic evaluations. That is, the current weight given to summative versus formative evaluation would actually be reversed, with more attention to formative, expertise-building assistance among peers and between teachers and supervisors.

Further, while most evaluation systems tend to place the onus for upgrading performance solely on the teacher (see Schlechty, 1989), a knowledge-based pay system would assign districts and schools a strong role in assisting teachers' skill development. A system that rewards the accumulation of professional skills and knowledge over a period of time would be concerned with providing the type of environment in which this development could take place (Hawley, 1985). In such systems, evaluations by school and district officials would not only identify teachers' respective strengths and weaknesses but also pinpoint school and district resources necessary to assist teachers to address weaknesses and capitalize on strengths.

Teachers' Career Development. A knowledge- and skills-based pay system would also align compensation with district expectations for teachers' career development. Burden (1982), for example, suggested that teachers who have taught for several years become more child-centered in their orientation and are able to experiment freely (see also Richardson, 1991). Similarly, Bacharach et al. (1986, 1987) suggested that as teachers progress in their careers they address different developmental goals. First, teachers concentrate on applying basic knowledge about instruction, classroom management, and student counseling in classrooms. Then, they build on this knowledge by acquiring a greater variety of methods for dealing with diverse classroom situations and for integrating different goals. For example, they become more adept at changing plans midstream in classroom instruction based upon their ongoing evaluation of students' needs and abilities. Finally, teachers concentrate on acquiring leadership skills and knowledge as they progress beyond their individual classrooms to making contributions to the school as a whole. Many districts lack specific expectations concerning teachers' career development despite literature suggesting that a definite pattern exists to the way teachers develop their skills over time (Burden, 1982).

A compensation system focused on improving professional skills and expertise should also concentrate on upgrading the professional induction process (and clarifying expectations for the subsequent progression of teachers' skills and knowledge). The career-development literature suggests that professional induction is most successful when teachers participate in an ongoing and substantive dialogue with teachers and supervisors in the school; such a dialogue is particularly helpful to beginning teachers (McLaughlin & Yee, 1988). A peer team of two to three teachers might be assigned to assist each beginning teacher (Conley & Bacharach, 1990). This peer team could provide formative assistance to the beginning teacher; it might also advocate the summative decision to retain a teacher (or to grant a teacher tenure). Such a structure would define district expectations for the skill development of beginning teachers as well as expand the role of experienced teachers in such development.

Pay-for-Performance

The major task for performance-based pay is to tie pay to performance. The major failing with most strategies—in the private sector as well as in education—is that this linkage has not been well developed. This section first discusses the problems with incentive and merit pay, individually based pay-for-performance strategies that have been tried unsuccessfully in the private sector and in schools, and then discusses a new approach to pay-for-performance that is linked to organizational performance. This new approach has been quite successful in the private sector and is increasingly being tried in public education.

Incentive Pay

Incentive pay is a system of compensation in which the individual is paid a predetermined sum for each unit produced. Summarizing from several research studies, Lawler (1990) identified several problems with this compensation structure:

- It encourages individuals to beat the system by establishing low norms for productivity so that most individuals can meet and surpass expectations.
- It divides the organization into workers who can make more by being more productive and workers such as support and secretarial workers who cannot. It thus produces an interworker division.
- It is more difficult to use with a highly educated workforce, which increasingly is the case in this country.
- It causes increasing numbers of problems in our employee-

rights–oriented society, with differential awards often leading to numerous and costly employee grievances.

Lawler (1990) concludes that incentive pay is appropriate
only where the work (1) is repetitive, (2) can be paced by the
worker, (3) is stable and simple, and (4) has easily measured
results. According to Lawler, most of this type of work already
has left the United States for developing countries with lower
workforce wage scales and education levels. Incentive pay is not
appropriate for knowledge work, high-technology work, high-
involvement management approaches, and work that requires
teamwork to be effective — characteristics also of the most effective elementary and secondary schools. As such, Lawler concludes that it is not a real option for the bulk of American
industries; by implication, he rejects it for schools as well.

Merit Pay

The more popular version of pay-for-performance in both corporations and the public schools has been merit pay. Merit pay is
a compensation system that links the salaries of employees to
evaluations of their performance. The idea is to pay the highest
performers the most money. To implement a merit pay plan
requires an aggressive individual performance appraisal system
that identifies each individual's contribution and pays those who
contribute more a higher salary. Merit pay has not been implemented well in either the private or public sectors. The Achilles'
heel of most merit plans has been their inability to effectively
evaluate performance and, thus, to produce a system in which
the high performers earn more in total compensation.

Lawler (1990) notes several problems with implementation of private-sector merit pay plans:

- The major flaw is the lack of credible, comprehensive measures of performance. Without such measures, the link between pay and performance cannot be made. The reasons
  for the lack of such measures in the private sector have been
  lack of managerial skill in developing and implementing

such measures; worker perceptions that management judgments on individual performance are invalid, unfair, and
discriminatory; and the fact that many jobs require teamwork to accomplish tasks, which makes it hard to single out
individual performance.

- Merit pay is usually only a small part of total compensation.
- Merit pay is usually rolled into an individual's base pay, so
  people who stay in the organization are paid primarily for
  past, not current, performance.
- Fixed pay ranges, which are part of job-based pay systems,
  usually force the best performers to top out on the pay
  schedule.
- Managers rarely recommend widely different pay increase
  differentials.

While some of these obstacles could be overcome with
better-designed merit pay structures, Lawler (1990) identifies
several points that argue against the use of merit pay structures:

- In complex organizations, which are increasingly the norm,
  it is difficult to identify individual performance.
- New high-involvement management structures, including
  the most effective schools, require highly interdependent
  teams, making it not only difficult but also counterproductive to separate out individual performance.
- Performance appraisal is counterproductive for organizations that attempt to improve quality (see also Deming,
  1987; Mohrman, 1989).

In short, Lawler concludes that merit pay is not a feasible option
for compensation in most private-sector organizations.

Merit pay has also been less than successful in public
education. Although many current merit pay proponents present it as a new concept, the idea actually dates to the early
1900s. However, most of the early merit pay plans did not last,
and another wave of interest in the 1960s was short-lived
(Murnane & Cohen, 1986). Despite this history of failure, merit
pay plans emerged in the early 1980s as one of the most popular
reforms. Although proposals in many states were not actually

implemented, merit pay often became embedded in other compensation systems, particularly career ladders (Schlechty, 1989).

A major problem with merit pay is that it is difficult and costly to administer. In Murnane and Cohen's (1986) field study of districts implementing merit pay prior to 1978, principals reported the administration of the merit pay program to be burdensome and time-consuming. Higher levels of administration exerted pressure on principals to give some teachers low ratings at the same time individual teachers pressured principals to justify those ratings (that is, to justify them relative to previous ratings or to other teachers). In any organization, when salary increases are linked to the performance appraisal system, employees are likely to closely scrutinize evaluation criteria, methods, and results (Porter, Lawler, & Hackman, 1975).

Murnane and Cohen's (1986) observations are consistent with this research. In addition, the Educational Research Service (1979) found that in the 1960s teacher dissension and problems in administration were the primary reasons districts abandoned such plans, just as Lawler (1990) found for most private-sector merit pay plans. More recently, observers (Popkewitz & Lind, 1989; Timar & Kirp, 1987) have criticized merit pay plans for promoting a bureaucratic and legalistic culture in schools when what is needed are more organic and flexible modes of management.

In sum, merit pay programs appear costly and difficult to administer. They create evaluation problems (or exacerbate existing ones) by giving evaluators incentives to provide broad judgments rather than helpful, diagnostic feedback to teachers. They cause dissension not only between teachers and administrators but among teachers themselves. Underlying much of the dissension is the fact that merit pay systems in education force teachers to compete for a fixed allocation of money; teachers are not, as in other occupations, such as sales, able to generate additional resources for the organization to finance their own pay increments.

Pay for Organizational Performance

While Lawler (1990) suggests that pay for individual performance is not feasible for most private-sector companies, he

argues that pay for organizational, division, and unit performance are all possible for most corporations. Lawler's reasoning
also applies in the main to education. Pay for organizational
performance, he suggests, should be provided in the form of
annual bonuses and not rolled into base pay. Thus, he argues
that bonus payments for organizational performance should be
included in compensation structures that seek to reinforce the
attainment of organizational goals.

Lawler concludes from research that bonus payments for
organizational performance:

- Improve employee motivation
- Help build a culture in which the individual cares about and
  is committed to organizational goals
- Help adjust labor costs to company profits for profit-making
  organizations

Three types of pay for organizational performance systems have been tried: gainsharing, profit sharing, and employee
ownership. All usually include some form of worker participation. Indeed, all types and forms of worker participation have
been connected to improvements in the productivity of the
company, organization, or division (Blinder, 1990).

School-Based Performance Systems. Employee ownership
and traditional profit sharing are not possible in public education. However, a customized version of profit sharing would be
possible. While the primary organizational goal in the private
sector is profits, the primary organizational goal in public education is student achievement. Other goals are also possible,
including good student attendance rates, high school graduation rates, postsecondary attendance rates, and parent and community satisfaction. These could be added to the above discussion. Nevertheless, student performance is one of the most
important education goals. Indeed, the nation's education goals
include having all students master complex thinking in reading,
language arts, history, geography, mathematics, and science and
having the United States rank first in the world in mathematics

and science. The design of a performance system would need to ensure that achievement gains were made across all levels of achievement, the bottom as well as the top. Gains by the lowest-achieving students could be rewarded more than gains by students in the top half; gains for students not proficient in English could be more highly rewarded to ensure that such a system had a student equity aspect to it.

A system could be devised to provide annual bonuses to staffs in schools that produce improvements in student achievement. While there are several design issues associated with school-based incentive programs (see Chapter Five), the key issue is that this component of teacher compensation is the analogue to profit sharing in the private sector, which has been shown across several types of private-sector organizations to improve productivity. Further, research has shown that teachers can respond positively to economic incentives (Jacobson, 1988b).

Albert Shanker (1990), president of the American Federation of Teachers, recently proposed a school-based incentive program, distinct from incentive pay, as a major force to restructure and improve America's schools. Shanker's proposal called for a voluntary, nationwide, multiyear school competition. Winners would be 10 percent of participating schools. He suggested using $500 million from the 1990 President Bush merit-school plan. That amount would be invested for five years. If all schools in the nation participated, the bonus would have yielded $15,000 for each staff in each winning school; if only half the schools in the nation participated, the bonus would have been $30,000. He claimed that such a school-based incentive program would "make the school staff into a team bent on achieving the goal of increasing student learning" (Shanker, 1990, p. 355).

South Carolina had individual-based teacher and principal bonuses in place for seven years that provided bonuses of between $2,000 and $3,000 for teachers and $2,000 and $5,000 for principals. The bonus system was criticized for pitting teachers against teachers. In 1991, the legislature consolidated the programs into one school-based program to provide bonuses for all faculty and administrators in schools showing exceptional improvement.

Gainsharing. Gainsharing combines a bonus plan with participative management. It typically uses measures of controllable costs or units of output, not profits, and is usually implemented at a subsystem level such as a plant or division. Gainsharing plans usually establish a base period when controllable costs (which include labor costs) and units of production are measured. When performance improves, that is, when unit costs are reduced or when more units are produced, the employees in the unit share in the gain.

In education the subunit would be a school, possibly a department in a secondary school, or a house within a restructured middle or high school. In schools, more units of production would mean improvements in student achievement; unlike the private sector, where more units of production produce a larger revenue stream, such improvements in the schools would not produce a larger revenue stream. However, the unit cost reduction could be incorporated into a gainsharing program for public schools. If teachers in a school could design approaches that reduced costs while maintaining or improving student performance, a gainsharing program could then have them share in the costs reduced. If increased student performance also occurred, teachers would benefit from the school bonus based on student performance improvements.

Gainsharing programs, according to Lawler (1990), are being adopted by many service organizations, types of organizations that include public schools. Further, improving productivity in the service sector, which now accounts for nearly 80 percent of the U.S. economy, is a key aspect of any long-term strategy to improve the productivity of the overall American economy. Thus, gainsharing may not only improve output but also help reduce costs.

Gainsharing programs, moreover, are more than pay-for-performance plans. According to Lawler (1990), they also are organizational development plans. By definition, they entail participative management, making them in tune with current trends of employee involvement. Research on gainsharing in the private sector shows that such programs:

- Enhance coordination, teamwork, and knowledge sharing at lower levels in the organization
- Focus attention on cost savings as well as on improved organizational outcomes
- Help with more rapid adoption of new technology and new methods and thus help improve efficiency, which produces bonuses in annual pay
- Strengthen unions because both employee pay and employee working conditions, the primary focuses of union actions, improve

Such impacts suggest that gainsharing plans have high saliency for use in education. As argued earlier, teamwork and knowledge sharing are characteristic of the most effective schools and the most effective teachers. Further, schools need to dramatically improve organizational outcomes—student performance—and use resources more effectively. Schools could benefit from more widespread use of microchip-based technologies to improve both cost structures and organizational effectiveness (Perlman, 1989). Finally, teachers are heavily unionized in most states. Any program that improves student performance, reduces costs, increases teacher pay, improves working conditions, and also strengthens unions ought to be considered for implementation.

Summary

For private-sector companies, Lawler (1990) concludes that it is wise to have an overall compensation structure that combines a variety of these elements:

- A knowledge- and skills-based pay component that would provide for the bulk of compensation, thus anchoring the compensation structure by providing a stable base pay, the

size of which would be determined by employees' initiative
to learn the specified knowledge and skills

- A systemwide profit sharing or employee stock ownership
  program, which in education would be a school-based bonus
  for improving specified outcomes
- Gainsharing in operating plants or organizational subunits,
  which in education would be schools or possibly departments in high schools

In addition, Lawler suggests strongly that such a compensation
system would need to be combined with a congruent management system that included fewer layers of organizational structure, worker participation, and high-involvement management.
In education, this would include real site-based management,
teacher involvement in professional decision making, development of norms of collegiality, and teacher participation in
schoolwide education improvement activities.

Lawler argues that such a multifaceted compensation
and management structure would focus individuals on organizational goals, improve productivity, foster improved interworker and worker-management interactions, and improve pay
for the most productive and skilled individuals and units. By
implication, such a teacher compensation structure would encourage teachers and administrators to develop expertise necessary to promote student higher-level thinking and problem-
solving skills; foster the continuous development of professional
and pedagogical knowledge; and stimulate teacher involvement
in schoolwide education improvement, including cost reduction strategies and productive uses of new and expensive technology. Finally, such a structure would support creation of a
school culture characterized by norms of collegiality and continuous improvement and strengthen union roles in supporting
the implementation of these objectives.

Total Compensation: Benefits and Pensions

Benefits and pensions are part of the total compensation package, and changes in them can provide further help in fostering

recruitment and retention of able individuals and educational improvements.

Benefits

Lawler (1990) states that employees typically desire a different mix of benefits than is provided in most fixed benefit packages and usually value fixed benefit packages at about 30 percent less than their actual cost to an organization. This produces a lose-lose situation. The solution, says Lawler, is to offer a flexible benefit package from which employees can pick the mix of benefits they prefer, subject to a cost constraint. Such flexible benefit options, now provided in over 30 percent of the Fortune 1,000 companies, produce a win-win situation. Individuals are pleased, and organizations do not have to increase benefit costs. In fact, many organizations have realized costs savings as they have switched to flexible benefit packages. Merging, and even expanding, health benefit coverage is less expensive than having two organizations provide a full, but narrower, range of health benefits.

Flexible benefit plans particularly fit the culture of knowledge-work organizations because such organizations are staffed largely by highly educated professionals who like to make decisions for themselves. Since education systems and schools are knowledge-work organizations, flexible benefit plans are likely to have similar positive outcomes. Thus, another change in the overall compensation structure would be to switch to a flexible benefit system. Further, since such plans improve the private sector's ability to recruit and retain productive workers (Lawler, 1990), the impact should be the same in education. Flexible benefit packages in education could help recruit and retain able individuals in teaching, improve teacher satisfaction with fringe benefits, and possibly reduce the cost of fringe benefits.

Pensions

Pensions also are an important component of total compensation. Current state approaches to teacher pensions are prob-

lematic on several grounds (McLoone, 1988). First, pension
benefits are inequitably available to teachers both within and
across states. Because of district hiring policies, as well as state
vesting and portability restrictions, state pension benefits can
vary widely for teachers who have taught for the same number of
years in the same state, but perhaps not in the same district.
Second, many state pension plans are drastically underfunded,
and teacher pension benefits are in some jeopardy.

Third, there is no portability of pensions across state
boundaries. Thus, teachers who move out of state literally have
to begin their pension program again in the new state. While
sometimes teachers can buy into the new state pension, it usually is expensive. Although teachers often are allowed to draw
out their pension contributions from the state from which they
moved, interest on their own contribution is usually low or
nonexistent, and they rarely have access to the state's contribution. The resultant sum they withdraw is usually much less than
the cost of buying into the new state's program. In short, teacher
pensions are low, are inequitably provided, and inhibit mobility
across state lines.

The solution, according to McLoone (1988), is a "defined-
contribution" pension program, similar to that provided to
professors by most colleges and universities. In a defined-
contribution pension program, organizations make an annual
contribution of money to a pension program that is usually
national in scope; the funds are usually immediately vested with
the individual. When the individual moves across district or
state lines, the new employer simply makes its contributions to
the same pension program, and the individual teacher is not
penalized for moving. The TIAA-CREF pension program, provided to most college professors, is one of the most well known
defined-benefit national pension programs. Such programs are
now provided by a wide range of institutions, and most colleges
and universities give professors a choice of national programs.

As is the case with most state pension programs, most
university programs require an employee contribution that is
matched at some rate by the university. Professors usually contribute 5 percent of their salary, which is then matched on a two-

to-one basis by the college; thus, many professors have 15 percent of their salary contributed to a pension program each year. This percentage compares quite favorably with the rate for most teacher pension programs, which can reach a level of 8 percent contributed by the employee and 8 percent by the education system.

There are two other advantages to this type of pension program for teachers. First, the liability is met annually as part of overall compensation costs; there are no unfunded future liabilities. Second, if the school district is required to pay the employee cost, the fiscal inequity of having states pay the pension costs for all teachers—in high- and low-expenditure–per-pupil, and thus high- and low-salary districts—is eliminated.

In short, switching to a defined-contribution pension program would add another attractive component to teachers' total compensation. Such a program would foster teacher mobility across district and state lines; eliminate potential unfunded, future state pension costs; and reduce current fiscal inequities in how states and districts pay teacher pensions.

Conclusions and Implications for State School Finance Policy

This chapter has shown how a redesigned education compensation system could undergird a goal-oriented education system; help produce high levels of student achievement in higher-level thinking and problem-solving skills; stimulate teachers' ongoing development of professional knowledge and skills; foster teacher involvement in professional decision making; spur development of norms of collegiality and continuous improvement; improve teachers' total compensation; and enhance the ability of education to recruit and retain more able individuals in teaching. As Lawler (1990) has noted, designing a compensation structure is more than just a pay issue; it is an activity that affects organizational goals, structure, culture, norms, and management strategy. This chapter has made several suggestions for rethinking how teachers are paid and, in the process, how schools are organized and managed.

Change in Teacher Compensation Structures

The proposed new compensation structure has been derived from research on compensation strategies that work in the private sector, especially for knowledge-production organizations (of which school systems are a prime example in the public sector), and from research on what has and has not worked in education. The proposed structure has six key components:

Recruitment into Training. Provision should be made for *inservice training fellowships* for 10 percent of the number of new teachers needed every year. Fellowships would provide for all college costs for a full four- or five-year preservice training program leading to a bachelor's degree and a beginning teaching credential. Fellowships would be available on a merit basis to individuals scoring in the top 25 percent of academic ability. Fellows would be required to teach in a public school for three to five years after completing training. Fellows would be required to pay back the costs of training on at least a one-to-one basis if they did not fulfill the teaching requirement.

Assuming the country needs about two hundred thousand new teachers each year, fellowships would be provided for about twenty thousand prospective teachers. At an average cost of $8,000 per teacher (at both public and private postsecondary education institutions), the annual cost would be $160 million. Since training takes five years, the total cost would be approximately $800 million. If the program were restricted to just a fifth-year program, that is, teacher training after earning a liberal arts degree, the program would cost only $160 million per year.

College work-study assistance should be provided for eligible students. The work would be performed in schools as teacher aides or in some other paraprofessional role. The cost could be part of the current work-study program, which would target a number of slots to teacher training programs.

Beginning Salaries. Beginning salaries would be set at a benchmark salary level. The minimum suggested benchmark is the average beginning salary for liberal arts graduates. Many states already have met this target. But states would be well advised to set their target as the average beginning salary for all college graduates in order to attract the large numbers of individuals with technical and scientific degrees and those liberal arts graduates who plan to enter other professions, such as law or medicine.

Base Pay. A redesigned compensation system would link pay to direct assessments of teachers' knowledge and skills, which would increase with experience. An analogy is the promotion and compensation system in higher education, where experience is a necessary but not sufficient criterion for promotion and additional compensation. Experience counts—one cannot advance to full professor and commensurate salary in one year—but promotion is based on direct indicators of professional accomplishment.

Thus, teachers would earn pay increments for increases in knowledge and skills they use in the classroom. While a skills-based compensation structure could be designed in a variety of ways, the following types of skills and knowledge are suggested as components of such a structure:

1. *Content knowledge.* Elementary, middle, and high school teachers teach content. Thorough and deep knowledge of content is a prerequisite for being able to help students think and problem solve in the subject matter domains (Smith & O'Day, 1988).
2. *Knowledge of how students learn.* Distinct from being able to use such knowledge to teach students effectively, it is a separate and identifiable area of knowledge.
3. *Knowledge of pedagogy.* This means knowledge of instructional and classroom management strategies effective with different types of students and, for elementary teachers, different content areas. Again, while this is different from being able to use such knowledge to teach students effectively, it is a separate and identifiable knowledge domain.
4. *Effective use of pedagogical skills.* This requires assimilation of

the first three sets of knowledge into action that is effective in producing student learning. While there has been disagreement in the past about how to assess different stages of proficiency in these skills, there is rapidly advancing knowledge that would make this feasible in the near future.

Indicators of professional skills other than direct classroom observation include the following:

1. *Board certification* from the National Board for Professional Teaching Standards, the National Association of Social Studies Teachers, or any other professional group that seeks to identify outstanding experienced teachers
2. *Performance assessments* to develop portfolios of student performance on a variety of tasks as the country moves to performance-based student assessments
3. *Schoolwide leadership skills* to participate effectively in schoolwide education improvement activities, in mentoring new and experienced teachers, in providing coaching and staff development assistance to teachers, and in a wide range of activities outside one's individual classroom

While other skill domains are possible, the idea is for education systems to identify the array of knowledge and skills they would like teachers to concentrate on acquiring, communicate those expectations to teachers, and provide a series of mechanisms, for example, professional development and peer assistance, to support such development. No quota should be placed on the amount of knowledge and skills that would qualify for extra pay.

Pay-for-Performance. There would be two components of pay-for-performance:

1. *Gainsharing.* For each school, a historical baseline of costs and performance would be calculated. Professional staff within the school would then share in any gain produced by jointly developed strategies to reduce the cost structure

while maintaining (or improving) performance. The staff could decide how the gain would be used: to purchase equipment, materials, or supplies; for a salary bonus; to lower class size; or to provide additional services. This would be a cost reduction and productivity improvement strategy, with gains to remain at the school for use at the discretion of school staff.

2. *School performance bonus.* An annual salary bonus for improving student performance in a school would be awarded. Such a system would need to be carefully designed. Improvements over a multiple-year time period would be preferable to annual improvements. Improvements for all students, rather than just an average level of improvements, would be needed. Improvements also would be broadly defined, focusing not just on student achievement (although that might be the primary area) but on a broad array of goals such as improvement in student learning climate, parent and student relations, student attendance, high school graduation rates, and community satisfaction. Improvements in certain subject areas, such as mathematics and science, or for special needs students could be valued more highly than other improvements. The school performance bonus could equal 20 percent of annual salary at its highest levels. Indeed, Kentucky is planning to provide up to 40 percent annual salary bonuses to faculty in schools that demonstrate comprehensive school improvement.

A Flexible Benefit Package. Teachers would be provided a flexible benefit package with a wide range of benefits from which they could choose, subject to current benefit cost constraints. The benefits would include a cafeteria-style benefit plan; perquisites such as reserved parking spaces and transportation now available only for senior managers; and expanded pension benefits, a privilege now reserved for senior managers.

Defined-Contribution Pension Plans. Pensions would shift from a defined-benefit, state-supported public pension to a defined-contribution, teacher- and district-funded pension program. Each year the employee would contribute a fixed amount, say 5 percent, and the district would contribute a fixed amount, say another 10 percent of salary, into a national pension program with both contributions fully vesting with the teacher. Programs such as TIAA-CREF, now used by colleges and universities, and those provided by Fidelity, for example, would be eligible. These programs would not penalize teachers for moving across district or school lines.

All of these components have been shown by research to help recruit and retain able and productive individuals into knowledge-work organizations such as schools; to foster teamwork, cooperation, collegiality, and professionalism; and to make organizations more productive. The proposed structure represents significant—but not radical—change from current pay structures. The proposed structure, moreover, reflects the changing nature of work organization that fits with a productive service economy that can adapt rapidly to technological change.

As school systems adopt such programs, they foster restructuring of schools to:

- Focus on the school's primary goals, which would include— but not be limited to—student learning
- Support continuous development of professional expertise, that is, the knowledge and skills needed to teach all students to think, problem solve, and communicate
- Incorporate high-involvement management techniques, including teacher participation in professional decision making
- Create norms of continuous improvement, collegiality, and teacher involvement in schoolwide issues

As the first section of this chapter showed, these are characteristics of the most effective teachers and the most effective schools.

Change in State School Finance Structures

The following eight changes in school finance structures could stimulate movement toward this revised manner of teacher compensation.

1. States, as well as the federal government, could create and fund the fellowship and work-study programs. Indeed, both of these areas are state and federal, rather than district, responsibilities. While the initial costs would be substantial, the long-term result— recruiting more able individuals into teaching— would make it a highly cost-effective strategy.

2. States could provide assistance to local districts to support a beginning teacher salary that would equal at a minimum the average beginning salary for liberal arts graduates and could well be targeted to match the average of all college graduates. Once states met their beginning salary benchmark, they could use the additional funds more productively for other components of the proposed new compensation structure.

3. States and the federal government could provide development funds for the design of alternative skill-based pay structures, including assessment structures. For the federal government, this would include support for the National Board for Professional Teaching Standards; states could support State Boards for Professional Teaching Standards. States also could provide incentive funds for districts that volunteer to begin such programs. States would want to ensure that the knowledge and skills identified would be strongly linked to curriculum frameworks that teachers would be expected to implement (Smith & O'Day, 1991).

4. States could directly fund major new staff development initiatives to spur development and expansion of teacher knowledge and skills. Indeed, massive professional staff development is needed to upgrade the expertise of teachers to enable them to

teach the thinking-oriented curriculum needed for all students
to achieve high levels of thinking and problem solving (Smith &
O'Day, 1988, 1991). Since staff development funds are usually
seen as extras and not part of programs, states could set aside
1 percent of the foundation or base program for staff development. That would provide between $30 and $75 per pupil for
local staff development, a sum well within the range needed to
change school curriculum and instruction to accomplish the
nation's bold education goals.

5. States and the federal government also could provide
development funds for designing gainsharing plans. There is a
well-developed technology for designing these programs in the
private sector (Lawler, 1990), but customized designs would
need to be developed in order to use them in schools and school
districts.

6. States could fund school-based–pay-for-improvement
bonus programs, similar in intent to those already implemented
in ten states. The Florida program provides a sum to districts,
and each participating district designs the school-based incentive program. By contrast, the South Carolina program is state
designed, and school improvement rewards are based on state-
set standards. States could make such programs a separate
categorical program, as all states have done so far. But the bonus
needs to be larger than what has been offered. While the Kentucky bonus of 40 percent might seem high, substantial bonuses
are needed in order to be effective motivators (Lawler, 1990).
Salary bonuses of at least 15 to 20 percent should be supported.
Over time, states could set aside a fixed percentage of the base
foundation program for such bonus schemes since such funds
provide the bulk of teacher salary dollars. If teacher salaries
consume about 45 percent of local district budgets and if 20
percent is allocated for bonus payments, then 9 percent of the
foundation level could be set aside by state law for either state- or
district-designed–school-based student performance improvement salary bonuses.

7. States could require all local districts to design and implement flexible benefit programs for teachers. States also could develop computer programs to help reduce the costs of implementing such programs.

8. States could, over time, change the entire teacher pension structure from a defined-benefit, state-funded public pension system to a defined-contribution, private-sector teacher pension program. This would likely enhance the equity of teacher pension benefits as well as reduce costs. Further, for states that now pay pension costs at the state level for teachers in all districts regardless of fiscal inequities and teacher pay differentials, decentralizing pension costs to teachers and local districts would improve the fiscal equity of this part of education costs. Districts could target a 5 percent contribution from employees and a 10 percent contribution from the district as the shared-cost goal over time.

As the private sector has learned over the last two decades, it is possible to dramatically restructure work, organization, management, and compensation in a manner that improves both productivity and worker satisfaction. Such changes were successfully implemented in numerous high-technology and knowledge-production organizations, the latter being the generic description of schools and education.

This chapter has proposed a six-point change in teacher compensation structures and eight complementary changes in state school finance policies to restructure teacher compensation, school management, and student learning. While the proposed changes allow for state and local tailoring of the specifics, the proposed structure would contribute substantially to the country's ambitious attempts to dramatically improve its education system. It would help recruit and retain more knowledgeable and more skilled individuals into teaching. It would foster characteristics of school organizations and cultures associated with the most effective schools and teachers. It would align pay with school productivity, that is, student achievement. It could even strengthen teacher unions. It is a plan worth discussing and trying.

References

American Federation of Teachers. (1990). *Survey and analysis of salary trends*. Washington, DC: Author.

Arfin, D. M. (1986). The use of financial aid to attract talented students to teaching: Lessons from other fields. *Elementary School Journal, 86,* 405–424.

Bacharach, S. B., Conley, S., & Shedd, J. (1986). Beyond career ladders: Structuring teacher career development systems. *Teachers College Record, 87,* 563–574.

Bacharach, S. B., Conley, S., & Shedd, J. (1987). A career development framework for evaluating teachers as decision makers. *Journal of Personnel Evaluation, 1,* 181–194.

Bacharach, S. B., Conley, S., & Shedd, J. (1990). Evaluating teachers for career awards and merit pay. In J. Millman & L. Darling-Hammond (Eds.), *The new handbook of teacher evaluation: Assessing elementary and secondary teachers* (pp. 133–146). Newbury Park, CA: Sage.

Bacharach, S. B., Lipsky, D., & Shedd, J. (1983). *Teacher compensation systems*. Manuscript submitted to the Research Division of the National Education Association, Washington, DC.

Bacharach, S. B., Lipsky, D., & Shedd, J. (1984). *Merit pay and its alternatives*. Ithaca, NY: Organizational Analysis & Practice.

Blinder, A. (1990). *Paying for productivity*. Washington, DC: Brookings Institution.

Bruno, J. (1981). Design of incentive systems for staffing racially isolated schools in large urban school districts. *Journal of Education Finance, 7,* 149–167.

Buchman, M. (1987). *Teaching knowledge: The lights that teachers live by* (Issue paper 87-1). East Lansing: Michigan State University, Center for Research on Teacher Education.

Burden, P. R. (1982, February). *Developmental supervision: Reducing teacher stress at different career stages*. Paper presented at the annual meeting of the Association of Teacher Educators,

Phoenix, AZ. (ERIC Document Reproduction Service No. ED 218 267).

Carnegie Forum on Education and the Economy. (1986). *A nation prepared: Teachers for the 21st century.* Washington, DC: Author.

Carnegie Task Force. (1989). *Turning points: Preparing American youth for the 21st century.* New York: Carnegie Corporation.

Carter, K. (1991). Creating a teacher work environment for the development of classroom knowledge. In S. C. Conley & B. S. Cooper (Eds.), *The school as a work environment: Implications for reform* (pp. 42–64). Needham Heights, MA: Allyn & Bacon.

Carter, K., Cushing, K., Sabers, D., Brown, P., & Berliner, D. (1988). Expert novice differences in perceiving and processing visual classroom information. *Journal of Teacher Education, 38,* 25–31.

Conley, S. C., & Bacharach, S. B. (1990). Performance appraisal in education: A strategic consideration. *Journal of Personnel Evaluation in Education, 3,* 309–319.

Conley, S. C., & Cooper, B. S. (Eds.). (1991). *The school as a work environment: Implications for reform.* Needham Heights, MA: Allyn & Bacon.

Cooper, J. M. (n.d.). *Differentiated staffing: Some questions and answers.* Unpublished manuscript.

Darling-Hammond, L. (1984). *Beyond the commission reports: The coming crisis in teaching.* Santa Monica, CA: RAND Corporation.

Deal, T. E., & Peterson, K. D. (1990). *The principal's role in shaping school culture.* Washington, DC: U.S. Government Printing Office.

Deming, W. E. (1987). *The merit system: The annual appraisal, destroyer of people.* Paper presented at A Day with Dr. W. Edwards Deming, University of Minnesota.

Dimensions. (1990, January 17). *Education Week,* p. 3.

Educational Research Service. (1979). *Merit pay for teachers.* Arlington, VA: Author.

Feiman-Nemser, S., & Buchman, M. (1985). Pitfalls of experience in teacher preparation. *Teachers College Record, 87,* 53–65.

Ferris, J., & Winkler, D. (1986). Teacher compensation and the supply of teachers. *Elementary School Journal, 86,* 389–404.

Firestone, W., Fuhrman, S., & Kirst, M. W. (1989). *Progress of reform*. New Brunswick, NJ: Rutgers University, Consortium for Policy Research in Education.

Freiberg, J. (1985). Master teacher programs: Lessons from the past. *Educational Leadership, 42*(4), 16–21.

Futrell, M. (1986). Career ladders: An NEA perspective. *Teacher Education Quarterly, 13*(4), 60–65.

Gitlin, A. (1990). Understanding teaching dialogically. *Teachers College Record, 91*, 537–563.

Goodlad, J. (1983). *A place called school*. New York: Macmillan.

Griffin, G. (1985). The school as a workplace and the master teacher concept. *Elementary School Journal, 86*(1), 1–16.

Gupta, N., Schweizer, T. P., & Jenkins, G. D., Jr. (1987). Pay-for-knowledge compensation plans: Hypotheses and survey results. *Monthly Labor Review, 110*(10), 40–43.

Hanushek, E. (1989). The impact of differential expenditures on school performance. *Educational Researcher, 18*(4), 45–51.

Hawley, W. D. (1985). Designing and implementing performance-based career ladder plans. *Educational Leadership, 43*(3), 57–61.

Hawley, W. D., & Rosenholtz, S. (Eds.). (1984). Good schools: What research says about improving student achievement [Special issue]. *Peabody Journal of Education, 61*(4).

Holmes Group. (1986). *Tomorrow's teachers*. East Lansing, MI: Author.

Jacobson, S. (1988a). Alternative practices of internal salary distribution and their effects on teacher recruitment and retention. *Journal of Education Finance, 14*, 274–284.

Jacobson, S. (1988b). The effects of pay incentives on teacher absenteeism. *Journal of Human Resources, 24*, 280–286.

Johnson, S. M. (1984). *The pros and cons of merit pay*. Bloomington, IN: Phi Delta Kappa.

Johnson, S. M. (1990). *Teachers at work: Achieving success in our schools*. New York: Basic Books.

Johnston, W. (1987). *Workforce 2000*. Indianapolis, IN: Hudson Institute.

Lampert, M., & Clark, C. M. (1990). Expert knowledge and

expert thinking in teaching: A response to Floden and Klinzing. *Educational Researcher, 19*(5), 21–23.

Lawler, E. E., III. (1986). *High-involvement management: Participative strategies for improving organizational performance.* San Francisco: Jossey-Bass.

Lawler, E. E., III. (1990). *Strategic pay: Aligning organizational strategies and pay systems.* San Francisco: Jossey-Bass.

Lawler, E. E., Ledford, G. E., & Mohrman, S. A. (1989). *Employee involvement in America.* Houston, TX: American Productivity and Quality Center.

Lieberman, A. (1988). *Building a professional culture in schools.* New York: Teachers College Press.

Little, J. W. (1982). Norms of collegiality and experimentation: Workplace conditions of school success. *American Educational Research Journal, 19,* 325–340.

Little, J. W. (1987). Teachers as colleagues. In V. Richardson-Koehler (Ed.), *Educators' handbook: A research perspective* (pp. 491–518). White Plains, NY: Longman.

Little, J. W. (1990). The persistence of privacy: Autonomy and initiative in teachers' professional relations. *Teachers College Record, 91*(4), 507–536.

Manassee, L. (1985). Improving conditions for principal effectiveness: Policy implications of research. *Elementary School Journal, 85,* 439–463.

McLaughlin, M. W., & Pfeifer, S. (1988). *Teacher evaluation: Improvement, accountability and effective learning.* New York: Teachers College Press.

McLaughlin, M. W., & Yee, S. M. (1988). School as a place to have a career. In A. Lieberman (Ed.), *Building a professional culture in schools* (pp. 23–44). New York: Teachers College Press.

McLoone, E. (1988). The changing conditions of teacher retirement systems. In K. Alexander and D. Monk (Eds.), *Attracting and compensating America's teachers* (pp. 223–248). New York: Ballinger.

Mohrman, A. M. (1989). *Deming versus performance appraisal: Is there a resolution?* Los Angeles: University of Southern California, Center for Effective Organizations.

Murnane, R. J. (1981). Seniority rules and educational productivity: Understanding the consequences of a mandate for equality. *American Journal of Education, 90,* 14–38.

Murnane, R. J. (1983). Quantitative studies of effective schools: What have we learned? In A. R. Odden & L. D. Webb (Eds.), *School finance and school improvement: Linkages for the 1980s* (pp. 193–209). New York: Ballinger.

Murnane, R. J., & Cohen, D. K. (1986). Merit pay and the evaluation problem: Why some merit pay plans fail and a few survive. *Harvard Educational Review, 56*(1), 1–17.

Murphy, J. (1989). Principal instructional leadership. In L. S. Lotto & P. W. Thurston (Eds.), *Recent advances in educational administration* (Vol. 1). Greenwich, CT: JAI Press.

National Commission on Excellence in Education. (1983). *A nation at risk: Imperative for reform.* Washington, DC: Author.

Perlman, L. (1989). *Closing education's technology gap* (Briefing Paper No. 111). Indianapolis, IN: Hudson Institute.

Popkewitz, T. S., & Lind, L. (1989). Teacher incentives as reforms: Teachers' work and the changing control mechanism in education. *Teachers College Record, 90,* 575–593.

Porter, A., & Brophy, J. (1988). Good teaching: Insights from the work of the Institute for Research on Teaching. *Educational Leadership, 45*(8), 75–84.

Porter, L. W., Lawler, E. E., & Hackman, J. R. (1975). *Behavior in organizations.* New York: McGraw-Hill.

Purkey, S. C., & Smith, M. (1983). Effective schools: A synthesis. *Elementary School Journal, 83,* 427–452.

Richards, C. (1988). State regulation of entry level teacher salaries: Policy issues and options. *Educational Policy, 2,* 307–322.

Richardson, V. (1991). How and why teachers change. In S. C. Conley & B. S. Cooper (Eds.), *The school as a work environment: Implications for reform.* Needham Heights, MA: Allyn & Bacon.

Rosenholtz, S. J. (1985a). Effective schools: Interpreting the evidence. *American Journal of Education, 93,* 352–388.

Rosenholtz, S. J. (1985b). Political myths about education reform: Lessons from research on teaching. *Phi Delta Kappan, 66,* 349–355.

Rosenholtz, S. J. (1989). *Teachers' workplace: The social organization of schools.* White Plains, NY: Longman.

Rosenholtz, S. J., & Smylie, M. A. (1984). Teacher compensation and career ladders. *Elementary School Journal, 85,* 149–166.

Schlechty, P. C. (1989). Career ladders: A good idea going awry. In T. J. Sergiovanni & J. H. Moore (Eds.), *Schooling for tomorrow: Directing reforms to issues that count* (pp. 356–375). Needham Heights, MA: Allyn & Bacon.

Schlechty, P. C., & Vance, V. (1983). Recruitment, selection and retention: The shape of the teaching force. *Elementary School Journal, 83,* 469–487.

Sedlak, M. W. (1987). Tomorrow's teachers: The essential arguments of the Holmes Group Report. In J. F. Soltis (Ed.), *Reforming teacher education* (pp. 4–15). New York: Teachers College Press.

Sergiovanni, T. (1990). *Value-added leadership.* New York: McGraw-Hill.

Shanker, A. (1990). The end of the traditional model of schooling—and a proposal for using incentives to restructure our public schools. *Phi Delta Kappan, 71,* 344–357.

Smith, M. S., & O'Day, J. (1988). *Teaching policy and research on teaching.* Palo Alto, CA: Stanford University, Center for Educational Research at Stanford.

Smith, M. S., & O'Day, J. (1991). Systemic school reform. In S. Fuhrman & B. Malen (Eds.), *The politics of curriculum and testing* (pp. 233–267). Philadelphia: Falmer.

Southern Regional Education Board. (1990). *Career ladder clearinghouse.* Atlanta, GA: Author.

Tennessee Education Association. (1988, January). The sublime has become the ridiculous. *Tennessee Education Association News,* p. 2.

Timar, T. B., & Kirp, D. L. (1987). Educational reform and institutional competence. *Harvard Educational Review, 57,* 308–330.

Tosi, H., & Tosi, L. (1986). What managers need to know about knowledge-based pay. *Organizational Dynamics, 14*(3), 52–64.

Von Glinow, M. A., & Mohrman, S. A. (1989). *Managing complexity in high-technology organizations*. New York: Oxford University Press.

Walberg, H. J. (1990). Productive teaching and instruction: Assessing the knowledge base. *Phi Delta Kappan, 71,* 470–478.

Watson, R. S., Poda, J. W., & Miller, C. T. (1987). What a state mandated merit pay plan taught us. *Executive Educator, 9*(7).

White House, The. (1990). *National goals for education.* Washington, DC: Author.

Wilson, B., & Corcoran, T. (1987). *Places where children succeed: A profile of outstanding elementary schools.* Philadelphia: Research for Better Schools.

Wilson, B., & Corcoran, T. (1988). *Successful secondary schools.* Philadelphia: Falmer.

Wise, A. E., & Darling-Hammond, L. (1985). Teacher evaluation and teacher professionalism. *Educational Leadership, 42*(4), 28–33.

Wise, A. E., & Darling-Hammond, L. (1987). *Licensing teachers: Design for a teaching profession.* Santa Monica, CA: RAND Corporation.

Wittrock, M. (Ed.). (1986). *Handbook of research on teaching* (3rd ed.). New York: Macmillan.

Yee, S. M. (1986, April). *Teaching as a career: Promotion versus development.* Paper presented at the annual meeting of the American Educational Research Association, San Francisco.

3

Financing Middle School Reform: Linking Costs and Education Goals

David D. Marsh
Jennifer M. Sevilla

Improving middle school education is a top priority for state and national policy makers. Whereas the 1980s education reform efforts focused on strengthening traditional education programs, the 1990s reforms have focused on what Cuban (1988) describes as second-order reforms aimed at the comprehensive restructuring of schools. Middle school reform provides a comprehensive view of restructuring that includes major revisions of curriculum and instruction, personalization of schooling for students, reorganization of time and resources, and increased teacher professionalism. The middle school concept is best summarized in the Carnegie Task Force report, *Turning Points: Preparing American Youth for the 21st Century* (1989), which synthesizes the research and experience on middle schools and organizes these as program components needed to make middle schools successful.

An analysis of middle school reform provides a powerful context for addressing a generic problem in education finance: how to conceptualize and calculate the costs of implementing and operating school restructuring reforms. This issue is relevant for several reasons:

- Significant education reform is needed in American schools.

- Fiscal resources, for both implementing new programs and operating schools, are limited.
- Current ways of conceptualizing education costs are inadequate for creating cost estimates regarding school restructuring.

The success of policy makers in enhancing American education reform is linked to their ability to understand and provide for the costs associated with such reforms.

This chapter examines the issue of conceptualizing the costs of comprehensive school reform, using the middle school reform effort as an example. The first section analyzes the middle school reform movement and summarizes its major components. The next section provides a set of principles for conceptualizing the costs of comprehensive school reform. The third section uses these principles to estimate the cost of comprehensive middle school reform. The following section reviews recent studies on the pattern of implementation needed for such reforms. The chapter concludes with an outline of key state and local strategies for implementation and a discussion of several alternative policy mechanisms for providing needed revenues and resources.

Research on the overall effectiveness of the middle school concept has been very limited. Most research has focused on the effectiveness of specific components of middle schools, such as cooperative learning or the advisory process for students. Consequently, this chapter does not attempt to relate costs to the possible benefits of comprehensive middle school reform or to describe potential returns on financial investments of this comprehensive reform.

Middle School Reform

Early in the development of the American system of education, educators realized that eight years of elementary school followed by four years of secondary school was an inappropriate way to organize the transition for an adolescent from the elementary to the high school level; as a result, around 1910 the concept of the junior high school evolved (Overly, Kinghorn, &

Preston, 1972). The original intent for the junior high school was to serve as a transition for adolescents, who were clearly becoming individualistic young adults. As time progressed, the age of puberty began to drop, and educators felt that the sixth-grade child would benefit from a program that included seventh- and eighth-graders undergoing similar social and physiological changes (Overly, Kinghorn, & Preston, 1972).

Junior high schools, with grade level combinations ranging 7–9, 8–9, 7–10, and 5–8 (Wiles & Bondi, 1981), were modeled after high schools and took on the atmosphere of the high school as well. Early reformers such as Gruhn and Douglass (1956) argued that junior high schools should differentiate themselves from high schools because the needs of their students were different.

It was not until the 1960s that the concept of the middle school, once popular in Europe and early American private schools, was reinstituted (Wiles & Bondi, 1981). According to Wiles and Bondi (1981), four factors led to the emergence of the middle school concept: (1) the need to provide a program for children undergoing physical and emotional changes, (2) the changed nature of the elementary school in the post-*Sputnik* era, (3) dissatisfaction with the nature of the junior high as an impersonal and formal organization, and (4) the need for a vehicle to foster education reform. In a more pragmatic vein, middle schools were created to make better use of existing physical facilities.

The 1980s was a decade of education emphasis on quality, partly in response to changes in the global marketplace (National Governors' Association, 1986). This emphasis on quality prompted improvements in curriculum and the overall instructional program (Marsh & Odden, 1988). The result was a return to traditional views of schooling, rather than a restructuring of the system itself. However, the resurgence of traditional schooling did not meet the needs of American preteens.

Current Focus

As summarized in two major reports (Carnegie Task Force, 1989; Superintendent's Task Force, 1987), current middle school reform features:

- An interdisciplinary curriculum that emphasizes for all students conceptual understanding, problem solving, and communication
- A set of innovative instructional strategies that support the student as an active learner and the teacher as the coach
- A personalization strategy that connects students to each other and to the learning process in ways appropriate for early adolescents
- An organizational structure that supports the new approach to curriculum and instruction

Middle school reform is not a separate and new reform; instead, it is a synthesis of important pieces. It is the synergism of the collection of innovations and their careful integration into the middle school concept that gives the ideas such power.

To date, there are estimated to be 10,857 schools using the middle school concept (Alexander & McEwin, 1989). However, many of the earlier models simply adopted the name *middle school* without adopting corresponding changes in their programs. These schools can be differentiated from true middle schools through a comparison of basic tenets. Table 3.1 summarizes the tenets of the traditional junior high school and the middle school.

Turning Points: A Synthesis of Middle School Reform

In 1987, the Carnegie Corporation established a Council on Adolescent Development, comprised of individuals representing education, research, government, health organizations, nonprofit groups, and philanthropists. This council began a careful analysis of the current status of adolescent education. It compiled data on the social, emotional, and academic development of adolescents, comparing thirteen-year-olds from five countries, including the United States, and four Canadian provinces in science and mathematics skills (LaPoint, Mead, & Phillips, 1989). The results of the international comparison revealed that thirteen-year-old students in the United States ranked at the

Table 3.1. A Comparison of Tenets from Middle Schools and Traditional Junior High Schools.

Middle School Tenets	Traditional Junior High School Tenets
• Recognize and respond to the uniqueness of the learner	• Treat learners uniformly
• Involve the student in the learning as an active partner	• Give the teacher all responsibility for the learning process
• Provide instructional balance in the emphasis given different realms of development	• Possess an overriding concern with intellectual capacity
• Integrate information/knowledge bases	• Emphasize the distinctiveness of subjects
• Present learning opportunities in many forms through many media	• Present learning opportunities in didactic forms
• Emphasize application of information and skill development	• Provide little opportunity for meaningful application
• Teach through student interests and needs	• Teach according to predetermined organization of information
• Define the purpose of instruction in terms of pupil growth	• Define the purpose of instruction according to organizational/administrative criteria such as units, credit, and graduation requirements
• View teachers as guides or facilitators of learning	• View teachers as subject matter specialists
• Utilize support staff as trainers of instructional personnel	• View support staff as specialists in narrowly defined roles
• Use an exploratory, inquiring, individualized approach to learning and evaluation	• Utilize standardized patterns of instruction and evaluation

Source: Compiled from Wiles, 1976, pp. 49–50.

bottom of comparative scales in mathematics and science proficiency.

These results led the Carnegie Middle School Task Force to a proposal for middle school reform known as *Turning Points* (Carnegie Task Force, 1989), which delineates the following essential principles:

- Large middle-grade schools are divided into smaller communities for learning.

- Middle-grade schools transmit a core of common knowledge to students.
- Middle-grade schools are organized to ensure success for all students.
- Teachers and principals have the major responsibility and power to transform middle-grade schools.
- Teachers for the middle grades are specifically prepared to teach young adolescents.
- Schools promote good health; the education and health of young adolescents are inextricably linked.
- Families are allied with school staff through mutual respect, trust, and communication.
- Schools and communities are partners in educating young adolescents (Carnegie Task Force, 1989, p. 36).

The task force authors further emphasized that "the middle grade school proposed here is profoundly different from many schools today. It focuses squarely on the characteristics and needs of young adolescents. It creates a community of adults and young people embedded in networks of support and responsibility that enhance commitment of students to learning. In partnership with youth-services and community organizations, it offers multiple sites and multiple methods for fostering the learning and health of adolescents. The combined efforts create a community of shared purpose among those concerned that all young adolescents are prepared for productive lives, especially those at risk of being left behind" (p. 36).

The authors envisioned a complex, integrated program — embodying both curriculum changes and school restructuring — that included eight key elements:

1. Create small communities for learning.

Schools should be a place where close, trusting
relationships with adults and peers create a climate
for personal growth and intellectual development
[p. 37].

The traditional junior high school is a large, complex, insensitive institution. Therefore, the task force suggested that "the middle grades must be restructured on a more human scale" (p. 37). In a middle school, students would feel more secure in an environment emphasizing friendly, family-like cohesiveness.

Further, each child would "be able to rely on a small, caring group of adults who work closely with each other to provide coordinated, meaningful, and challenging educational experiences" (p. 37). In this way, students would feel secure and adults would be better able to influence children's development.

Each student would also have at least "one adult who has the time and takes the trouble to talk with the student about academic matters, personal problems, and the importance of performing well in the middle grade school" (p. 37). Within the context of an education setting, all middle-level students need to find comfort for both successes and failures as they develop into productive adults.

2. Teach a core of common knowledge.

Every student in the middle grades should learn to think critically, through mastery of an appropriate body of knowledge, lead a healthy life, behave eth ically and lawfully, and assume the responsibilities of citizenship in a pluralistic society [p. 42].

The task force felt that all students should be taught a common, core curriculum. Students in the middle grades should be taught how to think critically through the development of an integrated subject matter core program. Further, emphasis should be placed on learning rather than on scoring highly on academic subject matter tests.

3. Ensure success for all students.

All young adolescents should have the opportunity to succeed in every aspect of the middle grade program, regardless of previous achievement or the pace at which they learn [p. 49].

The task force emphasized that students should be grouped, but not tracked, for learning, that scheduled classroom periods should be used to maximize learning, and that the structure of the education program should be expanded for an increased emphasis on learning. However, learning should not focus solely on the core program but should allow for success in other areas, such as athletics.

4. Empower teachers and administrators.

Decisions concerning the experiences of middle grade students should be made by the adults who know them best [p. 54].

The task force mentioned that our society "believes that an individual can be trusted to make decisions for themselves and for the common good" (p. 54). This has been practiced in business and industry but has yet to reach the public school system. Until the school staff is empowered, reform in the middle grades is hindered.

5. Select teachers trained for the middle grades.

Teachers in the middle grade schools should be selected and specially educated to teach young adolescents [p. 58].

The task force suggested that radical changes must take place in the training of teachers for the middle grade levels. Teachers must be trained in adolescent development, as well as in the strategies needed to make the students successful learners. Changes in the undergraduate education of middle school teachers are proposed, along with requirement of service in an internship program prior to licensing.

6. Improve academic performance through better health and fitness.

Young adolescents must be healthy in order to
learn [p. 60].

The task force suggested that a direct link exists between
the health of students and their ability to learn. Additionally, the
task force saw that the responsibility for student health and
accessibility to health care was a function of the school. As a
result, it proposed that each school should have a coordinated
health program to ensure identification of health problems and
their subsequent treatment and/or proper referral.

7. Reengage families in the education of young adolescents.

Families and middle grade schools must be allied
through trust and respect if young adolescents are
to succeed in school [p. 66].

The task force felt that many middle-level schools dis-
courage parental involvement. Offering parents meaningful
roles and keeping them informed about the learning process
will improve their engagement in education.

8. Connect schools with communities.

Schools and community organizations should
share responsibility for each middle grade student's
success [p. 70].

Community-school partnerships were seen as a viable
method of enhancing the education experiences of young
adults. The task force suggested five specific ways to involve
communities and schools: (1) placing students in youth services,
(2) ensuring students' access to health and social services, (3)
supporting middle-grade education programs, (4) augmenting
resources for teachers and students, and (5) expanding career
guidance.

Collectively, the components set forth by the Carnegie
Task Force in *Turning Points* establish a reform structure of

powerful dimensions. The middle school concept, if widely
implemented, could be successful in transforming the education of early adolescents from a system based on a teacher-
centered model to one based on the needs of adolescent youth.
In California, the Superintendent's Task Force (1987) produced
a report that came up with ideas similar to those of the Carnegie
Task Force. This excellent report is an integration of key ideas
and a useful guide to the operation and implementation of the
middle school approach.

Conceptualizing Costs: A Set of Guidelines

Conceptualizing the costs of education reforms is an important
policy problem. Reforms such as the middle school reform are
especially important because they are so clearly needed; yet
budgets are extremely tight. But concern about the costs of
major reforms is not limited to periods when budgets are tight;
such concern will be paramount over the next decade whatever
financial conditions may be.

    The following is a set of principles that can be used to
conceptualize the costs of education reforms:

1. Consider the new program design holistically (rather than
    as separable components) and as a set of alternative pro-
    gram scenarios rather than merely as a new program design
    compared against the old design.
2. Focus on additional costs for any of these alternative sce-
    narios rather than on total operational costs.
3. In considering alternative costs, focus first on the number
    of different school "ingredients" (such as the addition of a
    teacher, including benefits) rather than directly on the ac-
    tual cost of this teacher.

    The costs of major reforms, such as the middle school
concept, should be examined in a holistic manner for several
reasons. Research has established that these major reforms work
synergistically. In a study of California middle school reform,
Marsh and Crocker (1991) established that innovative curricu-

lum and instruction were intricately linked to the personalization of the schooling experience and to restructuring organizational elements of the school such as the budget and/or the master schedule. While various components of the middle school concept are important, it is the interaction of these components that makes the reform successful.

Variation between schools is usefully thought of as variation in the configuration of the different components of the middle school vision, which in this chapter is represented by alternative middle school scenarios. The difference between schools is not that one school has implemented all the components while another has implemented only a few of the components. Rather, the alternative scenarios reflect schools that have implemented a mild form of the middle school concept and others that have implemented a form much closer to the full middle school concept. Consequently, holistic scenarios, rather than analysis by component, is best suited to the analysis of costs.

The second guiding principle argues for conceptualizing costs for major reforms by examining additional costs rather than focusing on total operational costs. Determining the real cost of operating a school is extremely difficult, and examining total operating costs, while pertinent to the analysis of the efficiency of a school system or to the allocation of additional funds over a long period of time, is not relevant in the context of conceptualizing the cost of implementing a major reform. The pertinent policy issue for conceptualizing the costs of major reforms is how much more money the reform will cost than what is currently provided. Thus, the analytical task is to estimate the operating costs associated with each alternative scenario.

The third guiding principle focuses on calculating the additional cost of the new program by first estimating the *need* for additional ingredients of program operation, such as teachers, rather than calculating the *cost* of those teachers. Both policy makers and practitioners should plan programs in terms of units, which the specific program pieces to the overall design of the reform. The trend toward site-based management and local flexibility does not obviate this need to plan in program units; it just provides the local decision makers with a new sense of equivalent resources that is linked to the overall program design. Moreover, program units provide a consistent base for considering costs that vary across districts and states and over time.

Cost Analysis: Middle School Operations

Levin (1983) suggests the ingredients method of cost analysis, which includes personnel, facilities, equipment and materials, other program inputs, and student/parent inputs. Costs can be measured from two standpoints: operational costs and additional costs. *Operational costs* include those fixed and variable costs that vary from school to school, for example, teacher and administrator salaries, curriculum and instructional materials, bonded indebtedness, rental payments, depreciation, and insurance. Some fixed and/or variable costs may change, for example, plant maintenance or utility costs, in the transition from the junior high to the middle school. However, for this analysis, these costs are assumed to remain fixed. *Additional costs* are those costs over and above current operational costs. In the transformation to the middle school, these costs would include more teachers, counselors, materials and supplies, and capital expenditures. In Levin's terms, the following analysis includes the additional cost of ingredients needed to operate the middle school concept.

One of the major concerns for school districts is the effect of reorganizing students into housing arrangements as proposed by the Carnegie Task Force (1989). In general, organizing students in grades 6–8 in a separate physical plant reduces the size of the elementary school while increasing the size of the high school (Maurice, 1964). In stable or declining districts, this reorganization might be costly; in growing districts, the costs would remain relatively the same. The following analysis excludes only capital costs.

In order to consider how a school might reallocate its financial resources and redeploy its human resources, two scenarios are presented. Each scenario is a bundled set of components from the Carnegie Task Force report and is compared to a traditional junior high school model. The first scenario portrays a middle school that has only partially implemented principles discussed in *Turning Points*; it is called Modest Change Middle School. The second scenario describes a much more fully implemented version of the principles found in the Carnegie Task Force report and is called Major Change Middle School. Scenario three portrays a traditional junior high school.

Modest Change Middle School

Modest Change Middle School is representative of a typical U.S. junior high school that has made some changes to become a middle school. The school serves 1,000 students in grades 6–8 and has a professional staff of 56, including 48 teachers (4 are master teachers paid $4,000 per year over their current salaries), 3 guidance counselors, and a school librarian. The school administration includes a principal and two assistant principals. Student health care is provided by a licensed nurse.

Modest Change Middle School has incorporated several of the principles of *Turning Points* but on a modest level. The school has teamed teachers across disciplines on a small scale to utilize block scheduling, encouraged teacher empowerment, elicited community support, and used lead teachers. However, the master schedule still emphasizes fifty-minute classes and departmentalized subjects. The atmosphere is one in which learning occurs through teacher-directed, six-period, nonintegrated-subject classrooms.

The teacher-student ratio is 1:21, teacher contact minutes (the number of contact minutes of instruction a teacher has in a given day) are 250, class size is 25, and the teacher-student contact number (the number of students a teacher sees in a day) is 1:100. The administration of Modest Change Middle School is responsible for attendance, budgeting, and discipline. Teachers have limited decision-making power over the budget but retain individual decision-making power over their particular curriculum areas.

Major Change Middle School

Major Change Middle School has implemented all the components envisioned by the Carnegie Task Force (1989). The school services 1,000 students in grades 6–8 and has a professional staff of 57, which includes 52 teachers, 1 guidance counselor, and a school librarian. The administration includes 1 principal and 1 vice principal. Student health care is provided by a licensed nurse.

Major Change Middle School has redeployed its human resources so that it has developed a team of staff members to oversee a smaller number of students. In order to reduce teacher-student contacts, Major Change Middle School replaced 2 guidance counselors and 1 assistant principal with 4 additional teachers. This redeployment and subsequent hiring resulted in teams and houses becoming responsible for student attendance, counseling, and discipline.

In order to create small communities for learning, Major Change Middle School divided the entire enrollment into 4 houses with 13 teachers and 250 students each. Each house was further subdivided into 3 teams of 4 teachers and 83 to 84 students. (The remaining teacher in each house is a master teacher.)

The houses use the knowledge and skills of the master teachers to team teach, direct staff development, and work on curriculum design. To increase the decision-making capacity at the school, each house monitors one-fourth of the department-related expenditures. Teacher teams also participate in the hiring of new teachers and assume responsibility for student outcomes.

Flexible scheduling has been implemented, with an advisory period twice per week and one-half day per week used as a teacher planning day. The advisory period is accomplished with the use of all 58 staff members and serves as an academic and social counseling group. The advisor-student contact is reduced to 1:17 or 1:18.

A health coordinator is present on campus in the school-linked health center and works with the psychologist, food services personnel, teachers, and administrators to provide an integrated, well-developed physical and mental health care program. The health center is linked to community health services and provides integrated services to students on family planning, nutritional counseling, drug rehabilitation, and mental health care.

The health care center is staffed by a school nurse and/or a nurse practitioner (who serves as a health coordinator), a half-time health advocate, a half-time social worker, and student assistants. In school districts with access to a teaching hospital, interns may serve community time in the schools at no cost to the district.

The teacher-student ratio is 1:19, teacher contact minutes are 250, class size is 23, and the teacher-student contact number is 1:83.

Traditional Junior High School

The Traditional Junior High School model does not encompass any of the components of *Turning Points*. This model school serves 1,000 students in grades 6–8 and has a professional staff of 56, which includes 48 teachers, 3 guidance counselors, and a school librarian. The school administration consists of a principal and two assistant principals. Student health care is provided by a licensed nurse.

The Traditional Junior High School has no teaming of teachers and has a six-period student day (each period is fifty minutes long). Students move from room to room, and very little interactive dialogue occurs among staff members regarding either curriculum issues or student achievement. Learning takes place through teacher-directed, nonintegrated-subject classrooms.

The teacher-student ratio is 1:21, teacher contact minutes are 250, class size is 25, and the teacher-student contact number is 1:125.

The administration of Traditional Junior High School is responsible for attendance, budgeting, and discipline. Teachers have minimal decision-making power over budgetary items, and decision making tends to be top-down.

Changes in Teacher-Student Interactions

The middle school philosophy is that a child who has quality contact with a few teachers over the course of the day is more likely to feel part of a tightly knit environment that supports learning than does a student who has limited contact with several teachers. Table 3.2 summarizes four dimensions of teacher-student interaction. The first dimension is the teacher-student funding ratio, which defines the overall ratio of teachers and students assigned to the school. This ratio is often used by districts to determine the number of teachers assigned to the school, given the number of students enrolled.

The second dimension is the number of contact minutes of instruction a given teacher has with students over a school day. For this analysis, we hold this constant to show that teachers in all of our scenarios are seeing students for the same amount of time per week.

The third dimension, class size, is the number of students who are assigned to a teacher for a given class period. Within a school, class size can vary tremendously—especially for certain "advantaged classes." Adjusting the overall class size in a school is often quite costly because it involves changing the teacher-student ratio, that is, hiring more teachers to work with a given number of students. Yet some schools use flexible class size to provide time for more individual attention for some students or

Table 3.2. A Summary of Effects on Student Indicators
as a Result of Redeployment.

Student Indicator	Traditional Junior High	Modest Change Middle School	Major Change Middle School
Teacher-student ratio	1:21	1:21	1:19
Contact minutes	250	250	250
Class size	25	25	23
Teacher-student contacts	1:125	1:100	1:83

to lower the size of certain types of classes, such as English classes. Odden (1990) and Slavin (1984) question whether reductions in class size are positively related to student learning gains.

The final dimension of teacher-student interaction is the teacher-student contact ratio. This ratio shows the number of students a teacher sees in a day. Sizer (1984) argues that this ratio is the key to engaging students in powerful forms of conceptual understanding, problem solving, and communication. Shifts in the school schedule can alter this ratio dramatically, even when the teacher-student funding ratio does not change.

Through the redeployment of personnel and the establishment of 1 house for an entire grade level with 3 teams of 4 teachers each, Modest Change Middle School has maintained the teacher-student ratio, contact minutes, and class size. However, the teacher-student contact ratio has been reduced from 1:125 under the traditional junior high model 1:100, a reduction of 20 percent.

Major Change Middle School is comprised of 4 houses and a total of 12 teams, which serve the entire student body of 1,000. By replacing two counselors and one vice principal with four additional teachers, the number of teachers has increased by four. As a result, the teacher-student ratio and class size have decreased without a reduction in contact minutes. Further, teacher-student contacts have gone down to 1:83, a decline of 33.6 percent from Traditional Junior High School.

Additional Middle School Operational Costs

Table 3.3 presents total costs organized as sample budget comparisons among the traditional junior high school, Modest Change Middle School, and Major Change Middle School. Table 3.3 summarizes these costs in terms of traditional budget categories, such as personnel or instructional materials, to provide for easy direct comparison of the scenarios. The numbers show that the additional cost of operating Modest Change Middle School is very small. As a percentage of total operating costs for a traditional junior high school, the additional cost to operate Modest Change Middle School is less than 1 percent. The

Table 3.3. Sample Budget Comparisons Between Scenarios.

Ingredients	Type	Unit Costs	Traditional Junior High School		Modest Change Middle School			Major Change Middle School		
			Number of Units	Total	Number of Units[a]	Bonus[b]	Total	Number of Units	Bonus[b]	Total
Personnel	Teachers[c]	$ 33,000	48	$1,600,761	48	$16,000	$1,616,761	52	$16,000	$1,750,148
	Principals[c]	54,890	1	54,890	1		54,890	1		54,890
	Vice principal[c]	48,013	2	96,026	2		96,026	1		48,013
	Counselor[c]	38,364	3	115,092	3		115,092	1		38,364
	Nurse[c]	26,035	1	26,035	1		26,035	1		26,035
	Social worker[d]	0	0	0	0		0	.5		13,200
	Health advocate[d]	0	0	0	0		0	.5		9,600
	Librarian[c]	35,636	1	35,636	1		35,636	1		35,636
	Secretary[d]	21,600	4	86,400	4		86,400	5		108,000
	Substitutes[e]	26,025		26,025			26,025	0		0
Instructional material[f]		22,200		22,208			22,208			44,416
Nonadministration and noninstruction[g]		714,784		714,784			720,096			736,448
Total			60	$2,777,857	60		$2,799,169	63		$2,864,750
% Change				0%			0.76%			3.12%

[a] Based on 25 students per class. Calculated at: 1,000 students × 6 periods/25 students × 5 periods.
[b] Based on $4,000 in bonus paid per qualified teacher.
[c] Based on national averages + 20% fringe benefit. *Source:* National Education Association, 1990.
[d] Based on national averages + 20% fringe benefit. *Source:* U.S. Department of Labor, 1990.
[e] Based on $75 per substitute.
[f] Based on approximately 8.2% of above total.
[g] Based on approximately 33% of above total.

only cost difference is the bonus paid to senior teachers for their leadership in curriculum and teacher development.

For Major Change Middle School, the cost increase is just over 3 percent, an astoundingly small amount considering the major changes reflected in the school's program. The major changes include increasing the teaching staff by 10 percent (to lower class size) and operating a health clinic that includes new half-time positions (a social worker and health advocate). The changes also include hiring an additional secretary and doubling the instructional materials budget. These additional costs are offset by redeploying administrative and counseling personnel to the classroom and saving the costs of substitute teachers because of the new instructional team configuration.

The above analysis uses average national data that do not exactly fit any particular state or school setting. The cost of implementing middle school reform would be much higher in some states given their larger class size combined with high teacher salaries. California is just such a case. Operational costs for middle school reform in California would be 12 percent higher in order to initially reduce class size from twenty-eight to twenty-five students across the state. Thus, the total additional cost for a school like Major Change Middle School would be 15 percent more. Of course, the absolute dollars required would vary depending on current levels of expenditures per pupil and teacher salaries.

Implementation Costs for Middle School Reform

The analysis of implementation costs for middle school reform is guided by two design principles.

1. Match the nature of implementation needed to the nature of the reform undertaken; adjust the development cost accordingly.
2. Include the cost of implementing each of the alternative program scenarios of the new program design but as development rather than operational costs.

For most schools, comprehensive reform such as middle school reform will require a more substantial and extensive implementation process than was required for earlier education reforms (Odden and Marsh, 1987; Odden, 1990; Fullan, 1990). There are several reasons for this. First, secondary schools are more difficult to change. Fullan (1990, p. 251) puts the issues this way: "Secondary schools are more complex and address a wider range of goals and agendas than do elementary schools. They contain many more structural and normative barriers to organizational change, such as departmentalization, individual teacher autonomy, physical isolation, and size. On the other hand, they are more loosely coupled and more impervious to simple (and incorrect) solutions than are elementary schools." Middle schools suffer from many of these organizational and normative problems.

Second, middle school reforms are difficult to implement. Marsh, Brown, Crocker, and Lewis (1988) studied middle school reforms in California using the Superintendent's Task Force report *Caught in the Middle* (1987) as their vision of a middle school. They found:

1. Most schools studied had begun to implement all program elements found in *Caught in the Middle*.
2. Most schools had made substantial progress in actually implementing the curriculum and instructional features of the middle school concept, especially those concerning character development and learning to learn. Schools typically had made moderate progress in implementing a core curriculum, a focus on thinking and communication skills, and use of active learning strategies. For every school in the sample, the problem was not a uniformly mediocre program across the school. Instead, in every case, the problem was lighthouse programs within the school that were not extended to the entire school. Each school had very advanced and sophisticated program elements in core curriculum, student knowledge, critical thought, and innovative/active instruction for some aspect of the school. But these

lighthouse efforts were not the norm for all parts of the school.

3. While the schools had adopted many of the features designed to enhance student potential, implementation of these elements was less extensive. Equal access, attention to student diversity, and at-risk programs were extensively implemented. Attention to the physical/emotional needs of the student body was addressed in the schools where this was part of the vision, but three schools had given this only recent attention—their implementation was less advanced. Finally, the marginal implementation of academic counseling programs was a surprising finding.

4. All schools in the study had given extensive attention to improving school culture in their school vision. This effort, which typically occurred early in the sequence of the reform, focused on creating a safe school environment, student accountability, rewards and incentives for student accomplishment in areas other than (or in addition to) athletics, affective support for students, and stronger school spirit. These aspects of school culture reflected a sense of order and purpose and "student centeredness" found in *Caught in the Middle*, which also emphasized commitment to high academic standards and high standards of personal and social behavior. While most schools reflected the standards dimension, only two had strong emphases on the "jointly developed and enforced" dimension reflected in *Caught in the Middle*.

5. Organizational changes involving school structure, student transition between elementary, middle, and high schools, school scheduling, and student assessment were desired by the schools but were often not implemented very extensively.

These results suggest that implementing the middle school elements found in *Turning Points* will not be easy. Specifically, the partial implementation found in the Marsh et al. study (1988) parallels Modest Change Middle School described above.

In short, schools will find it fairly easy to implement the middle school concept when it affects only part of the school (Modest Change) but will have difficulty extending middle school ideas to the whole school (Major Change).

Moreover, the Marsh et al. study (1988) points to a major stumbling block in implementation—the organizational structure of the school. This finding confirms what Fullan (1990) found in his review of ten recent studies of secondary school reform: organizational change was both very important and very difficult to obtain.

Important Implementation Factors

Schools that have implemented principles from *Caught in the Middle* provide insights about the process needed to implement ideas from *Turning Points*. Marsh et al. (1988) found that successful implementation at the school level happened in two ways: through schoolwide change processes and through processes related to the successful implementation of a specific middle school program element. At the schoolwide level, all schools in the sample featured a strong principal leadership role with a middle school vision that was often developed through networking with other lighthouse middle schools, through reading, or by attending conferences featuring exemplary middle school practice. Each school typically had an external network that provided ideas to the principal and key staff. Within the school, the principal typically pushed groups of key teachers to implement program components and then formed schoolwide discussions of the middle school concept.

Critical to the implementation of individual program elements was the development of lead teachers. At each school, there were at least two lead teachers who had become highly competent, within their content area, in innovative middle school program directions. This competence typically was developed through attendance at regional workshops such as the California Writing Project. These workshops emphasized in-depth discussion and practice of new approaches (in this case, to writing) and fostered weeks and months of staff development rather than hours of workshop practice. Lead teachers often were able to develop networks with effective teachers at other schools and were able to provide help to other teachers as a function of their own professional growth.

Lead teachers then typically had the time and energy to try out these new approaches in their own classrooms. At the schools studied by Marsh et al. (1988), this phase of professional growth usually lasted from one to three years. At the same time, these teachers were providing informal staff development for friends and colleagues at the home school. This represented a new phase of activity in staff development at the school. The first phase entailed nurturing the lead teachers; the second phase involved lead teachers working with other teachers at the school to disseminate effective practices.

The Marsh et al. study (1988) provides several other lessons. First, the implementation period is not short; three to five years are needed to fully implement the middle school concepts, especially the major changes required for implementation. Second, regional networks of schools working on middle school concepts can be very helpful and should be included in the overall implementation design. Third, progressive state policies can help in many ways. They can provide curriculum direction and appropriate assessment and accountability, and can enhance development of lead teachers (Smith & O'Day, 1991). Finally, state-funded school improvement programs, which feature site-directed development, can provide only limited help. They can be the flypaper that catches and funds the middle school vision.

Cost Analysis

In analyzing the cost of implementing middle school reform, it is assumed that full schoolwide implementation is the ultimate goal and that that level of implementation will take three to five years. For cost analysis purposes, there are four key implementation factors:

- Principal leadership development
- Lead teacher development

- Schoolwide faculty/curriculum/culture development and collaboration
- Regional networks supporting organizational structure improvement as well as other local development

Schools are at several different stages of readiness for implementing major reforms such as the middle school concept. One set of middle schools can be called "readiness" schools because they already have demonstrated a capability to undergo sustained change and have achieved at least some recognition for their instructional programs. A second set of middle schools are schools typically facing difficult challenges, such as serving a large population of disadvantaged students. These schools can be called "need" schools and usually are located in districts that are less effective in carrying out reform.

Readiness Middle School Implementation Process. Readiness Middle School already had implemented some program pieces prior to the beginning of the five-year development process. It also had a strong school culture and a safe environment. Implementation during years one and two created a strong sixth grade with all the middle school curriculum and instructional elements. Pilot teams next focused on the seventh grade. By year three, middle school features characterized all three grade levels, and the health/community connection clinic was in place. Years three through five emphasized organizational changes to accommodate the new class schedule and improvements in the curriculum/instructional process. A consultant team from the school's network helped the leadership team make these organizational changes.

In year one, a leadership team from the school visited other middle schools and participated in a series of workshops offered by the regional network of middle schools on aspects of overall program development. The principal also participated in a regional network series on the role of the principal in implementing major school reform; triads of principals also shadowed each other and studied the methods of a lead principal who worked with the network. In a similar way, the network helped six lead teachers from Readiness Middle School become experts at aspects of the new curriculum and instructional program and the advisory process.

The lead teachers—along with network leaders—then helped all teachers at the school to understand the middle school concept. This was followed by a set of summer curriculum institutes where teams of teachers developed and tested curriculum and advisory approaches. The summer institutes continued all five years. Moreover, the new class schedule and the shortened Wednesday afternoon provided more time for teachers to revise and implement curriculum and solve problems on an ongoing basis.

Need Middle School Implementation Process. Need Middle School required a longer and more intense development process. The school began by developing capacity in its school leaders and implementing the advisory process and the health clinic during the first year. In years two and three, the sixth-grade program was initiated and implemented; the seventh-grade program began in year three, and the eighth-grade program started in year four. At the end of year four, the program was revised to address some serious problems, and a new principal came to the school. By the end of year five, the entire program was in place but was of mixed quality. Years six and seven were needed to refine the program.

Need Middle School used the same set of regional workshops and summer institutes as did Readiness Middle School. In addition, it used a set of urban school consultants to focus more directly on school-neighborhood relations, the health clinic, and issues of student engagement in the small communities of middle school learners.

Readiness Middle School had a number of advantages that Need Middle School did not. These advantages can be seen as advantages of capacity and/or will, as defined by McLaughlin (1991). Enhanced capacity can be seen in the strength of lead teachers who already know how to operate the new curriculum in their areas; for example, some teachers might have had extensive experience in the national writing project and be doing process writing/core literature in their own classrooms. Readiness Middle School also was experienced at bringing about major change, which translates into both capacity and increased confidence or will. The development process for Need Middle School is shown in Table 3.4.

Costs. The implementation costs for Readiness Middle School and Need Middle School are presented in Table 3.4. These costs are reported as additional costs, following the model established by Little et al. (1987). For example, when the principal participates in a day-long regional workshop held during the work year, the cost of attending the workshop is included but the principal's salary for that day is not. Conversely, teacher stipends for attending the school's summer institute are included because these stipends are in addition to the regular salary for the teacher. The cost of salary credits, that is, increases in a teacher's future salary obtained from inservice training education credits, has not been included. Little et al. (1987) found these salary credit costs to be substantial.

Table 3.4 illustrates several important patterns in implementing the middle school concept:

1. The implementation process for *readiness* schools will last five years and cost approximately $120,000 per year, an amount equivalent to 4.6 percent of the operating budget for the school ($120,000 is 4.3 percent of $2,777,857, which is the estimated operating budget presented in Table 3.3).
2. For *need* schools, the implementation process will take longer and cost slightly more, averaging $161,140 per year. This amount is equivalent to approximately 6 percent of the estimated operating budget for the school.
3. For both readiness and need schools, the major items in the implementation budget are teacher development costs. These costs include both development of lead teachers (who can help other teachers at the school) and schoolwide faculty/curriculum/culture development. These two teacher development items constitute at least 85 percent of the

Table 3.4. Development Cost Per Year for Readiness Middle School and Need Middle School.

Development Factor	School	Years					Total Dollars	
		1	2	3	4	5	Readiness	Need
Principal leadership development	Readiness	$2,500	$2,500	$2,500	$2,500	$2,500	$12,500	
	Need	3,500	3,500	3,500	3,500	3,500		$17,500
Lead teacher development	Readiness	49,500	49,500	49,500	49,500	12,000	210,000	
	Need	49,500	49,500	49,500	49,500	49,500		247,500
Schoolwide faculty/curriculum/culture development	Readiness	65,500	65,500	65,500	65,500	65,500	327,500	
	Need	92,140	92,140	92,140	92,140	92,140		460,700
Regional network/organizational change	Readiness	10,000	10,000	10,000	10,000	10,000	50,000	
	Need	10,000	10,000	10,000	10,000	10,000		50,000
Other	Readiness						–0–	
	Need	10,000	10,000	10,000				30,000
Totals	Readiness	127,500	127,500	127,500	127,500	90,000	600,000	
	Need	165,140	165,140	165,140	155,140	155,140		805,700

development costs associated with implementing the middle school concept.

The implementation costs presented are not necessarily
expenses that are beyond what a school currently is spending for
development efforts. For example, if a readiness school were
spending $127,500 for teacher and program development, the
additional resources needed for implementation would be zero
if all development resources could be targeted toward middle
school reform. Moreover, these program development resources
could come from several sources: state, district, school, or outside funding.

Conclusions and Implications for School Finance

Several conclusions can be drawn from this analysis. First, the
cost of operating a middle school is not much different from
that of operating a traditional junior high school. Even for the
full-blown version of the middle school concept represented by
Major Change Middle School, the additional costs were only 3
percent above the costs of operating a traditional program. In
short, the shift to a middle school concept is not constrained by
operating costs. Second, the costs of implementing middle
school reform are not overwhelming when viewed as a percentage of the operating budget. These development costs range
from 4.6 percent for schools with well-established capacity to 6
percent for schools with less well-established capacity for these
changes.

In absolute terms, the operational and development costs
for middle school reform are not overwhelming. Both additional costs have been shown to represent a small percentage of
the current operating costs of schooling for early adolescents.
When these resource requirements, however, are viewed in the
current context of limited fiscal resources, the costs of implementing and operating middle school reform appear to be
significant. Fortunately, an analysis of fiscal resource trends over
the last forty years shows that resources significantly increased

(in real dollars) over each of the last decades and are likely to do the same in the 1990s (see Chapter One of this book).

Consequently, the more important problem for this next decade is to link fiscal and human resource development strategies so as to enhance major education reform. The development costs are primarily ones of administrative and faculty development and would be incurred over a five-year period. Several alternative policy mechanisms could provide the resources to support this development. First, many schools are already spending considerable resources on staff development. One policy strategy would focus on redirecting and extending these expenditures. The problems will be to focus resources on the comprehensive nature of the reform and to build sufficient teacher capacity to carry out the major changes that are needed.

A second policy mechanism would be to link middle school reform to the curriculum/textbook adoption cycle found in many districts and states. Since curriculum and instructional changes are a necessary aspect of middle school reform, combinations of incentives and mandates could be used to build teacher capacity linked to the implementation of the new curriculum.

Finally, states and districts could lengthen the professional school year for teachers so as to directly support the teacher development needed for major education reforms. This mechanism could provide the implementation support for achieving major education goals. The state might focus on coordinating the policy levers such as education goals, student assessment, curriculum adoption, and preservice teacher training, while the extended professional school year could provide ways for teachers to carry out the extensive teacher development needed to achieve these goals.

References

Alexander, W., & McEwin, C. K. (1989). *Schools in the middle: Status and progress*. Macon, GA: Panaprint.

Carnegie Task Force. (1989). *Turning points: Preparing American youth for the 21st century*. New York: Carnegie Corporation.

Cuban, L. (1988). A fundamental puzzle in school reform. *Phi Delta Kappan, 70,* 341–344.

Fullan, M. G. (1990). Change process in secondary schools: Toward a more fundamental change. In M. McLaughlin, J. Talbert, & N. Bascia (Eds.), *The contexts of teaching in secondary schools: Teachers' realities* (pp. 224–255). Columbia, NY: Columbia Teacher's College.

Gruhn, W., & Douglass, H. (1956). *The modern junior high school.* New York: Ronald Press.

LaPoint, A., Mead, N., & Phillips, G. (1989). *A world of differences: An international assessment of mathematics and science.* Princeton, NJ: Educational Testing Service.

Levin, H. M. (1983). *Cost effectiveness: A primer.* Newbury Park, CA: Sage.

Little, J. W., Gerritz, W., Stern, D., Guthrie, J., Kirst, M. W., & Marsh, D. (1987). *Staff development in California* (Report No. PC87-12-15-CPEC). Berkeley, CA: Policy Analysis for California Education.

Marsh, D., Brown, E., Crocker, P., & Lewis, H. (1988). Helping middle schools improve: A study of middle school implementation in California. *California ASCD Journal, 2*(3), 14–22.

Marsh, D., & Crocker, P. (1991). School restructuring: Implementing middle school reform. In A. R. Odden (Ed.), *Education policy implementation* (pp. 259–278). Albany: State University of New York Press.

Marsh, D., & Odden, A. R. (1988). Local response to the 1980s state educational reforms: New patterns of local and state interaction. In J. Murphy (Ed.), *The educational reform movement of the 1980s: Perspectives and cases* (pp. 167–186). Berkeley, CA: McCutchan.

Maurice, T. (1964). The real meaning of a school budget. *School fiscal problems and procedures.* Pittsburgh, PA: University of Pittsburgh.

McLaughlin, M. W. (1991). The Rand change agent study: Ten years later. In A. R. Odden (Ed.), *Education policy implementation* (pp. 143–156). Albany: State University of New York Press.

National Education Association. (1990). *Data search: Estimates of school statistics.* West Haven, CT: Author.

National Governors' Association. (1986). *Time for results*. Washington, DC: Author.

Odden, A. R. (1990). Class size and student achievement: Research-based policy alternatives. *Educational Evaluation and Policy Analysis, 12*, 213–227.

Odden, A. R., & Marsh, D. (1987). How comprehensive reform legislation can improve secondary schools. *Phi Delta Kappan, 69*, 593–598.

Overly, D., Kinghorn, J., & Preston, R. (1972). *The middle school: Humanizing education for youth*. Washington, OH: Charles A. Jones.

Sizer, T. (1984). *Horace's compromise: The dilemma of the American high school*. Boston: Houghton Mifflin.

Slavin, R. (1984). Meta-analysis in education: How has it been used? *Educational Researcher, 13*(8), 6–15.

Smith, M. S., & O'Day, J. (1991). Systemic school reform. In S. Fuhrman & B. Malen (Eds.), *The politics of curriculum and testing* (pp. 233–267). Philadelphia: Falmer.

Superintendent's Task Force. (1987). *Caught in the middle*. Sacramento: California State Department of Education.

U.S. Department of Labor. (1990, April). *Occupational outlook handbook, 1990–1991 edition* (Bulletin No. 2350). Washington, DC: Author.

Wiles, J. (1976). *Planning guidelines for middle school education*. Dubuque, IA: Kendall Hunt.

Wiles, J., & Bondi, J. (1981). *The essential middle school*. Columbus, OH: Merrill.

4

Promoting School-Based Management: Are Dollars Decentralized Too?

Priscilla Wohlstetter
Thomas Marshall Buffett

Decentralizing school district management has emerged in the 1990s as a popular cornerstone of education reform. Local school districts, as well as state legislatures across the nation, are giving schools more decision-making authority as a way to improve school productivity. Indeed, seven out of the eight largest urban school districts in the United States are in various stages of implementing school-based management.[1]

The school-based management movement grew out of research suggesting that school autonomy is associated with school effectiveness (Purkey & Smith, 1985). Advocates argue that those most closely affected by school-level decisions — teachers, students, and parents — ought to play a significant role in making decisions about the school's budget, curriculum, and personnel (Carnegie Forum on Education and the Economy, 1986). Support for school-based management has also come from studies that found education reform was most effective and sustained when implemented by people who felt a sense of ownership and responsibility for the reform (Fullan, 1991).

Note: The authors would like to thank the policy makers and educators who were interviewed for this study and Ronald Boggs, who helped to conduct the interviews. Special thanks are due to G. Alfred Hess, Jr., who provided useful comments on an earlier draft.

While many districts are moving rapidly toward a decentralized management style, little has been written on the financial dimensions of school-based management. This chapter explores different ways local school districts and states have encouraged school-based budgeting and offers policy makers new alternatives for designing this dimension of school-based management.

We studied five school districts and three states in different stages of implementing school-based budgeting. The five school districts were Chicago, Dade County (Florida), Detroit, Edmonton (Canada), and Los Angeles. These districts were selected by asking a panel of experts familiar with school-based management to nominate any large urban school district where budgetary allocations were made to the school site.[2] Panel members also were asked to nominate states that had policies to encourage school-based budgeting in local schools. This request produced a list of three states: California, Florida, and Kentucky. Members of the panel also suggested that we study England, which in 1988 mandated comprehensive school-based budgeting in all local schools by 1993.

Data for this study were collected primarily from telephone interviews with staff involved in implementing school-based budgeting reforms. At the district level, respondents usually included central administrative staff (for example, associate superintendent for school-based management); in state departments of education, program staff most often provided information about state-level reform. At least two people were interviewed about each reform, and the interviews, which lasted for sixty to ninety minutes, were conducted using structured protocols.

The following discussion is divided into four sections. The first reviews the knowledge base related to school-based budgeting: what do we know about how school-based budgeting works, and what are the key financial issues? The second and third sections analyze the organization and design of different approaches to school-based budgeting and highlight various ways local school districts and states encourage school-based budgeting. This chapter concludes with a proposal for a set of

initiatives for state and local policy makers to enhance implementation of school-based budgeting while maintaining fiscal
accountability.

School-Based Budgeting: Lessons from the Field

Under school-based budgeting, resource allocation decisions
are transferred from the central administration to a smaller
decision-making arena—the school. Thus, a key concern for
policy makers is the balance between central authority and
school powers. Greenhalgh (1984, p. 5) offers the following
comparison between a centralized and decentralized budgeting
system: "In a centrally administered school district, the finaliza-
tion of a budget is buried deep within a central office accounting
complex. In a decentralized school district, the budget of each
instructional center is developed by building leaders, staff members, parents, students, and community members." School-
based budgeting, at least in theory, should

- Provide greater efficiency in allocating resources because
  decisions are placed close to those who are affected (Levin,
  1987)
- Increase flexibility in the instructional program by broaden-
  ing schools' spending authority (Clune & White, 1988)
- Direct accountability to the school and away from the central administration and board of education (Ornstein, 1974)

Pierce (1977) has argued that school-based budgeting is the
most responsible way to control the costs of public education,
especially during times of fiscal retrenchment.

Clune and White (1988) concluded from their survey of
over 100 school districts that in the context of school-based
management, budgetary decisions were decentralized most
readily, followed by personnel and then curriculum decisions.
Furthermore, most (about 60 percent) of the districts Clune and
White studied in depth incorporated school-based budgeting
into their reform. As the superintendent of schools in Edmonton, Canada, explained, "It's the 'golden rule': whoever has the

gold rules." In big-city school districts, Clune and White found that school-based budgeting tended to be part of a comprehensive reform where decisions over all three areas (budgeting, curriculum, and personnel) were decentralized. Smaller school districts tended to tackle selected areas of decision making. Some districts focused exclusively on school-based budgeting, while other districts delegated budget and personnel decisions, for instance, but retained curriculum decisions centrally. Thus, evidence from the field suggests few consistent patterns in the scope of decisions given to schools under school-based management.

Other studies conclude that general approaches to decentralization also vary (Ornstein, 1974; Wohlstetter & McCurdy, 1990). Some school-based budgeting reforms are state-directed—initiated at the state level by policy generalists (often governors and legislatures)—but implemented at the local level by school administrators and teachers. Other reforms, by contrast, are the result of negotiations at the district level between administrators and teachers.

Whether state-imposed or locally developed, education reforms historically have used different policy instruments to bring about change. According to McDonnell and Elmore (1987, p. 134), there are four types of policy instruments:

- *Mandates* are rules governing the action of individuals and agencies and are intended to produce compliance.
- *Inducements* transfer money to individuals or agencies in return for certain actions.
- *Capacity-building* is the transfer of money for the purpose of investment in material, intellectual, or human resources.
- *System-changing* transfers official authority among individuals and agencies in order to alter the system by which public goods and services are delivered.

In the context of school-based management, all policies are fundamentally system-changing. School-based budgeting changes the education system so that the main budgetary function of the central administration is to allocate funds to individual schools. At the same time, schools, usually through site councils representative of various school constituencies (administrators, teachers, students, parents, and the community), are empowered to decide how allocated funds will be spent.

Prior research on school decentralization (Wohlstetter & McCurdy, 1990) further suggests that *within* the category of system-changing policies there is considerable variation depending upon the mechanism used to change the system. Wohlstetter and McCurdy found that in Chicago, where the school-based management reform was imposed from outside the school district by the state legislature, the policy instrument used mandates to bring about school decentralization. By contrast, in Dade County and Los Angeles, school-based management plans were negotiated internally as part of collective bargaining, and the reforms relied on inducements to encourage participation.

In a recent study, Hentschke (1988) proposed that for restructuring to be effective, authority relationships must change within school districts. He argued that school-based budgeting requires changing the rules about who has what kinds of decision-making authority over the use of resources. According to Hentschke, only changes in the district's authority relationships will produce changes in budgeting practices and ultimately lead to improved school productivity. Hentschke suggested five areas of change:

1. Authority over utilities and substitute teachers:
    Traditional schools: District office provides goods free to schools on an as-needed basis.
    School-based budgeting: Schools receive an allocation to use as their needs arise.
2. Authority over staff development, curriculum development, and other central office support:
    Traditional schools: District office provides services free to schools whether or not the services are needed.
    School-based budgeting: Schools buy services from the district office on an as-needed basis.
3. Authority over the mix of professionals:

Traditional schools: District office specifies the quantity and mix of personnel at schools.

School-based budgeting: Schools receive an allocation and can decide the quantity and mix of personnel at the school.

4. Authority over the source of supply:

Traditional schools: District office limits services and supplies available to schools to what the district office can provide.

School-based budgeting: Schools can purchase services and supplies from nondistrict providers.

5. Authority to carry over resources:

Traditional schools: District office receives all unspent appropriations from schools at the end of the fiscal year.

School-based budgeting: Schools can carry over unspent appropriations into the next fiscal year.

Changing relationships in these five areas means that resource decision-making authority is redistributed from various functional authorities in the central administration to individual schools, with the effect that accountability and the balance of power within districts shift to the school site. Schools benefit from their decisions and also bear the risks associated with their decisions (Hentschke, 1988).

Based on information from Clune and White's 1988 survey, districts have experimented with only a few of these changes in authority relationships. Some school-based management programs gave schools authority over the mix of professionals, allowing schools to choose the number of teachers, aides, and full-time and part-time positions. Some schools also were given authority to carry over resources. However, few districts in the Clune and White survey changed authority relationships in the other three areas.

Hentschke (1988, p. 333) observed that part of the reason for this is the lack of evidence linking school-based budgeting to increased school productivity: "[T]here is no guarantee that localized discretion leads to more productive schooling. . . [and] for district-level policymakers to delegate such authority to school building educators, they have to be convinced that such an act will increase the productivity of schools."

In addition, Clune and White (1988) observed that school-based management programs evolved over time, with districts switching their focus to different dimensions of decentralization depending on such factors as a change in the district's financial situation or the arrival of a new superintendent. Consequently, another reason for limited implementation may be the learning curve phenomenon — the idea that districts apply an incremental approach to school-based management. As an observer of England's 1988 decentralization reform commented: "In the first year, the school people were like rabbits with headlights in their eyes: They were caught by surprise. But evidence from pilot tests suggests that three or four years down the road, as people get confident, they will begin to take on a zero-based budgeting view and make choices" (Davies, 1990).

Finally, Malen and Ogawa (1988) suggest a third set of implementation factors, based on case studies of school-based management in Salt Lake City. The researchers found that even when formal authority was delegated to the building level, factors such as the composition of school site councils, the power and role orientations of principals, and the nature of district oversight and support "operated to maintain rather than alter traditional decisionmaking relationships at the site level." Consequently, the school site councils "did not wield significant influence on significant issues" in the areas of budget, personnel, or programs (Malen & Ogawa, 1988, p. 266).

The most recent literature on school-based management has focused on improving implementation by advising educators on how to organize for school-based management. The guidebooks by Brown (1991) and Prasch (1990) offer practical examples of ways to implement school-based management in local school districts. In Prasch's section on budgeting, for example, he creates sample district policies and regulations to suggest how to transfer budget control to individual schools. Both guidebooks try to translate the theory of school-based management into practical advice, based on the conviction that full implementation is a prerequisite for evaluating the effects of school-based management on school productivity.

District Approaches to School-Based Budgeting

In contrast to Pierce's (1977) assertion that the catalyst for school-based budgeting is cost savings, the common goal across the five school districts in our sample was to increase school productivity. As they stated in interviews, policy makers did not adopt school-based budgeting as a mechanism to reduce costs; their focus was on improving school performance through providing greater flexibility in the use of resources at the school level; schools would be able to target resources to meet local needs. Although the purposes of the policy makers were similar, the reforms originated in different ways and featured varied strategies, as previous research has concluded (Clune & White, 1988; Wohlstetter and McCurdy, 1990).

Initiation and Scope of School-Based Budgeting

Table 4.1 provides a summary of key features of the sample districts and their reform strategies. The push for school-based management in Detroit came from a school board directive (the Empowered Schools program); in Edmonton, reform was initiated by the superintendent. Community groups and citizen reformers appealed to the Illinois state legislature to decentralize the Chicago public schools (Hess, 1991b; Rollow, 1990). In Dade County and Los Angeles, school-based management was developed jointly by the teachers' unions and school districts as part of the collective bargaining process.

As noted earlier, the intent behind all school-based management policies is to improve the education system by altering authority relationships within the district. Across the sample districts, different mechanisms were used to accomplish that goal (see Table 4.1). Chicago and Edmonton mandated that all schools in the district plan and control their budgets, while in Dade County, Detroit, and Los Angeles, participation is volun-

Table 4.1. Characteristics of Sample School Districts: 1989–1990.

	Demographics				School-Based Budgeting Reform		
School District	Student Enrollment	Total District Budget (U.S. $)	Per-Pupil Expenditures	Total Schools (#)[a]	School-Based Budgeting Schools (#/%)	Year School-Based Budgeting Began	Policy Mechanism
Chicago	404,409	2.3 billion	$5,583	610	610/100%	1990	Mandate
Dade County	281,403	2.1 billion	7,462	271	151/56	1986	Capacity-building
Detroit	182,000	1 billion	5,495	248	8/3	1990	Inducement
Edmonton	73,670	305 million	4,133	194	194/100	1979	Mandate
Los Angeles	647,787	3.9 billion	6,021	535	4/1	1990	Capacity-building

[a] The number of schools includes elementary, junior high, and high schools and excludes specialized schools (for example, for handicapped students and adult education).

tary. Districts in the sample usually provided some additional resources or special training to help build the capacity for decentralization at the school level. Schools that participate in Dade County, for example, have received $6,000 to bring in experts to assist with implementation.

There also is considerable variation in terms of the scope of the reforms. With the exception of Edmonton, where the reform has a single focus, school-based budgeting in the other sample districts has been implemented within the context of more comprehensive decentralization efforts. Thus, at the same time schools gained authority over the budget, most also have increased responsibility for staffing and curriculum decisions. The scope of the reforms also varies in terms of the number of schools involved. In the two districts using mandates—Chicago and Edmonton—school-based budgeting was adopted simultaneously by all schools in the district (see Table 4.1).

In the districts where participation is voluntary, decentralization was encouraged in different ways. In Dade County and Los Angeles, the reforms had strong support from the teachers' unions, and the promise of greater discretion over decisions affecting classrooms served as an incentive for participation. On the other hand, Detroit schools that join the program are eligible to receive financial incentive awards for demonstrated performance. In all three districts where participation is voluntary, implementation has been incremental, with the number of school-based management schools increasing as the reforms age. After nearly five years, Dade County's participation rate is at 56 percent; in Detroit and Los Angeles, fewer than 5 percent of schools in the district have moved to school-based management, and the reforms were adopted only within the last year.

As noted earlier, changes in budgeting require changes in the formal authority of educators involved in budgeting decisions. The remainder of this section examines the budgeting process and budgeting practices in the sample schools to highlight changes in the traditional roles of educators, at both the building level and central office.

Variations in the Budgeting Process

The budgeting process consists of three sequential components: formulation, adoption, and monitoring. In traditional school districts, all phases of the budgeting process are largely centralized, with the locus of control in the central office. By contrast, in decentralized districts, individuals at the school site, usually through elected councils, are the key players, and when it comes to central office staff, schools in decentralized districts "look for helpers, not tellers." Table 4.2 compares the roles of educators in traditional districts with educators in the sample districts where budgeting is decentralized.

Budget Formulation. When a traditional school district formulates its budget, the school board sets district goals and the central administration, by estimating revenues from various sources and projecting expenditures, builds a budget that reflects these goals. Once the school board approves the budget, schools then receive various allocations for use in centrally specified areas. While traditional schools have always maintained control over some pool of discretionary resources, the school's influence over the education program offered to students remains marginal.

The role of site personnel in schools where budgetary authority has been decentralized is considerably different. In these districts, the school board and central office staff forecast revenues that will be available to the district and then decide how much of those revenues will be made available to schools. The central administration also determines which areas of authority will be placed under school control and which under central control. Revenues earmarked for school discretion are then distributed—either by staff units or actual dollars—based on some measure of pupil count. Each school receives an estimate of its revenues based on the number and type of students it has and the number and type of staff for which it is eligible. Next, schools budget the available resources in accordance with a plan that is typically developed by the school-site council. These plans go by different names—school-based management plans

Table 4.2. Budgeting Processes in Sample School Districts.

	Participants				
	School Board	Central Office	Area Superintendent	Principal	School-Site Council
Formulation					
Traditional schools	Moderate	High	Moderate	Moderate	None
Chicago	Low	Low	None	High	Moderate
Dade County	Low	None	None	High	High
Detroit	Low	None	Moderate	High	High
Edmonton	Low	Moderate	Moderate	High	a
Los Angeles	Low	Low	None	High	High
Adoption					
Traditional schools	High	High	Low	Low	None
Chicago	Low	Low	Moderate	None	High
Dade County	Low	Moderate	Moderate	None	None
Detroit	High	High	Moderate	None	None
Edmonton	High	None	High	None	a
Los Angeles	None	High	High	High	High
Monitoring					
Traditional schools	Moderate	High	High	Moderate	None
Chicago	None	High	None	High	High
Dade County	None	High	Moderate	High	High
Detroit	Moderate	High	Moderate	Moderate	Moderate
Edmonton	None	Low	Moderate	High	a
Los Angeles	None	Low	None	High	High

a In Edmonton, principals are responsible for constructing the school budget in consultation with staff, parents, and community members. Principals are not required to establish school-site councils.

in Los Angeles and school-improvement plans in Chicago—but all encompass locally developed performance goals and therefore reflect the budgetary priorities of individual schools. Thus, instead of goals being determined centrally, each school has the responsibility to develop its own.

As shown in Table 4.2, the school board, the central office, and area superintendents play limited roles in the budget formulation process for individual schools. In school-based budgeting districts, the primary central function is to set parameters for allocating district revenues. Other central activities focus on providing services directly to schools. In Chicago and Los Angeles, the central office provides mostly information and technical assistance, such as helping schools project their revenue estimates or translate performance goals into budget items. In Detroit, the principal and school-site council work with the area superintendent to formulate the budget. In Edmonton, the area superintendent and school principal, in consultation with staff, students, parents, and the community, establish the school's goals for student achievement. In Dade County, school resources are budgeted at the building level in accordance with individual school plans developed jointly by the principal and school-site council.

Budget Adoption. In traditional school districts, budget adoption also is a centralized process. After the central office plans the district budget, the school board approves it and line-item resources are dispersed to the schools. By contrast, the budget adoption process in decentralized school districts begins at the school level. As suggested by Table 4.2, the main difference between traditional and decentralized schools is the directional flow of the adoption process: school budgets in decentralized schools move upward through the district hierarchy, from the building level to the school board, rather than down the hierarchy.

Some of the sample districts are more specific than others regarding who must approve budgets at the school level. In order to adopt a budget in Los Angeles, the principal, union steward, and a parent or community representative must sign a

Certification of Participation. Edmonton's reform, which has been labeled "principal-based decisionmaking" (Brown, 1990, p. 166), simply requires that the principal *consult* with school constituents during the adoption process. Principals in Edmonton schools are not required to create formal school-site councils, as is the requirement in the other sample districts.

While final adoption of the budget is still a centralized function in school-based budgeting districts, reviews by the district administration are largely focused on compliance, not substantive issues. School budgets must comply with district, union, state, and federal regulations (unless waivers have been obtained), but within these parameters decentralized schools are free to propose their own educational programs. In the sample districts, for example, the role of area superintendent has changed dramatically under school-based budgeting (see Table 4.2). In most of the sample districts, area superintendents used to be able to dispense services from their large staffs and funds for special projects to individual schools. Under school-based budgeting, area superintendents have little control over school budgets, except for acting as conduits to central staff. In effect, the area superintendents serve as checkpoints for ensuring that school budgets are in compliance with contract and regulatory obligations before the budgets are submitted for approval.

It is important to note that the budget formulation and budget adoption processes for school-based budgeting districts are fundamentally different than for organizations in other spheres of the public sector. While school-based budgets reflect the financial implications of institutional goals, as is the case for budgets of public institutions generally, school budgets are not requests for money. The total value of resources available to the school is set before the budget formulation process begins at the school site. In the budget adoption phase, central district staff do not evaluate local plans on the basis of affordability but rather, as stated earlier, on the basis of compliance with existing policies. In sum, traditional public-sector budgeting entails institutional requests for financial resources that are needed to meet stated goals. By contrast, school budgets in decentralized districts demonstrate how the school will operate in the upcoming fiscal year, given an amount of resources that has been centrally determined and allocated (irrespective of school-based plans).

Monitoring. Monitoring the budget also has changed with the adoption of school-based budgeting. However, the nature of monitoring activities has changed more than the actors who are involved. In most of the districts, the central administration has retained a prominent role in the monitoring process (see Table 4.2). But instead of focusing on compliance issues, the new role of the administration is to provide information feedback to schools. In three districts, Chicago, Dade County, and Edmonton, the central office maintains automated financial systems and provides financial information to school-site personnel. In Edmonton, schools can opt to go on-line and create their own accounting codes for the central office to use in preparing monthly financial reports to schools. Across most of the sample districts, money has been invested to develop technology at individual school sites so that each school has a management information system for monitoring (and staying within) its own budget. Where automated systems are maintained centrally, schools simply cannot spend beyond the amount budgeted; requests from depleted accounts are rejected. In this way, accountability has been pushed down the professional bureaucracy to the school level but monitored by a computerized, central control mechanism.

Variations in Budgeting Practices

Budgeting practices encompass how funds are allocated and the amount of spending discretion schools have. A main concern of policy makers is the relationship between the two, that is, the extent to which allocations control spending. In traditional schools, funds are allocated by category (function or unit), and the categories prescribe school spending.

In theory, a school under school-based budgeting is allocated a lump sum and has control over its share (however defined) of *every* district resource. While this form is not currently in place anywhere, the sample districts generally have moved in this direction; as shown in Table 4.3, discretion over some traditionally centralized resources has been transferred to the school level.

Allocation Rules. The allocation rules used by the sample districts are surprisingly uniform, and all entail some measure of the number of students (for example, average daily attendance, average daily membership, number of full-time-equivalent students). In fact, typical allocation mechanisms have not changed substantially under school-based budgeting. Standardized norm tables are created and resources are distributed according to school eligibility. The primary difference is that with school-based budgeting more of the allocated resources are under the control of school personnel.

As noted earlier, school resources are allocated by either staff units or actual dollars. In all of the sample districts, individual schools are allocated personnel resources by staff units or positions. If a school decides to convert the resources associated with optional personnel positions for use in other areas (see section below on expenditure authority), staff units are exchanged on an average-cost basis. With such exchange possible, the decision to allocate personnel resources by position rather than dollars is of symbolic but not fiscal importance.

Whereas the allocation rules used by the districts are similar, the sample differs in the extent of resources that are delegated to schools. In Chicago, Dade County, and Detroit, discretion over all resources that are committed through district contracts, including teacher salaries, is maintained centrally. In Chicago, between 72 and 76 percent of the annual budgets of the Chicago public schools is devoted to salaries, pensions, and medical benefits (Hess, 1991a); in Detroit, salaries account for about 80 percent of school budgets. In practice, the site councils in all three districts think they have some control over these traditionally nondiscretionary funds because the councils can alter staffing arrangements and even increase class size by seeking waivers from contracts, categorical restrictions, or state laws.

Table 4.3. Budgeting Practices in Sample School Districts: Areas of Authority for School Sites.

School District	Leaky Roofs, and so on	Utilities and Substitute Teachers	Staff Development, Curriculum Development	Mix of Personnel	Contracting Outside District	Carrying Over Funds
Traditional schools	District	District	District	District	No	No
Chicago	District	District	School	School	Yes	Yes[a]
Dade County	District	School[b]	School	School	Yes	Yes
Detroit	District	School	School	School	Yes	No
Edmonton	District	School	School	School	Yes	Yes
Los Angeles	District	District (utilities) School (substitute teachers)	School	School	No	Yes[c]

[a] Schools can carry over discretionary funds provided under the state compensatory aid program.

[b] Savings from utilities (difference between amount budgeted and amount spent) accrue to the school site for use the following year.

[c] The only account that can be carried over is for teacher illness days. Any money that is saved through lower-than-average teacher absenteeism is carried over for one year and can be spent in any area.

School sites in the three districts also receive funds designated discretionary that are allocated based on student enrollment. Thus, in both direct and indirect ways, school-based budgeting brings more fiscal responsibility to the local level. For example, it was estimated that during the first year of the Chicago reform the average elementary school received about $90,000 in new discretionary funds (Hess, 1991a).[3] Dade County reported that schools participating in school-based management have control over approximately 70 percent of their budget, largely through the site councils' authority over personnel decisions.

The other two districts in the sample—Los Angeles and Edmonton—are at opposite ends of the spectrum in terms of the amount of the total district revenues allocated to school sites. Los Angeles gives schools control over considerably less than 25 percent of their budgets. All schools in the district have control over resources for instructional supplies, and the only additional area that school-based budgeting schools can choose to have responsibility for is that of substitute teachers. Schools that choose this option are allocated the dollar value of the number of teachers they have multiplied by the average number of sick days per teacher per year in the district (currently ten). At the other extreme is the district office in Edmonton, which allocates 80 percent of the total budget to schools through an elaborate funding formula that has thirteen different categorizations of students (by grade level, handicapped status, program, and so on). Each school receives a lump-sum allocation based directly on weighted student counts. As in Chicago, Dade County, and Detroit, schools in Edmonton receive some of their discretionary authority indirectly through control over personnel decisions.

Expenditure Authority. Whereas the resource allocation mechanism—per-pupil formulas—for traditional and decentralized schools is essentially the same, schools under school-based budgeting have more discretion over areas usually under the purview of the central office. Consequently, spending authority formerly held by central and area district offices has shifted to the school level and increased local site autonomy. In particular, the school-based budgeting districts have expenditure authority in five areas: (1) the mix of teachers and other professional staff, (2) substitute teachers, (3) staff development, (4) purchase of goods and services, and (5) budget balances.

While assembling the pool of qualified applicants remains largely a central function, decentralized schools can, within certain parameters, decide whom to hire. By allowing the purchase and/or exchange of staff units on an average-cost basis, sample districts afford schools a specific kind of staffing flexibility. When making hiring decisions, schools can select any potential candidate they want and not worry about the budgetary effect because they are allocated a position, not dollars. The result is that schools can hire the most experienced teacher they want but cannot make a trade-off to take two "cheap" (that is, inexperienced, thus lower on the salary scale) teachers.[4] The total costs of staff (and thus of the school budget), therefore, float depending on the experience levels of the teachers who are employed.

The alternative to average-cost distribution and exchange, having schools make budgetary decisions based on real costs, provides a different type of flexibility. This strategy allows schools more discretion over the number of positions filled. Schools can opt to hire relatively inexperienced teachers and use the savings for additional personnel (or in other areas). Conversely, schools that allocate resources on an average-cost basis have flexibility in choice of personnel irrespective of cost. In sum, there are two alternative forms of flexibility for schools embarking upon school-based budgeting: flexibility in experience and flexibility in the number of positions. Schools in the sample districts were given the flexibility to determine the experience levels of their teachers but not the discretion to decide the number of positions. As one of the reformers in Chicago commented, "Since we'd seen rural school districts constantly turn over their new teachers to keep costs down, we opted for flexibility in experience."

While allocation based on average cost can afford schools greater flexibility in terms of staff experience, realization of this benefit can be hindered by the rights associated with tenure. In most school districts, as teachers gain seniority within the system, they earn the right to transfer from one school to another. Because teachers frequently perceive their success to be closely linked to the social status of their students (Pierce, 1977), teachers tend to transfer away from poor schools. Thus, while personnel decisions can be made irrespective of actual cost, the availability of more experienced teachers may be limited for less affluent schools. Because salaries are commensurate with experience, the migration of more seasoned teachers away from poor schools can create substantial disparities in real instructional expenditures at the schools (despite equal allocation of staff units), as well as in the amount of teacher experience. Although experienced teachers do not cost any more, poor schools may have a more difficult time recruiting and retaining them. Thus, with traditional benefits accruing to seniority, average cost distribution and exchange may threaten intradistrict equity. This remains a policy concern for decision makers in districts considering school-based budgeting.

Across the sample districts, the parameter that most greatly influences resource expenditure is class size. Unless a waiver has been obtained, the number of teachers hired must accommodate the student-teacher ratio set for that grade level. In Edmonton, schools must report and receive approval when class size exceeds thirty; however, the only requirement is that the needs of students are met. Schools in Chicago are free to choose the mix of professionals "within applicable laws and contract agreements." In Los Angeles, the district adopted a "hold harmless" provision: no one can lose his or her job as a result of the decentralization effort. By contrast, in Dade County and Edmonton, schools can declare staff surplus to their needs, and it is the district's responsibility to relocate the employee.

The differences in personnel policies across sample districts underscore an important point: the amount of fiscal discretion a school has can be increased or decreased through the collective bargaining process. McDonnell and Pascal (1988) conclude that collective bargaining agreements can be either an effective vehicle for implementing reform or a major obstacle to change. Because personnel salaries consume the largest portion of the school budget, the rules that govern salary schedules and reductions in force have important implications for budgetary autonomy and school-based management. School-based management also raises an interesting policy dilemma for teachers' unions, one not yet explored. Union strength is dependent on centralization and uniformity of policies among schools within a district. Policies are negotiated for an entire district, with little room for schools to deviate. Under school-based management, schools often are permitted to seek waivers to union bargaining agreements, and policies among schools become differentiated according to site-based plans. Will unions gain or lose strength if school policies are negotiated separately at the building level? Many union grievances relate to perceived inequities that result from procedural differences from school to school (starting and ending time of work day, for example). On the other hand, to the extent that decentralization empowers and professionalizes teachers, it deserves union support and seems to have had it to date. Consider, for example, decentralization reform in Dade County and Los Angeles (Wohlstetter & McCurdy, 1990).

Across the sample districts, there are certain positions that are mandatory "buy-backs" for every school; for example, every school must have a principal. Los Angeles and Dade County are similar in that required positions are specified by the central administration. When personnel positions are allocated, they come as either convertible or inconvertible. Convertible positions give schools more discretion over personnel decisions: if someone in such a position retires or is transferred, the school council has the option of converting that position to cash for some other purpose. Hentschke (1988) found, moreover, that when building-level educators in Dade County were allowed discretion in spending for personnel, they tended to employ part-time employees in order to save and redeploy some of the costs for fringe benefits.

A second personnel area under school control is discretionary positions. These may be purchased from the central administration, and schools under school-based budgeting are able to divert available funds (as determined by the average cost for the position in the district) to any other expenditure category. Because expenditure decisions in the sample districts are based on average unit cost (not real cost), school-level decision makers now can select personnel on the basis of merit, not seniority. Personnel hirings in the sample districts must comply with all contractual and state guidelines unless the appropriate waivers have been requested and secured. Experience from the field suggests that most waiver requests are granted and that the few that are not approved often are turned down for procedural reasons (for example, the principal applies for a waiver without allowing teachers to vote).

Expenditure authority over substitute teachers also has been decentralized in some of the sample school districts. In Dade County and Los Angeles, for example, schools under school-based budgeting can receive the dollar amount of the cost for substitute teachers in exchange for assuming responsibility over this expenditure area. If a school has a low rate of teacher absenteeism, the savings accrue to the school the following year for use in other areas. Likewise, if a school has a higher-than-average absentee rate, other funds will have to be tapped in order to balance the account. (Both Dade County and Los Angeles have policies whereby the district pays for substitutes in the event of catastrophic illness.)

Financial resources for staff development and curriculum development, traditionally centralized functions, have been decentralized in the two districts that have moved all schools to school-based budgeting (Chicago and Edmonton). Whereas traditional districts provide the services at no charge to schools, the schools in Chicago and Edmonton have discretion over the resources for such services. Depending on their individual needs, schools can decide, based on real costs, whether to send staff to professional development activities or to hire a curriculum consultant. Money not used in these areas can be used in other areas to purchase equipment or provide more planning time for staff, for instance. In the sample districts where participation in school-based budgeting is voluntary, participating schools still have free access to professional development and curriculum development services that are available to traditional schools.

Another expenditure area that has devolved to decentralized schools is the purchase of goods and services from
vendors outside the district. In traditional schools, the range of
services available to schools is limited to what the central office
can provide. Schools under school-based budgeting generally
have more flexibility and can make purchases from nondistrict
providers. In Dade County most purchases are made from district suppliers; however, one school has contracted with Berlitz
to teach Spanish because building-level educators thought that
the private firm would do a more cost-effective job than the
district (Hentschke, 1988). In Detroit and Edmonton, schools
can contract with outside vendors but do not receive full-dollar
value when goods or services are purchased from nondistrict
suppliers. Thus, there is a clear incentive to use district providers. In Detroit and Edmonton, as well as Chicago (which does
give schools full-dollar value), purchases must be made from a
preapproved list of vendors unless a waiver has been obtained.

The last area of budgetary practice that was examined is
the authority to carry over unused resources to the next fiscal
year. In traditional schools, any unspent funds are returned to
the district coffers. Detroit has not changed this practice. However, in Edmonton, school surpluses and deficits are carried
forward to the next fiscal year. During the first year of school-
based management, the total budget in Edmonton was $165
million, and surpluses amounted to $3 million, about 2 percent
(Brown, 1990). Dade County also allows schools to carry over all
unused funds, including 100 percent of savings realized through
utility conservation (compared to 80 percent for traditional
schools in the district) and all of the unspent salary funds for
convertible positions. In Los Angeles, the district decided that,
due to its poor financial condition, the only resources that can
be carried over (with the exception of a few state textbook
accounts) are unspent funds in the substitute teacher account.
Chicago schools can carry over their state compensatory aid
funds; if schools underspend one year, they can have the leftover
funds on top of their new allotment for the next year. When
district funds are carried forward, they become discretionary

the following year whether or not they were during the year they were allocated.

In sum, a considerable amount of resources has been rolled into the site allocation formula, and decisions on how to use them have been substantially delegated to schools. System-wide data from Chicago reveal how schools are spending their new discretionary money: "Schools have added educational support staff, relatively equally across the system, an average of about two additional teachers at each school. It appears that schools with heavier concentrations of low income students have chosen to focus on adding aides. In addition, they may have made more material purchases of computers, copy machines, books, and supplies" (Hess, 1991a, p. 24). Notwithstanding this new authority, some important fiscally oriented decisions have been retained by central offices. In addition to the areas already cited, external building maintenance (for example, fixing the leaky roof) and payment for utilities have remained largely central office responsibilities (see Table 4.3).

Along with the expenditure authority given to schools is the issue of the schools' willingness to take advantage of the flexibility. This is largely an implementation question beyond the scope of this chapter; however, given what we already know about the incremental nature of budgeting, districts may have to set up alternative mechanisms, such as zero-based budgeting, to help schools feel more comfortable redirecting resources toward the purposes, programs, and objectives expressed in their site-based plans. According to Guthrie, Garms, and Pierce, "Zero-based budgeting assumes that annually, or at least regularly, an entire budget can be built from the ground up with few assumptions regarding existing obligations" (1988, p. 233). Consequently, if a purpose is agreed to by the school site and included in the site-based plan, then the school would devote considerable resources toward accomplishing this purpose. On the other hand, if a program is no longer aligned with the purpose of the school, then its expenditure base would be reduced or eliminated. In sum, zero-based budgeting, or a similar mechanism, might be needed to encourage schools to make resource allocation changes at more than just the margins.

State and Central Government Approaches to School-Based Budgeting

Across the sample, state and central government approaches to decentralization, like the district strategies, share the goal of increasing school productivity through greater local autonomy. Another similarity among the subjects of the study was the catalyst for the reform: all reforms were produced by legislative bodies, state legislatures in the United States and Parliament in England.[5] Table 4.4 summarizes key features of the four approaches to school-based budgeting that were studied.

In other ways, the reforms are quite varied. Florida adopted an incremental approach to decentralization. The state's first school-based budgeting initiative (Accountability Act of 1973) was adopted nearly two decades ago; since then, the legislature has enacted six other reforms aimed at strengthening school-site management. By contrast, England and Kentucky moved to decentralize very recently, included decentralization as part of a comprehensive reform program, and required all schools to participate.

The three states and England also have employed fundamentally different policy mechanisms to bring about change (see Table 4.4). Two of the central governmental bodies, Kentucky and England, used mandates that required all schools to move into school-based management by a specified date (1996 in Kentucky and 1993 in England). Florida invested money in the area of capacity-building by sponsoring staff development activities for participating districts. The California reform used an inducement mechanism that provided additional resources to schools on the condition they move toward school-based budgeting. The remainder of this section, which is organized by type of policy mechanism, highlights the primary elements and expected effects of the different approaches to school-based budgeting.

Mandates

In a sense, mandates are inimical to school-based management. There is a paradox of sorts when a central authority, through legislation and bureaucratic initiatives that appear to seek uniformity, orders schools in a particular direction while, at the same time, advocating school-based decision making. As adopted in England and Kentucky, the division of authority (which provides a partial answer to the paradox) vests central authorities with the responsibility for setting outcome measures and performance objectives and schools with the responsibility for operational management decisions. In other words, schools are free to choose the means for accomplishing centrally speci fied ends.

While the goal of education reform in England and Kentucky is enhanced decision-making authority at the school site, the initiatives were enacted in the context of large-scale education reform efforts that go well beyond governance. The Kentucky Education Reform Act of 1990 included changes in the way schools are financed, teachers are certified, and students are evaluated. Kentucky's reform also required development of student learning goals, state curriculum frameworks, and a performance-based student assessment program. School-based management was mandated as an implementation strategy, but it clearly was *not* intended to decentralize authority over what students learn. England's Education Reform Act of 1988 (ERA) is similarly comprehensive. The ERA established provisions for a national curriculum and a national assessment program, with performance standards for each subject. In both England and Kentucky, core values (that is, student outcome goals) were centralized, while decision-making authority over how to teach those values was decentralized to the school level.

The Kentucky Education Reform Act contains rules that specify the composition of school councils and the rate at which school-based management should be implemented. School councils are required to include parents (elected by the school's parent-teacher organization), teachers (elected by teachers at the school), and an administrator. By the 1991–92 school year,

Table 4.4. Characteristics of Sample State/Central Government Approaches to School-Based Budgeting.

State/ Central Government	Year School-Based Budgeting Began	Number of School-Based Budgeting Schools or Districts	Percent of School-Based Budgeting Schools or Districts	Policy Mechanism	Primary Elements	Expected Effects		
						State	Local	
California	1981	4,300 schools	61%	Inducement	• Staff development days • Flexibility in use of categorical money • Waivers	• No change in relationship	• Increased budgetary flexibility • Reduced paperwork	
England	1988	104 districts	100%	Mandate	• Rules: all schools must participate; district must delegate money to schools • Money to district for management information systems	• More interventionist (for example, national curriculum) • More direct contact with schools	• Spending priorities established by schools	
Florida	1989	40 districts	60%	Capacity-building	• Training on restructuring • Technical assistance • Waivers • Money for experts	• Less sanction-oriented • More direct contact with schools • More service-oriented	• Increased evaluation role • Increased paperwork	

| Kentucky | 1991 | [a] | Mandate | • Rules: all schools must participate; school-site councils must have set composition
 • Technical assistance
 • Money for staff development | • More interventionist (for example, state-identified learner outcomes)
 • More direct contact with schools
 • More service-oriented | • Implementation strategies designed by schools
 • Increased paperwork |

[a] By the 1991–92 school year, each district must have at least one school participating. By 1996, all the schools in the state must participate in school-based decision making unless granted an exemption by the State Board for Elementary and Secondary Education.

every district in the state must have at least one school in school-based management, and all schools must participate by July 1996. The intent of policy makers, according to the interviews, was to create some uniformity in council operations across school districts in the state.

England's reform, which prescribes full implementation by 1993, also defines which aspects of school governance should be controlled by individual schools and which should be retained by the district office. In what has been likened to a landlord-tenant relationship, the ERA specifically required that "the LEA [Local Educational Agency] must retain funds to cover major capital works, central administration, advisory services and legal and medical services. . . [and] the rest of the money must be allocated to the schools by a formula so that in a typical LEA about two thirds of funds will be allocated directly to schools and one third retained centrally" (Davies & Ellison, 1990, pp. 18–19). Two years after passage, Parliament, disturbed by the continued dependency of schools on LEAs, amended the ERA to restrict LEAs to planning and building activities and to boost the amount allocated directly to schools to 85 percent (up from two-thirds).

In sum, the decentralization reform in England targets financial issues directly, requiring that all local districts develop plans for delegating financial responsibility to the building level. Furthermore, if individual schools feel that LEA fiscal policy is too restrictive, they can opt out of local authority and receive funding directly from the national government. By contrast, the Kentucky reform does not offer schools this option. In fact, the section of the Kentucky reform authorizing school-based decision making contains no specific mention of finance; rather, it contains a mandate to decentralize management in general.

Mandates, according to McDonnell and Elmore (1987), assume that the required action—in this instance, school-based management—is something all school districts can be expected to do, regardless of their differing capacities. In England and Kentucky, where there existed high levels of political support for education reform, policy makers nevertheless recognized the burden the new policies imposed on districts and schools and provided some resources for implementation.[6]

Both mandates were accompanied by capacity-building activities (see Table 4.4). The Department of Education and Science in England offers education support grants to local districts to assist with training and computer costs. In Kentucky, the state board of education has allocated resources to school districts to cover staff development costs in a variety of topical areas, including school-based management. The state board also has required that each local board of education appropriate to the school level not less than $75 per full-time-equivalent (FTE) student. Local decision-making councils can decide how to spend most of the money (about $60 per FTE); however, the state requires some support in certain areas.

Responsibility for enforcing compliance with the two mandates was vested in state/central government agencies. Consequently, the roles of Kentucky's state board and department of education and the Department of Education and Science in England were expected to become more influential and more interventionist. As an observer in England commented, "Before the Education Reform Act, the Department of Education and Science had a hands-off policy toward education: there will be schools, and it is the Local Educational Agency's (LEA) responsibility to run them. Now, the department prescribes explicit guidelines for LEA school-management plans, approves the plans, and offers LEAs support grants to assist with implementation." Respondents in both England and Kentucky also expected state/central government agencies to become involved more directly with schools, since schools — not districts — were the targets of reform.

Capacity-Building

Florida has approached decentralized budgeting in a very different way. Instead of requiring that all districts and schools embrace a single reform, the state enacted legislation to promote local efforts. By helping to increase the decision-making capacities of schools in human resources and technology,

Florida's District School Site Restructuring Incentive Program aims to change how education systems make fiscally oriented decisions.

The state of Florida invested money in the area of capacity-building by offering professional development activities and technical assistance to school districts that want to restructure. The broadest impact of the program comes from statewide and regional training conferences that are designed to help local restructuring efforts by reviewing what is currently known about restructuring, providing restructuring models and a standard evaluation plan for restructured schools, and facilitating the development of networks for restructured schools. In sum, Florida's reform is an investment in the future. By helping schools build the capacity to manage themselves, the reform is expected to produce future returns, including improved school productivity.

In Florida, as in California, there are both state and local policies to encourage school-based budgeting; evidence from the interviews suggests that the two types of policies, which were developed independently, remain largely uncoordinated. For example, schools in Dade County that are in the process of restructuring have not made use of all the state reform funds available to them.

Another interesting result of Florida's restructuring program is that the state role in education policy changed. The reform led to an increased emphasis on cooperation between state and district policy makers and school administrators. Specifically, the state moved from being more sanction-oriented to providing services directly to the schools.

Inducement

California's School-Based Coordination Act, which preceded the Los Angeles reform by nine years, offers an inducement (eight funded staff development days) to schools on the condition they move toward school-based budgeting. Participating schools can combine funds from different categorical programs and also do not have to track for reporting purposes where funds have been spent. The intent of the reform was to provide schools with greater flexibility in how resources from state categorical funds were spent so that schools would make decisions based on student needs, rather than on the funding source.

While participation has grown considerably in the past few years, about 70 percent of the participating schools are coordinating only one categorical program with their core program. Because there is no penalty for minimal participation — and since minimal participation is sufficient to obtain the inducement (eight funded staff development days) — most schools have opted for the minimum. Another implementation problem, discovered during inteviews, was the existence of districts in California (as in Florida) that had initiated school-based management reforms of their own but had not taken advantage of complementary state reforms, such as the School-Based Coordination Act.

Conclusions and Policy Implications

Conclusions

The purpose of this study was to examine notable or exemplary approaches to school-based budgeting. Previous research on school-based management (Clune & White, 1988; Malen & Ogawa, 1988) found that traditional patterns of decision making were difficult to alter and that school-site councils rarely made "real" or substantive decisions. By contrast, the findings from this study propose new patterns of decision making that effectively empower building-level educators with substantial discretion over some resources. The evidence suggests the following conclusions:

- The intent of policy makers in adopting school-based budgeting was to improve school productivity, not to reduce costs. Consequently, locally developed school plans focused on achieving educational goals (for example, reducing dropout rates), rather than reducing the costs of schooling.
- School-based budgeting often was adopted as part of a

comprehensive school-based management plan. In the few instances where reforms focused exclusively on decentralizing budgeting, there were spillover effects into curriculum and personnel decisions.

- State/central government and local initiatives to encourage school-based management (and budgeting) were developed independently and remained largely uncoordinated. As a result, decentralized schools are often not taking advantage of higher-level reforms, and schools participating in such reforms are not often in districts that have adopted school-based management.

- Participation in school-based budgeting was typically on a voluntary basis. However, four (of nine) reforms mandated school-based management for all schools in the district or all school districts in the state/country.

- School-based budgeting reforms transferred authority in budget formulation and adoption from the central office to individual schools and allowed schools, primarily through site councils, to create their own budgets to meet locally developed needs.

- Schools, to varying degrees, received lump-sum allocations and were allowed to decide the mix of personnel at the site, to purchase services (for example, staff development) from the central office or nondistrict providers, and to carry over unspent funds into the next fiscal year.

- Educators at the building level have become increasingly involved in monitoring expenditures, with the effect that accountability, in terms of budgetary control, has shifted to the school.

Policy Implications

In her recent article on restructured schools, David (1990) concluded that there are significant parallels in the actions districts and states can take to promote change. In the specific case of school-based budgeting, we agree. States and districts, moreover, are in strong positions to influence schools; both have sufficient financial and regulatory leverage to bring about change (Elmore & Fuhrman, 1990).

Thus, we believe that each state and its local districts can enter into a friendly partnership to help schools adapt to school-based management. The division of responsibility within each partnership should not be uniform across states nor compartmentalized as in a hierarchy. Rather, responsibility should be allowed to vary to match states' different political cultures. Consequently, many of the initiatives offered below may be taken by only one member of the partnership, depending on whether the state has strong local control norms or a tradition of state-directed reform. A few of the initiatives, at the discretion of the partners, probably should be taken jointly by states and local school districts.

- Establish standards or guidelines to help define the outcomes of budgeting in restructured schools (for example, a fixed percentage of the total budget must be spent at the discretion of the school). The outcomes ought to be measurable to allow for assessments of progress.
- Encourage "systemic reform" (Smith & O'Day, 1991) in which school-based management is joined in a coordinated effort with curriculum and instruction reforms to improve school productivity.
- Systematically review existing education policies and regulations to determine whether there are impediments to school-based budgeting and to better coordinate various state and district policies.
- Utilize zero-based budgeting or a similar mechanism to encourage schools to redirect expenditures toward the purposes, programs, and objectives of locally developed site-based plans.
- Where participation in school-based budgeting is voluntary, expand the use of inducements to raise participation levels. For example, grantors could award an up-front school improvement grant of $50–$100 per pupil.
- Establish set-asides for evaluation activities to aggressively

monitor the impact of school-based management on student performance and on school productivity in general.

In conclusion, the idea of a fluid and interdependent partnership between the state and local districts is very promising as an aspect of school-based budgeting. The partnership ought to be responsible, in effect, for accountability—specifying the goals of the education system—and furnishing resources to inspire change and manage information feedback. Based on the experiences of the school districts in this study, budgeting processes and practices have been decentralized to a limited extent. In order to fully test the efficacy of school-based budgeting, additional fiscal responsibility and authority ought to be further devolved to the school-building level.

Notes

1. Based on 1989–90 student enrollment data from the Council of Great City Schools, the largest urban school districts are: New York City (939,500), Los Angeles (610,000), Chicago (404,991), Dade County (278,789), Philadelphia (193,588), Houston (191,284), Detroit (172,033), and Dallas (132,730). Of the eight, Houston is the only school district that has not moved toward school-based management.
2. Respondents included national associations (Education Commission of the States and the National Governors' Association), national teachers' unions, educational consultants, and deans and professors of education in major universities.
3. Across the district, the amount of discretionary money varies considerably depending upon the extent to which schools qualify for four different pots of money: (1) percentage of students who are poor (eligible for free lunch), (2) state and federal compensatory education funds for improving reading achievement, (3) racial isolation, and (4) bilingual education. Consequently, an integrated school with no poor children and no bilingual children would receive nothing. On the other hand, a school that is mostly

Hispanic, poor, and low achieving with a high percentage of limited-English-speaking students would qualify for all pots. Although most of the Chicago public schools receive some discretionary money, the amount varies from zero to $1.2 million (Sebring, personal communication, May 1991).

4. Prasch (1990) warns that although the cost of a category of employee must bear a relationship to the salary paid, it should not be a straight-line relationship to the salary of each individual employee; such a formula likely would encourage the problem of trading "cheap" for expensive staff.

5. The specific legislative reforms discussed in this section are the District School Site Restructuring Incentive Program of 1989 (Florida), the Education Reform Act of 1988 (England), the Kentucky Education Reform Act of 1990 (Kentucky), and the School-Based Coordination Act of 1981 (California).

6. Education reform in England, which Prime Minister Thatcher championed, benefited directly from her widespread popularity. The Kentucky Education Reform Act was enacted in response to a state supreme court decision that ruled the state education system unconstitutional.

References

Brown, D. J. (1990). *Decentralization and school-based management.* Philadelphia: Falmer.

Brown, D. J. (1991). *Decentralization: The administrator's guidebook to school district change.* Newbury Park, CA: Corwin Press.

Carnegie Forum on Education and the Economy. (1986). *A nation prepared: Teachers for the 21st century.* Washington, DC: Author.

Clune, W. H., & White, P. A. (1988). *School-based management: Institutional variation, implementation, and issues for further research* (Rep. No. RR-008). New Brunswick, NJ: Rutgers University, Consortium for Policy Research in Education.

David, J. L. (1990). Restructuring in progress: Lessons from pioneering districts. In R. F. Elmore & Associates, *Restructur-*

ing schools: The next generation of educational reform. San Francisco: Jossey-Bass.

Davies, B. (1990, December). Personal interview with authors.

Davies, B., & Ellison, L. (1990). Local management of schools: The current revolution in English education. *School Business Affairs, 56,* 16–23.

Elmore, R. F., & Fuhrman, S. (1990). The national interest and the federal role in education. *Publius, 20,* 149–162.

Fullan, M. G. (with S. M. Stiegelbauer). (1991). *The new meaning of educational change* (2nd ed.). New York: Teachers College Press.

Greenhalgh, J. (1984). *School site budgeting.* Lanham, MD: University Press of America.

Guthrie, J. W., Garms, W. I., & Pierce, L. C. (1988). *School finance and education policy* (2nd ed.). Englewood Cliffs, NJ: Prentice-Hall.

Hentschke, G. C. (1988). Budgetary theory and reality: A Microview. In D. H. Monk & J. Underwood (Eds.), *Microlevel school finance: Issues and implications for policy* (pp. 311–336). New York: Ballinger.

Hess, G. A., Jr. (1991a, April). *The reallocation of funds under the Chicago School Reform Act.* Paper presented at the annual meeting of the American Educational Research Association, Chicago.

Hess, G. A., Jr. (1991b). *School restructuring, Chicago style.* Newbury Park, CA: Corwin Press.

Levin, H. M. (1987, June). *Finance and governance implications of school-based decisions.* Paper presented at the National Advisory Committee of the Work in America Institute, New York.

Malen, B., & Ogawa, R. T. (1988). Professional-patron influence on site-based governance councils: A confounding case study. *Education Evaluation and Policy Analysis, 10,* 251–270.

McDonnell, L. M., & Elmore, R. F. (1987). Getting the job done: Alternative policy instruments. *Education Evaluation and Policy Analysis, 9,* 133–152.

McDonnell, L. M., & Pascal, A. (1988). *Teacher unions and educational reform.* Santa Monica, CA: RAND Corporation.

Ornstein, A. C. (1974). *Race and politics in school/community organizations.* Pacific Palisades, CA: Goodyear.

Pierce, L. C. (1977). *School site management.* Unpublished manuscript, Aspen Institute for Humanistic Studies, Program in Education for a Changing Society, Cambridge, MA.

Prasch, J. (1990). *How to organize for school-based management.* Alexandria, VA: Association for Supervision and Curriculum Development.

Purkey, S. C., & Smith, M. S. (1985). School reform: The district policy implications of the effective schools literature. *Elementary School Journal, 85,* 353–389.

Rollow, S. G. (1990, April). *Populism and professionalism: School reform in Chicago.* Paper presented at the annual meeting of the American Educational Research Association, Boston.

Smith, M. S., & O'Day, J. (1991). Systemic school reform. In S. Fuhrman & B. Malen (Eds.), *The politics of curriculum and testing* (pp. 233–267). Philadelphia: Falmer.

Wohlstetter, P., & McCurdy, K. (1990). The link between school decentralization and school politics. *Urban Education, 25,* 391–414.

5

Using Incentives
to Promote School Improvement

Lawrence O. Picus

During the 1980s, states devoted large sums of new money to education. Much of this increase occurred after the publication of *A Nation at Risk* in 1983 (National Commission on Excellence in Education). Nationwide, total school funding rose 83 percent in nominal terms between 1980 and 1988 and 43 percent between 1983 and 1988 (Odden, 1990). When adjusted for inflation, real spending for K–12 education increased 30 percent in the 1980s. This increase occurred on top of real dollar increases of 35 percent in the 1970s and 67 percent in the 1960s (National Center for Education Statistics, 1990). The hope was that more money combined with the 1980s reforms would improve student performance. These overall funding increases were accompanied by a series of new, school-based incentive programs created to encourage improved school performance.

Incentives are popular among education policy makers and have been promoted by the National Governors' Association in recent reports on the status of education reform (David, Cohen, Honetschlager, & Traiman, 1990; National Governors' Association, 1990). However, incentives are still in the early stages of development. Policy makers view incentives as an alternative to regulatory approaches used in the past to stimulate local response to state education goals. Incentives are seen as more effective in ensuring local responsiveness to state reform goals than the mandates and sanctions used in the past. Many policy makers stress the "moral superiority" of voluntary compliance and argue that incentives minimize the need for "coercion as a means of organizing society" (Church and Heumann, 1989). There is also a growing sense that it is more appropriate for the state to monitor district performance in meeting established goals, while leaving specific program decisions to local officials most familiar with the realities of their situation.

The current political movement to decentralize government generally has made this argument popular. By shifting decision-making authority from the state to local school districts, incentive proponents can claim that spending changes result from locally established priorities, and are not part of a growing and "bloated" bureaucracy. Some dispute the voluntary aspects of incentive plans because the withdrawal of previously awarded incentives looks like punishment. Supporters of incentives claim that incentives are more effective in attaining the ends of public policy than regulation or mandates. Unfortunately, there have been few empirical studies of this claim — in or out of education (Church and Heumann, 1989).

The most recent education incentive programs began with merit pay and career ladder programs. The intention was to reward individuals in the education system who were doing an especially good job. Merit pay and career ladder programs have been studied extensively and their problems documented in studies by Richards (1985), Murnane and Cohen (1986), and Johnson (1986). Other studies have proposed new approaches for rewarding productivity (Lawler, 1990; Blinder, 1990), including paying teachers for productivity (Chapter Two of this book). But teacher compensation need not be the only domain of incentive programs. There are numerous incentive options available to state policy makers.

The purpose of this chapter is to describe alternative incentive options available to policy makers and delineate the circumstances under which each would be effective in achieving state policy goals. Two general categories of incentives are described. They are (1) incentives built into a state's education finance formula and designed on the basis of intergovernmental grant theory and (2) state-financed incentives provided directly either to districts or to individual schools. These incentives can be designed to spur specific actions on the part of recipients or to reward outcomes.

This chapter has three sections. In the first section, traditional intergovernmental grant models are examined, and the expected effects of general and categorical grants on school district spending are described. Another intergovernmental grant mechanism, the matching grant, is also discussed. Matching grants are really a special form of either general or categorical grants, depending on the purpose of the grant. The second section analyzes specific state-financed incentive programs. These incentives can be directed toward either districts or individual schools, reward specific actions or inputs (such as increasing time spent on instruction), or reward specific outcomes (such as performance). The third section provides a summary of findings and discusses the implications of those findings for school finance policy.

Intergovernmental Grants: Theory and Incentives

State policy makers have two primary options for directly influencing local school district spending decisions. They can mandate changes in the way school services are provided or they can use intergovernmental grants to influence local behavior. While mandates offer the most direct way of achieving legislative goals, they carry with them political and financial problems. Consequently, state legislatures often rely on intergovernmental grants to stimulate desired school district action. Two basic grant instruments—general grants and categorical grants—are available to state policy makers. Past empirical research shows that each of these two grant instruments has a different impact on local spending decisions. This section begins with a brief discussion of mandates and then reviews the two types of intergovernmental grant mechanisms and their expected impact on school district spending decisions.

Mandates

A state's authority to impose mandates on local governments has long been recognized. This authority stems from "Dillon's Rule," an 1868 court ruling by Iowa judge John F. Dillon, which holds that local governments owe their origin to and derive their powers from state legislatures (Advisory Commission on Intergovernmental Relations, 1989). This principle was upheld by the United States Supreme Court in *City of Trenton* v. *New Jersey* in 1923 and is used by state courts today.

Opponents of mandates claim that local governments are in the best position to respond in flexible and diverse ways to community problems and issues. They argue that if revenue and expenditure decisions are mandated, local officials' flexibility to respond is constrained. If local and state policies are not aligned, these constraints become divisive. The resulting loss of local control is the most frequently voiced criticism of mandates. Another argument against mandates is that they are often enacted with little or no information about the costs being passed on to local governments. This makes it difficult for mandate sponsors to consider the benefit-cost trade-offs of their proposals.

Proponents of mandates argue they are a legitimate tool to spur governmental action by local governments. Mandates also make it possible to move in the direction of uniform levels of service across an entire state. Many mandated programs fall within areas affecting more than one local jurisdiction. Highways, education, and welfare are three examples. Proponents of mandates say that for programs over which the state has considerable responsibility, the reordering of local priorities through the use of mandates is appropriate state action.

One of the major concerns about mandates is their cost. Today, fourteen states require mandate reimbursements. As a result, reliance on mandates to achieve legislative goals is very costly to state governments. A total of forty-two states require an estimate of the local cost burden of new state mandates (Government Accounting Office, 1988). Because of these requirements, state policy makers often choose to use intergovernmental grants rather than mandates to influence school district spending. The following section describes the expected response of local school districts to different types of intergovernmental grants.

The Incentive Properties of Traditional Intergovernmental Grants

State school finance systems have always used a variety of intergovernmental grants to distribute funds to local school districts. *General,* or *block, grants* are usually used to provide the bulk of state support to districts. Funds allocated through general aid formulas have few restrictions on their use, and their purpose is twofold: (1) to provide general assistance and support for financing education and (2) to equalize variations in local fiscal capacity. When used for equalizing fiscal capacity, general grants distribute aid (at least to some extent) inversely to local districts' ability to raise revenue from their own sources.

State and federal policy makers also use *categorical grants* to encourage school districts to undertake desired actions or to provide services to groups of children viewed as needing additional education resources. Federal categorical programs provide funds to school districts to help children with special needs (for example, Chapter 1 funds for disadvantaged children, special education funds for handicapped children, and bilingual grants to districts with high concentrations of limited-English-proficient children). Other federal categorical programs compensate districts for factors largely out of their control (for example, impact aid, which compensates school districts for loss of tax revenue due to a large federal presence, such as a military base, within the district's boundaries). Many states also have categorical grant programs designed to encourage local actions that are in line with established state policy goals.

States rely on both grant mechanisms to distribute state funds to school districts and to influence their spending behavior. Research on the response of local school districts to state intergovernmental grants has focused on the local trade-off between additional spending for education and other uses of the funds, including tax relief. Research has reached a remark-able consensus about the effects of these two grant mechanisms.

General Grants. State school finance equalization for-mulas rely extensively on general grants to local school districts. These dollars can be used as the local district chooses. The two most common school finance general grant mechanisms are foundation programs and guaranteed tax base, or power-equal-izing, programs. Each of these provides support for local school district operations and helps equalize disparities in district revenue-raising capabilities. Foundation programs distribute funds to districts through block grants that are used for general operations. Guaranteed tax base programs can be thought of as a matching grant, where the state guarantees a certain level of funding based on the district's local school tax rate. Thus, the state "matches" the district's contribution. For both mechanisms, the state's share of total expenditures is a function of local district capacity. The greater a district's capacity to raise funds on its own, the lower the state share. (See Odden and Picus (1992) for a discussion of state general aid formulas.)

Research on the effects of general grants for education has shown that school district spending increases by only a portion of the increase in general aid, with the balance devoted to local property tax relief. Studies of unrestricted or general state grants to school districts consistently find that a portion of the increased grant amount is used for tax reductions (or for spending on other government programs). For the most part, local school districts use between 50 and 80 cents of a state general grant dollar increase on educational programs, with the balance devoted to other uses. Policy makers planning to use general grants to achieve desired education policy goals should note that only about half of the funds distributed to school districts will be spent for the intended purpose. (See Miner (1963); Struyk (1970); Stern (1973); Grubb and Michelson (1974); Ladd (1975); Bowman (1974); Grubb and Osman (1977); Black, Lewis, and Link (1979); Park and Carroll (1979); Vincent and Adams (1978); and Adams (1980).) Of course, if the policy goal is to reduce local property taxes, general grants are an appropriate mechanism.

In summary, general grants are a powerful tool for increasing local spending capacity and for providing local property tax relief for school districts. However, their unrestricted nature makes it difficult for state policy makers to ensure local participation in programs they think should receive priority. Thus, the best use of general aid is to support overall education programs and fiscal capacity equalization. The unrestricted nature of general grants may make them useful in financing site-based management programs. Policy makers interested in stimulating specific actions on the part of local school districts need to consider alternative funding instruments such as categorical grants. These tools are described below.

Categorical Grants. In contrast to general aid, categorical grants are offered to school districts for a single reason or purpose and often come with strict application and reporting requirements. Categorical grants are used to ensure that school districts provide services deemed important by the state or federal governments. For example, school districts in several states receive funds from both the federal government and the state to provide services for disadvantaged and poor children. The federal program, Chapter 1, provides additional funds to school districts that must be directed toward children identified as economically disadvantaged. Several states have similar programs that provide aid to school districts on the basis of low-income students. Services supported through categorical grants are often provided more efficiently at the local level. Without assistance, however, school districts may not provide the desired level of service.

Many categorical grants are available automatically to recipient governments on the basis of predetermined formulas or characteristics. For example, the federal compensatory education program, Chapter 1, provides dollars to all districts on the basis of the number of children enrolled who come from families with poverty-level incomes. Funds appropriated for this program are distributed to the qualifying districts on a per-pupil basis. Other categorical programs have specific application procedures. Districts wishing to participate in a program must apply for funds, usually through a competitive process. Awards are made to districts submitting the most highly rated plans. Federal bilingual grants under Title VII are an example of this type of categorical grant.

Categorical grants can be designed to fully fund the desired program, or they can include a matching component whereby the local district must pay for a portion of the program from its own revenues. Some matching programs are designed so that over time the state or federal share of the cost of the program declines, leaving the district responsible for maintaining the program. In some instances, districts qualify for more funds than the state has appropriated for the program. The usual solution to this problem is to proportionately reduce each district's grant.

To ensure that categorical grants are used for the intended purpose, states and the federal government have developed a complex system of rules to monitor compliance. For example, Chapter 1's "Supplement Not Supplant" requirement is designed to make sure the recipient district uses its Chapter 1 funds on the children who qualify for assistance and that spending on the supported program district funds does not decline as a result of the grant. Other enforcement mechanisms include audits and evaluations to ensure that recipients establish programs designed to meet the grant's purpose. Many categorical grants have specific reporting requirements that help the state monitor the use of categorical funds. These enforcement mechanisms add to the cost of administering the grant program.

Empirical findings about categorical grants indicate that, unlike general grants, categorical grants stimulate local education expenditures by more than the amount of the grant. Although an early pre–Chapter 1 regulation study by Feldstein (1975) indicated that districts were not using all of their federal Title I funds on services for disadvantaged children, research in the late 1970s found these regulations had succeeded not only in directing the full amount of the grant toward its intended purpose but in stimulating additional local spending on the program in many cases. As a result, researchers found districts increased spending on categorical programs by as much as $1.10 to $1.20 for each categorical grant dollar they received. (See Grubb and Michelson (1974); Ladd (1975); Vincent and Adams (1978); and Tsang and Levin (1983).)

Categorical grants are a powerful tool for state and federal policy makers who want to encourage specific actions on the part of local districts. By focusing resources on targeted populations or programs, categorical grants not only get used for their intended purpose but frequently stimulate local districts to provide additional funding from their own resources.

Summary

As this discussion shows, there are a variety of grant mechanisms available to states. The type of grant instrument chosen, as well as the distribution mechanism used, can affect how the funds are spent by local districts. General grants are most effective when the state's goal is to provide districts with general revenue to support education or to equalize fiscal capacity. These grants leave allocation decisions up to the district; consequently, they are often not effective if the state's goal is to get districts to offer specific services or programs. Given the opportunity to use the new dollars as they see fit, districts are likely to make different spending decisions than ones the state would choose. Indeed, districts often use half of an increase in state aid to support education and the other half to reduce local taxes.

Categorical grants can be given to school districts to serve a specific population or to implement a particular program. These grants are considered categorical rather than general grants because they are distributed to a limited number of districts. Categorical grants designed to meet a specific purpose frequently include one or more mechanisms to ensure compliance with the grant's goals. Research shows these grants not only are spent for the intended purpose but often stimulate district spending from other sources as well.

An alternative to these types of grants is to provide financial incentives to school districts or schools that undertake desired actions or that meet certain performance goals. These fiscal incentives are the topic of the next section.

The Use of Incentives to Implement State Policy Goals

An alternative to using grants to stimulate school district behaviors is to offer incentives for districts or schools that undertake desired actions or meet certain performance standards. While still somewhat of a novelty in education today, incentives are increasingly being used in the private sector and in some other public sectors. The approach is to provide incentives for operational units (production divisions or departments—the analogue in education is schools) rather than for individuals. There is increasing recognition that individual performance incentives can work at cross-purposes to the kind of team efforts required to develop and sustain a productive organizational climate (Swinehart, 1986; Conley & Bacharach, 1990; Rosenholtz, 1989; Lawler, 1990). In the private sector, incentives are often linked to the productivity of individual units, which are rewarded on the basis of performance over a multiple-year time period (Blinder, 1990; Goggin, 1986; Stansberry, 1985; Swinford, 1987).

There are two design elements that need to be considered in establishing an incentive program. Incentives can be directed toward either districts or individual schools, and they can reward specific actions or inputs (such as increasing time spent on instruction) or outputs (such as improved performance). In effect, policy makers can choose among four possible incentive options, which are summarized in Table 5.1.

Table 5.1. Alternative Incentive Models Available to State Policy Makers.

Award Distribution	Level	
	District	School
Inputs	1	3
Outputs	2	4

To date, only two of these options have been used in education, and little research on their effectiveness has been conducted. California has experimented with output incentives to school districts (model 1), while a number of states have begun experimenting with school-based incentive programs, designed to reward schools on the basis of outcomes (model 4). This section begins with a discussion of California's incentive program to lengthen the school day and year and to increase beginning teacher salaries, a model 1 incentive program where school districts received additional funds for meeting certain organizational and salary requirements. The second part of this section reviews the growing use of school-based outcome or performance incentives in a number of states, a model 4 incentive program.

District-Based Input Incentive Programs

One option is for states to use incentives to get local school districts to offer desired service levels. States offer incentive grants to districts with the condition that certain service levels be achieved. In exchange, the district receives additional funding, usually in the form of a general grant. Decisions on how the incentive funds will be spent are up to the recipient government, as long as the service requirements of the grant are met.

The advantage of an incentive grant is that it allows the district considerable latitude in determining how to provide the new level of service. However, because school districts are not required to accept the incentive funds, it is unlikely such incentives will produce compliance by all districts with established state policy goals. Assuming incentive grants are available to all districts that elect to comply with the incentive, or that are already in compliance, the following effects of an incentive grant can be identified:

I.   The district currently operates the program.
    A.   The district is in compliance with the requirements of the incentive. It takes the money and uses it as a

general grant. The state has spent money and not accomplished anything.

B. The district is not in compliance with the requirements.

1. The cost of compliance is less than the amount of the grant. The district complies, takes the grant, and uses the excess as a general grant. The state has accomplished compliance, but the cost is greater than if the state had mandated compliance and paid for it.

2. The cost to the district is greater than the amount of the grant.

a. The district complies and accepts the grant. Extra district money is used to comply. The grant has had a multiplier effect.

b. The district does not comply and does not take the grant. The state has failed in getting the district to accept the requirements, but there has been no cost to the state.

II. The district does not currently operate the program.

A. The cost of compliance is less than the amount of the grant. The district complies, takes the grant, and uses the excess as a general grant. The state has accomplished compliance, but the cost is greater than if the state had mandated compliance and paid for it.

B. The cost to the district is greater than the amount of the grant.

1. The district complies and accepts the grant. Extra district money is used to comply. The grant has had a multiplier effect.

2. The district does not comply and does not take the grant. The state has failed in getting the district to accept the requirements, but there has been no cost to the state.

Because these incentives are a relatively new school finance concept, little empirical research on their effectiveness is available. In one California study, Picus (1988) analyzed the effect of formula-based incentives for a longer school year and longer school day in that state's 1982 education reform act. The study found that incentives of this type had a stimulative impact on district spending for instructional programs.

Under Senate Bill (SB) 813, California school districts were eligible for incentive payments of $35 per student in 1984–85 if they increased the length of the school year to 180 days. Districts that already had 180-day school years also received these incentive payments. In addition, districts that increased the length of the school day to a state-established minimum received incentive payments of $20 per pupil in grades K–8 and $40 per pupil in grades 9–12 for each of three school years beginning in 1984–85. Almost all districts in the state took advantage of these incentives. Another incentive program designed to increase beginning teacher salaries paid districts the cost of increasing teacher salaries to a minimum of $18,000 per year. Only about half of the districts in the state took advantage of this part of the program.

An important component of these incentive programs was that once a district met the time requirements and received the incentive payments, future payments were rolled into the district's revenue limit. Including the payment as part of a district's (block grant) revenue limit ensured continued funding for the program. To keep local districts from receiving the funds and then reverting back to old schedules that did not meet the incentive program's minimum requirements, the legislature enacted a penalty provision that reduced a district's state aid by an amount greater than what it received through the incentive program. This penalty is still in effect today to ensure compliance. As a result, districts that elected to extend their school days and years to receive the incentive funds have not reduced school time.

Picus (1988) notes that the legislature expected districts to use the incentive funds to increase spending on direct instructional programs. Table 5.2 shows Picus's estimates of changes in spending by program area that resulted from a one-dollar increase in incentive revenue for California unified districts. For every incentive dollar a district received, the district

Table 5.2. Estimated Impact of a One-Dollar Increase in Incentive
Revenue on School District Spending by Expenditure Category:
California Unified School Districts, 1984–85 to 1985–86.

Expenditure Classification	Incentive Revenue
Instruction	$2.05
Administration	0.78
Auxiliary	−0.36
Instructional support	−1.18
Maintenance and operations	0.24
Transportation	−1.09
Pupil services	−0.04

Source: Data from Picus, 1988.

increased spending on instruction by over $2.00. In addition,
Table 5.2 shows other changes in district spending patterns as a
result of the incentive program. For example, a one-dollar increase in incentive funds led to an increase of approximately
seventy-eight cents in spending on administration and a smaller
increase in spending on maintenance and operations. On the
other hand, spending for instructional support, transportation,
and auxiliary and student services declined in response to the
incentive funding.

Picus concluded that the California incentives were effective in getting school districts to implement legislatively established goals. By offering funding incentives to increase the
length of the school day and school year and to increase beginning teacher salaries, the legislature stimulated local districts to
increase the share of total expenditures devoted to instructional
programs. Although increased spending on instruction does
not guarantee that student performance will improve or that
dropout rates will decline, interviews with state legislators and
other participants in the education policy arena indicated that
increased spending on instruction was viewed as one measure of
the success of the reform components of SB 813. Picus' analysis
also found that by the end of the six-year study period, district
spending decisions across functions began to return to the
pattern observed prior to enactment of SB 813's incentive
components.

Picus also found that SB 813's incentive grants were more successful in directing expenditures toward instruction than other grant instruments have typically been. School districts responded to the incentive grants by increasing the percentage of total expenditure devoted to instruction; the response to general and categorical grants has been smaller spending increases in instruction and relatively larger increases in other program areas. It is possible that state categorical programs designed to increase instructional spending might have been equally successful, but no such programs were enacted.

Picus' findings have a number of important implications for the design of district-level input incentive programs financed through state school finance formulas. They include the following:

- Formula-based incentive programs can be an effective grant mechanism, stimulating school districts to implement legislative goals. Incentives are a powerful tool for gaining local acceptance of state-established goals. Incentives do not carry the negative connotations associated with mandates, and their voluntary nature makes it possible for school districts or local governments to opt out of programs they dislike. More important, carefully designed incentives make substantial compliance with legislative goals a real possibility.
- Incentive programs are most effective when the funding represents a small portion of a school district's budget. If incentives represent a substantial share of district budgets, they effectively become mandates since districts have to use a larger portion of their budget to meet the incentive requirements.
- Incentives can be expected to achieve higher participation rates in times of fiscal constraint. School districts facing revenue shortfalls may be more willing to accept funds, even if they come with strings attached, than will districts with adequate fiscal resources.
- Rolling incentive funds into general assistance programs in future years may limit the effectiveness of the incentive. School districts may modify their spending patterns to

qualify for the grant but over time return to previous patterns. Even when incentive programs require maintaining service levels once implemented, it may be possible for districts to use some of the funds in other program areas.

- The harder it is for school districts to retreat from the grant requirements, the greater the long-term success of the incentive program. The ability of a school district to retreat from the grant requirements depends on how difficult and costly it is to do so. Incentives that require major reorganizations, although they may be less successful in gaining compliance, are more likely to have a lasting impact on school districts. On the other hand, incentives that are easily implemented at relatively low cost may gain greater compliance, but maintaining that compliance may be more difficult.

School-Based Fiscal Incentives

A second incentive program that has been tried and studied in a number of states is school-based fiscal incentives designed to reward outputs, or school performance (model 4 incentive program). These incentive programs pose a host of different issues. While still something of a novelty in education today, a number of states have experimented with site-based incentive programs with varying degrees of success.

This section of the chapter contains two parts. The first describes site-based incentive programs, focusing discussion on programs in South Carolina and California. Next, there is an analysis of the design issues states need to consider in establishing site-based incentive programs.

State Programs. A number of states have experimented with a variety of site-based incentive programs. These programs have taken a number of forms. Some reward schools directly for performance, while others provide funds to districts and allow the districts to distribute the rewards to schools. In some programs, the state determines the eligibility criteria for the program and sets the standards by which performance is judged. In other programs, performance is measured on the basis of how well a school or district meets self-determined educational goals. Current school-based incentive programs in the states are summarized in Table 5.3. Some programs have enjoyed greater success than others. Two specific school-based incentive programs are described more fully below.

South Carolina's school incentive reward program is one part of what Peterson (1988) refers to as South Carolina's "carrot and stick" approach to school accountability. A school must meet student achievement goals to qualify for any award. Eighty percent of the annual per-pupil award is based on the achievement standard. The program provides rewards to roughly 250 schools making the largest achievement gains. In addition, bonuses are available for student and teacher attendance. The attendance incentives are based on fixed standards, and schools can get an additional 10 percent of the per-pupil award for each attendance standard it meets. If a school meets all three outcome standards it can receive about $30 per student. In addition to financial rewards, schools receive flags and certificates signifying their performance. Honorable mention awards are presented to schools with performances approaching the standards required for a monetary reward.

Richards and Shujaa (1990) show that the schools gaining the most from this program are in poor districts. They cite South Carolina Department of Education reports that schools with fewer resources and historically lower achievement show the greatest support for the program. Moreover, Richards and Sheu (1991) show that by relying on gains in student achievement, the impact of background factors in award assignment has been significantly reduced.

Cibulka (1989) concluded that the program has proven to be a source of motivation for schools and teachers. He indicated that there is a great deal of support for the program among educators, and that the greatest support has been found among schools with fewer resources and historically lower achievement gains. Because of the program's success, legislation was introduced to release schools that won awards two years in a row from state regulations. Richards and Shujaa note this may complicate analysis of the South Carolina program's success because the most successful schools will be able to escape requirements that limit their performance. If deregulation really does promote higher levels of performance, then repeat winners will have an advantage over other schools for future incentive payments.

South Carolina also has a school district intervention program (Peterson's "stick") to help poorly performing schools and districts. South Carolina districts that have low performance levels on achievement tests, poor student or teacher attendance, high dropout rates, or problems meeting accreditation standards are declared to be impaired districts (Peterson, 1988). Impaired districts are then visited by a team of educators, who issue recommendations that, once approved by the State Board of Education, must be implemented by the local school district. Districts failing to comply with the recommendations face withholding of funds or removal of the district superintendent. State technical assistance is also provided to impaired schools. By 1988, only nine districts in the state had been identified as impaired.

California's program to provide schools with cash awards for high performance on the California Assessment Program (CAP) test did not fare as well as South Carolina's program. While South Carolina's school-based incentive program appears to be a success, not all state incentive programs have been as fortunate. In addition to the formula-based incentives described above, California's SB 813 included a provision to award cash to high schools on the basis of increases in the standardized achievement test scores obtained on the twelfth-grade CAP test.

The program was funded in both 1984–85 and 1985–86 but eliminated the following year. In the first year of operation, approximately 49 percent of the state's high schools received awards, ranging from $5 to $192,000 and averaging $26,047. In the second year, 48 percent of the state's high schools received awards. Awards were discretionary and could be used in any manner determined by the school—except to increase salaries.

The program appeared to be successful; senior test scores improved, and the number of seniors taking the test increased. However, there were a number of serious implementation problems. Some schools managed to artificially lower the CAP scores

Table 5.3. Summary of Current School-Based Incentive Programs by State.

State	Year Implemented	Program Description	Award Criteria	Eligibility Criteria	Size and Type of Awards
California	1985	California School Recognition Program	California Assessment Program test scores; student attendance; number of writing and homework assignments; enrollments in core curriculum and courses required for university admission at high schools; SAT and ACT scores; dropout rates; and locally defined indicators for K–8	Elementary and secondary schools compete in alternate years; nomination, application, and site visit required.	Nonmonetary (flags and plaques).
Florida	1984	The District Quality Instruction Program (Merit Schools)	Performance criteria locally defined and approved by the state	All Florida school districts are eligible to submit a plan. Schools must meet their district's performance criteria to be eligible.	Awards made to districts, which distribute funds to qualifying schools according to prorated student FTE scale. Largest amount received by a district in 1988–89 was $328,000; smallest amount was $5,700.
Indiana	1988	The A-Plus Program for Educational Excellence (Public law 390, 1987)	Pupil attendance rate; English/language arts proficiency; math proficiency; and average total battery score on state achievement test	Schools must show overall improvement statewide against the previous year's performance. Schools are automatically included if they meet improvement criteria on any two of the four indicators.	Two tiers of monetary awards (1989): 1. All eligible districts share $4 million. 2. All schools receive a weighted share of $6 million according to size of gain.

State	Year	Program	Measures	Eligibility	Award
Kentucky	1983	Flags of Excellence and Flags of Progress	Annual dropout rate; scores on state-mandated test; pupil attendance; and performance on state accreditation monitoring.	All schools are eligible. Awards are based on overall performance statewide and annual improvement on performance indicators.	Nonmonetary (flags and plaques).
Louisiana	1988	School, District, and State Progress Profiles/School Incentive Awards	As of 1989–90, state had not decided on indicators. Measures under consideration include school achievement on state norm-referenced test and Louisiana Educational Assessment Program.	All public schools.	Monetary awards to begin in 1991, details not yet determined.
Mississippi	1990	Mississippi's BEST Education Act of 1990	Achievement scores; dropout rates; student attendance; teacher attendance and participation in professional development; parental/community involvement; student involvement in extracurricular academic and community activities; and ratio of administrators to instructional budget.	Schools divided into three categories: improving schools, better schools, and lighthouse schools.	*Improving Schools* — Up to $200 per certificated employee (CE) and up to $100 per noncertificated employee (NCE). *Better Schools* — Up to $400/CE and $300/NCE. *Lighthouse Schools* — Up to $800/CE and $400/NCE. 70 percent of the funds will be used for salary expenses for existing personnel. Use of the remaining 30 percent will be determined by a vote of all school personnel in the school. May not be used for athletics.

Table 5.3. Summary of Current School-Based Incentive Programs by State, Cont'd.

State	Year Implemented	Program Description	Award Criteria	Eligibility Criteria	Size and Type of Awards
Missouri	1986	Incentives for School Excellence	Public schools compete within four regions on the basis of performance criteria established in grant applications, which must describe the school's goals for improvement.	Each application must address one or more of the following: cognitive improvement, effective improvement, or effective schools criteria.	Monetary awards of up to $30,000 per school.
Pennsylvania	1988	Act 110 of 1988	Annual performance improvement on statewide test scores; dropout rates; proportion of students taking the SAT; and increase in average SAT scores.	Schools are automatically included in the program.	Monetary awards.
South Carolina	1984	Education Improvement Act of 1984	Annual improvement in three categories: achievement test scores (80%); pupil attendance (10%); and teacher attendance (10%).	Automatic inclusion, no application required.	Largest award about $59,000; average is about $1,500. Funds awarded on a per-pupil basis. Nonmonetary awards also granted to schools that don't quite qualify for monetary awards.
Tennessee	1986	Ten Great Schools Program (governor's initiative with corporate financing for first three years)	Schools selected by Department of Education; no specific criteria specified. One elementary, one middle, and one high school from each of three regions, plus one at-large school.	"High standards and quality results in student achievement, community involvement, overall curriculum and their instructional programs."	Each of ten schools receives an unrestricted cash gift of $10,000 from a private company (Northern Telecom, Inc.).

Washington	1988	Schools for the 21st Century	Proposals submitted to State Board of Education and reviewed. Twenty-one schools are funded.	Schools submit application with information on: project objectives; technical assistance needed; budget; staff incentive pay plan; evaluation and accountability process; collective bargaining contract modifications; modification of waiver of school district rules; modification of waiver of state rules; ten-day supplemental contracts for project-related instructional employees; assurances of cooperation and support from the local school board, parents, businesses, and community organizations.	Each school selected receives $50,000 per year plus funds to cover the ten supplemental days for instructional staff.

Source: Compiled from Richards and Shujaa, 1990, Table 1; Demarest (1990); and phone calls to state representatives.

in the base year to maximize their improvement during the award years. Other schools tried to change the definition of a senior so that those most likely to do poorly on the test would not have to take it, thus raising the gain score above what it otherwise would have been. There is also anecdotal evidence of high school seniors threatening to do poorly on the test unless administrators agreed to spend the award funds as designated by the students. There also appear to be cases where students intentionally failed the test to purposely lower their school's gain score.

As these two state examples show, the design of an incentive program plays a crucial role in the success of that program. The next part of this section discusses the design elements that must be considered in establishing a school-based incentive program.

Design Elements for School-Based Incentive Programs. In designing a school-based incentive program, policy makers need to consider five general areas: (1) eligibility requirements, (2) the size of the incentive programs, (3) the distribution mechanics, (4) how incentive funds can be used by recipients, and (5) alternatives to direct financial incentives.

Eligibility requirements. Policy makers first need to consider eligibility requirements for an incentive program. Among the issues that must be addressed are the performance measure that will be used, the level for measuring performance, the period of performance, and the standard for which an incentive award is received.

1. *Performance measure.* The most common measure of performance is student achievement as measured through some kind of achievement test. Incentives can then be based either on a school's overall achievement level or, more often, on some measure of improvement. Other testing issues must be resolved, including what kind of test to use and what score to consider. There is growing interest in using performance-based tests that assess abilities to think and solve problems rather than multiple-choice tests that assess basic skills. Using average test scores for

all students in a school could result in decreased attention to low achievers and more attention for high achievers. To resolve this problem, test scores across all levels of student achievement would be needed. Improvements for students in the bottom half, or for limited-English-proficient students, could even be weighted more heavily.

Research has found that socioeconomic status is consistently correlated with student achievement. As a result, systems that reward absolute levels of student achievement may be biased toward high socioeconomic areas, often the areas least in need of additional recognition or assistance. Rewarding improvements or gains in student achievement would ensure that incentives did not have a high socioeconomic bias since low-performing schools often show larger gains than high-performing schools.

There is a great deal of concern over the use of standardized tests to measure student performance and a growing feeling that schools should move to performance assessment instruments that rely more heavily on demonstrations of what students know and can do. Tests that require students to solve problems, apply knowledge to new and different situations, and include direct writing samples are much preferred over norm-referenced tests. As states move more toward performance-based testing, which relies heavily on teacher evaluations of students, the design of school-based performance awards will need to be revised.

In addition to test scores, other measures that have been used in school-based incentive programs include enrollment measurements such as the number of students in advanced placement courses and the number in core academic programs. Teacher and student attendance rates are also used as a basis for incentive programs in some states, as in South Carolina. Finally, other measures could be used, including lowering the dropout rate, improving postsecondary enrollments, and measuring community satisfaction.

2. *Level.* A number of existing incentive programs are directed at the school level. For example, the U.S. Department of

Education's outstanding school awards are based on the performance of school sites, as are many state programs. However,
incentives can also be focused more broadly at school districts
or more narrowly by grade or department (at the high school
level). In Table 5.3, which summarizes existing incentive programs in the states, the fifth column indicates the level incentives are directed toward in each of those states. Since the school,
or the department or "house" within a school, is the production
unit, most incentives should be targeted at that level.

　　　3. *Performance period.* The period of performance is also a
critical policy variable in the design of incentive programs:
should schools (or other units) be rewarded for performance on
an annual basis or for their performance over a period of time,
say two or three years? Often, single-year gains are achieved at
the expense of future performance. Thus, using a two- or three-
year average might encourage long-term development of successful educational practices rather than implementation of
quick fixes designed to rapidly improve test scores.
　　　Table 5.3 shows that most state programs offer rewards
based on annual performance, rather than relying on multiple-
year assessments of progress. One of the concerns of local officials has been whether the program will continue to receive
funding at the state level. There is little incentive to develop a
three-year improvement plan if there are no assurances that
program funding will not be eliminated before the end of the
second year. Consequently, there are substantial incentives on
the part of local districts to support annual assessments for
award determination. Similarly, legislators faced with multiple
requests for program funds (both within and outside of education) may prefer to appropriate funds to incentive programs on
an annual basis rather than commit scarce state resources two,
three, or more years into the future. The immediacy of annual
awards focuses more attention on the program and on the
problems it is designed to solve and provides at least the sense of
greater accountability. Annual awards could be made, though,
on the basis of a multiyear record of performance.

4. *Performance standard.* Another important allocation issue is the performance standard chosen. Richards and Shujaa (1990) describe two such standards: fixed and competitive. In either case, the standard can be based directly on a measure, such as a test score, or on improvement in that measure. A fixed performance standard provides incentive awards to all schools that meet some predetermined criteria for receiving an award, while a competitive standard requires that schools compete with other schools to receive awards. Theoretically, all schools in a state could receive incentive awards under the fixed criterion if they all met the established standard. On the other hand, only a certain percentage of the schools in a state could receive an incentive reward based on a competitive performance standard.

Further modifications often must be considered. The demographics of a school's population can make a substantial difference in the school's competitiveness, whether the standard is based on total performance or on improvement. Schools unable to compete because they have a large population of minority, poor, or language-disadvantaged children could be at a substantial disadvantage. Moreover, if per-pupil spending variations exist across a state, those districts with additional funds may be in a better position to implement programs viewed as successful and hence be able to show greater improvements in student achievement. To resolve this problem, a number of states, including South Carolina, have established programs where schools are grouped into bands, configurations of similar schools. Then incentives are offered to schools showing the best performance or improvement within their grouping. While this strategy addresses the issue of achievement variation by socio-economic status, the technical issues entailed in designing such programs can be controversial.

Program size. The second design issue policy makers must consider is the size of the program in comparison to the state's overall school finance system. If the award is too small, schools may choose not to compete for the incentives; if it is too large, other components of the finance formula may suffer. South

Carolina provides approximately $30 per pupil in incentive funds. While this amounts to a relatively small portion of the total state funding for education, the award level seems to be large enough to generate considerable interest among schools in that state.

There is limited evidence that recognition of achievement is by itself adequate incentive for schools to participate in state incentive programs. Table 5.3 shows that rewards in many states are nonmonetary and include such things as plaques and flags signifying the school's performance.

Many—perhaps most—argue, however, that even larger incentives are needed if an incentive program is to succeed. Odden and Conley (Chapter Two of this book) suggest that incentives for improved teacher skills and performance should be as high as 20 percent of teacher salaries. In Kentucky, there are plans to provide salary bonuses of up to 40 percent in schools that improve student achievement.

Distribution mechanics. The monetary rewards of most school-based incentive programs are distributed through separate categorical programs. The issues surrounding the distribution of incentive funds through the state aid formula are discussed above. In general, incentives for performance appear to be better distributed through separate programs, while incentives designed to encourage districts to enact certain types of programs may be better distributed through the general aid formula. The discussion on general grant programs above reviews the effects of general grants on the equalization functions of general aid programs. At present, most incentive programs are small enough that they do not pose a significant threat to the equalization component of state school finance structures.

Use of incentive funds. Another issue concerns how incentive funds can be used by recipients. For example, can the funds be used to give teachers bonus payments? If so, all teachers would share equally in those payments. In California's Cash for CAP program, schools were not allowed to use the funds they received for payments to teachers. Instead, the funds had to be used for instructional materials and supplies. The same is true for the South Carolina incentive program. There seems to be no a priori reason why awards could not be used for salary bonuses; indeed, that is the primary use of production unit incentive awards in the private sector, including knowledge-production organizations (Lawler, 1990).

Alternatives to direct financial rewards. School-based incentive programs do not have to provide fiscal rewards to be successful. In fact, the incentives do not necessarily have to reward good performance. Alternatives to the fiscal approach described above include relaxing state regulations and establishing programs whereby the state takes over the operation of school districts that do not perform up to state-established minimum standards.

An option available to designers of school-based incentive programs is to reward schools or school districts that perform well by exempting them from state regulations (Fuhrman, 1989). This approach offers schools the opportunity to experiment with programmatic approaches often considered unavailable due to state regulations. While this approach is attractive on the surface, it does not appear to have been as successful as one might expect. This lack of success probably stems from a number of factors. First, even if state regulations are relaxed, district policy and union contract agreements must often be adhered to. While many districts are willing to relax their own policies and regulations along with the state, it is often more problematic to change contract agreements with the teachers' bargaining units.

Second, given that the school has to show success under the state requirements before deregulation is granted, school officials may believe the program they offer is the best possible to meet the needs of their students and may not be particularly interested in making dramatic changes of the type implied by the relaxation or elimination of state regulation. Moreover, if deregulation is a key to the success of local schools, why should only the successful schools be given this opportunity? Is it possible that those schools that are not performing well within the framework of state requirements would benefit more from deregulation? This question has not been addressed in the literature on school-based incentive programs.

Finally, states can enact negative incentive programs where the price of poor performance is substantial state intervention, often including state takeover of the school or school district. New Jersey and Kentucky have both taken over school districts that were not meeting state-established minimum levels of performance. In California a number of districts have run into financial problems. The state has bailed them out but at the same time appointed a trustee who must approve all school board decisions. A program to take over districts that are not meeting minimum academic performance does not exist in California. While negative incentives such as state takeover may not result in school districts joining the ranks of the highest-performing schools overnight, such disincentives to poor performance may have enough of an impact to at least marginally improve the schools in those districts. What we do not yet know is whether these state takeovers also result in more dollars going to the affected school districts. The few instances to date where states have taken over the operation of a district need to be tracked to determine whether there was an infusion of new dollars and, if so, what impact those dollars had on school improvement.

Conclusions and Implications for State School Finance Policy

This chapter shows there are a wide range of incentive instruments available to state policy makers interested in stimulating certain actions on the part of local school districts. The incentives range from the use of traditional school finance general and categorical aid formulas, to incentive funding programs that operate through the school finance formula, to performance-based school-site incentives. Choice of a policy instrument depends on the programmatic goals of state policy makers and how directly they wish to control local behavior. In general, the more specific the program requirements, the more influence the state has on local decisions.

If state policy makers are concerned with resource allocation issues and want to influence how local school districts spend available funds, the following considerations are important:

- General grants can be expected to have limited success in encouraging school districts to allocate resources in specific ways. Empirical research has found that, in general, fifty cents of each dollar granted to local school districts through general grants are used for noneducational purposes such as tax relief or spending in other areas. Consequently, general grants are of little or no value as incentive tools. They are effective, however, in compensating for variations in the local property tax base and should continue to provide the bulk of state education aid.
- Categorical grants offer state policy makers greater opportunity to influence local spending patterns. Categorical grants usually include substantial compliance requirements and have been found to actually stimulate district spending on the supported program. Districts not only spend all of the grant funds on the program but supplement those funds with their own resources as well. Categorical grants, perhaps with even greater fiscal capacity-equalizing components, are appropriate for such services as compensatory, special, and bilingual education and transportation.
- Direct financial incentive programs are effective in getting school districts to meet specific program or spending requirements. The incentives are designed to encourage districts to devote additional resources to supported programs by providing funds only to districts that meet the minimum requirements. An empirical study of this type of incentive in California showed that local school districts responded to incentives to increase the length of the school day and school year by spending an extra $2.00 per pupil on instruction for each dollar of incentive revenue received from the state.

Incentives to change the mix of inputs used by the school district rely on an indirect link between the incentive and improved student performance. While the incentives have been successful in increasing spending for instruction, there is no clear evidence for related gains in student performance. A problem with input-based incentives is that they usually reward districts that already meet program objectives. This reduces the effectiveness of the program by giving funds to school districts that do not need the incentive to change.

Policy makers have attempted to resolve these problems by developing school-based incentive programs that reward outputs rather than inputs. Under this model, schools are rewarded for improvements in performance. Consequently, funds are targeted to schools that show results, which provides incentive for local officials to implement programs that meet established state goals. Decisions about which programs will best meet policy goals are left to local district and school leaders. A number of important issues must be considered if these site-based incentive programs are to succeed. They include:

- An adequate performance measure must be established. Tests that assess student abilities to think and problem solve are preferred over tests that only assess basic skills. The program should reward schools for *improvement* in student performance, not "raw" scores or total achievement levels. This will ensure that all districts, including the most disadvantaged, have the opportunity to earn incentive payments. Finally, test scores should include more than average scores. Greater rewards could be provided for increased performance by the bottom half.

- Measures other than test scores can be used, but there must be enough variance in measured outcomes across schools or school districts to make the incentive appear worthwhile. For example, Richards and Sheu (1991) found the component of South Carolina's incentive program that rewards attendance to be less successful than other parts of the program. Since almost all district attendance rates were within one or two percentage points, the distinctions between districts that received rewards and those that did not were very small.

- The size of the reward must be large enough to encourage

participation. While some have found small awards—$30 per pupil—and nonmonetary rewards successful in fostering participation, many others have proposed more substantial incentives. Kentucky, for example, is suggesting teacher bonuses of as much as 40 percent of salary.

- Annual rewards provide immediate incentive to help focus schools on the problems the program is designed to resolve and provide a greater sense of accountability. Annual awards could be based on multiple-year improvement data.
- Because financial support for school improvement does not come until after the fact, some schools' ability to establish programs designed to meet the state goals may be impaired.
- All incentives need not be in the form of fiscal rewards for success. Some states have experimented with exemptions from state regulations for districts that succeed in improving student performance; other states have created disincentives for poor performance by threatening to take away control from districts that are perceived as failing.

The choice of incentive policy instruments at the state level should be driven by the extent to which policy makers want to control local program decisions and provide capacity to improve. Policy makers desiring a prescriptive incentive program can rely on traditional categorical grants to achieve their goals. Policy makers wanting to increase local capacity to improve student achievement will want to consider formula-based incentives and, possibly, general grants. And policy makers who want to reward strong local performance and leave the decision as to how that performance is achieved up to the local authorities may want to use some kind of school-based incentive program.

References

Adams, E. K. (1980). *Fiscal response and school finance simulations: A policy perspective* (Report No. F80-3). Denver, CO: Education Commission of the States.

Advisory Commission on Intergovernmental Relations. (1989).

Significant features of fiscal federalism: 1989 (Vol. 1) (Report M-163). Washington, DC: Author

Black, D. E., Lewis, K. A., & Link, C. K. (1979). Wealth neutrality and the demand for education. *National Tax Journal, 32,* 157–164.

Blinder, A. (1990). *Paying for productivity.* Washington, DC: Brookings Institution.

Bowman, J. H. (1974). Tax exportability, intergovernmental aid, and school finance reform. *National Tax Journal, 27,* 163–173.

Church, T. W., & Heumann, M. (1989). The underexamined assumptions of the invisible hand: Monetary incentives as policy instruments. *Journal of Policy Analysis and Management, 8,* 641–657.

Cibulka, J. G. (1989). State performance incentives for restructuring: Can they work? *Education and Urban Society, 21,* 417–435.

City of Trenton v. *New Jersey,* 262 U.S. 182 (1923).

Conley, S., & Bacharach, S. B. (1990). Performance appraisal in education: A strategic consideration. *Journal of Personnel Evaluation in Education, 3,* 309–319.

David, J. L., Cohen, M., Honetschlager, D., & Traiman, S. (1990). *State actions to restructure schools: First steps.* Washington, DC: National Governors' Association.

Demarest, S. (1990). *Outline: School incentive programs.* Unpublished manuscript, Rutgers University, New Brunswick, NJ.

Feldstein, M. S. (1975). Wealth neutrality and local choice in public education. *American Economic Review, 65,* 75–89.

Fuhrman, S. (with P. Fry). (1989). *Diversity amidst standardization: State differential treatment of districts.* New Brunswick, NJ: Rutgers University, Consortium for Policy Research in Education.

Goggin, Z. (1986). Two sides of gain sharing. *Management Accounting, 68,* 47–51.

Government Accounting Office. (1988). *Legislative mandates: State experiences offer insights for federal action.* Washington, DC: U.S. Government Printing Office.

Grubb, W. N., & Michelson, S. (1974). *States and schools: The political economy of public school finance.* Lexington, MA: Lexington Books.

Grubb, W. N., & Osman, J. (1977). The causes of school finance inequalities: Serrano and the case of California. *Public Finance Quarterly, 5,* 373–392.

Johnson, S. M. (1986). Incentives for teachers: What motivates, what matters. *Educational Administration Quarterly, 22,* 54–79.

Ladd, H. F. (1975). Local education expenditures, fiscal capacity, and the composition of the property tax base. *National Tax Journal, 28,* 145–158.

Lawler, E. E., III. (1990). *Strategic pay: Aligning organizational strategies and pay systems.* San Francisco: Jossey-Bass.

Miner, J. (1963). *Social and economic factors in spending for public education.* Syracuse, NY: Syracuse University Press.

Murnane, R. J., & Cohen, D. K. (1986). Merit pay and the evaluation problem: Why some merit pay plans fail and a few survive. *Harvard Educational Review, 56,* 1–17.

National Center for Education Statistics. (1990). *Digest of education statistics: 1989.* Washington, DC: U.S. Department of Education.

National Commission on Excellence in Education. (1983). *A nation at risk: Imperative for reform.* Washington, DC: Author.

National Governors' Association. (1990). *Educating America: State strategies for achieving the national educational goals.* Washington, DC: Author.

Odden, A. R. (1990). School funding changes during the 1980s. *Educational Policy, 4,* 33–47.

Odden, A. R., & Picus, L. O. (1992). *School finance: A policy perspective.* New York: McGraw-Hill.

Park, R. E., & Carroll, S. J. (1979). *The search for equity in school finance: Michigan school district response to a guaranteed tax base* (R-2393-NIE/HEW). Santa Monica, CA: RAND Corporation.

Peterson, T. (1988). *New education accountability measures focusing on results: School incentives, district intervention and state oversight of reforms.* Paper prepared for the Texas Governor's Select Committee on Education.

Picus, L. O. (1988). *The effect of state grant-in-aid policies on local government decision making: The case of California school finance* (P-7492-RCS). Santa Monica, CA: RAND Corporation.

Richards, C. (1985). The economics of merit pay: A special case of utility maximization. *Journal of Education Finance, 11*, 176–189.

Richards, C., & Sheu, T. M. (1991). *The South Carolina school incentive reward program: A policy analysis.* New Brunswick, NJ: Rutgers University, Consortium for Policy Research in Education.

Richards, C., & Shujaa, M. (1990). State-sponsored school performance incentive plans: A policy review. *Educational Considerations, 17*, 42–52.

Rosenholtz, S. J. (1989). *Teachers' workplace: The social organization of schools.* White Plains, NY: Longman.

Stansberry, J. W. (1985). New productivity incentives for defense contractors. *Harvard Business Review, 65*, 156–160.

Stern, D. (1973). Effects of alternative state aid formulas on the distribution of public school expenditures in Massachusetts. *Review of Economics and Statistics, 55*, 91–97.

Struyk, R. J. (1970). Effects of state grants-in-aid on local provision of education and welfare services in New Jersey. *Journal of Regional Science, 10*, 225–235.

Swinehart, D. P. (1986). Compensation: A guide to more productive team incentive programs. *Personnel Journal, 65*, 112–117.

Swinford, D. (1987). Unbundling divisional management incentives. *Management Review, 76*, 35–38.

Tsang, M. C., & Levin, H. R. (1983). The impacts of intergovernmental grants on education spending. *Review of Educational Research, 53*, 329–367.

Vincent, P. E., & Adams, K. (1978). *Fiscal response of school districts: A study of two states — Colorado and Minnesota* (Report No. F78-3). Denver, CO: Education Commission of the States.

6

Investing Education Dollars: Do We Need a "Dow Jones Index" for America's Schools?

James W. Guthrie

It is difficult to envision a people more preoccupied with performance than Americans. Keeping records, shattering records,
breaking world records, setting national records, establishing
personal records, or being the first, the best, or the most are all
part of our national obsession with measuring individual and
institutional performance. Almost every American city, whether
it is a metropolis or a hamlet, has some claim on a record. It
somehow possesses the largest, oldest, longest, heaviest, slowest,
tallest, greatest, smallest, tastiest, deepest, quietest, fastest, highest, noisiest, or prettiest something. It is little wonder that the
Guinness Book of Records is regularly among the best-selling pub-
lications in the United States. (We know because we keep records.) People even invent activities so that, even if only for a
short time, they can hold the new record for doing them.

Some of this measurement is frivolous. Some is fundamental to human survival, for example, measurements of global
warming or infant mortality. Some measurement is straightforward and easily understood, such as annual rainfall records.
Other measures are abstract, esoteric, and highly specialized,
such as the Federal Reserve System money supply indicator M3.
Some measurement is remarkably precise, such as lifetime
major league baseball batting averages. Other measures are

continuously controversial and subject to constant revision, for example, international indices of civil liberties. Some measures are easily calculated and popularly understood, such as athletic team won-and-lost figures. Other measures, while perhaps widely accepted, are only vaguely understood by laypersons, for example, the consumer price index (CPI). Of course, some measures are neither widely known nor widely understood. For example, the U. S. Government's Information Security Oversight Office keeps annual records on the number of "new" government-created secrets (6,796,501 in 1989).

Regardless of complexity or simplicity, advantages or disadvantages, confidence or controversy, there is hardly a nook or cranny of everyday American existence that goes unmeasured: life, death, sex, taxes, crime, athletics, economics, transportation, health, commerce, and so on. There exist a huge number of performance measures to which we as a people have grown accustomed; they appear regularly on our television, in our newspapers, and in our conversations. They have even become embedded in our contractual agreements for day-to-day activities such as pay raises, home loans, and divorce settlements.

No doubt the ultimate explanation for this measurement mania resides somewhere deep within our national character or collective psyche. Meanwhile, suffice it to say that these measures also serve many practical purposes. They enable us to chart trends on dimensions important for everyday existence; they enable us to make informed predictions regarding important future events; they enable us to plot progress toward significant goals; they enable us to quickly convey complicated information to a wide audience; they enable us to reach agreement on controversial issues in a relatively short period of time. In short, Americans find performance measures to be a major asset in plotting and planning our personal lives, private-sector endeavors, professional activities, and public policy.

Measuring Education

Education is no exception to the American fascination with measurement. Probably no other public-sector endeavor is characterized by as much record keeping, measurement, and assessment as public schooling. Records are kept from the time a child is first enrolled in school until he or she graduates. Teachers and textbooks, administrators and athletics, courses and counselors, buildings and budgets, taxes and tests, assets and attitudes are all systematically measured and recorded for public schools. A recent California study of children found education data to be far more available than data from other sectors, such as criminal justice, foster care, mental health, health, and welfare (Kirst, 1989), but not everyone believes that all available education data are useful (Weiss & Gruber, 1987).

Moreover, education measurement is multifaceted. Individual schools, local school districts, county agencies, state education departments, federal government agencies, professional associations, numerous research organizations, and private-sector companies are engaged in gathering and compiling these measurements. No one appears ever to have assigned a dollar figure to these local, state, and federal education data-gathering efforts, but surely it must be expensive.

However, simply because education measurement occurs on a broad scale does not mean that the efforts are accurate, understandable, or useful. Figure 6.1 illustrates the point. It shows data that strongly suggest that public schools (presumably) are inefficient. As resources (spending) have increased, productivity (student achievement) has remained the same.

The graph in Figure 6.1 shows a historical comparison of what is said to be U.S. school spending levels with nationwide student achievement. We are not told how school spending is measured, whether it includes capital outlay as well as recurring expenses. We do not know if this graph includes nonpublic as well as public elementary and secondary education (presumably it does not). We do not know if the spending figure is on a per-pupil basis or is simply a total amount. (Enrollments have been increasing since 1983. It is possible for aggregate spending to increase, while per-pupil spending stays even.) We are not told if the expenditures are adjusted for inflation.

However, regardless of the problems on the expenditure side, the measurement of student achievement is sufficiently

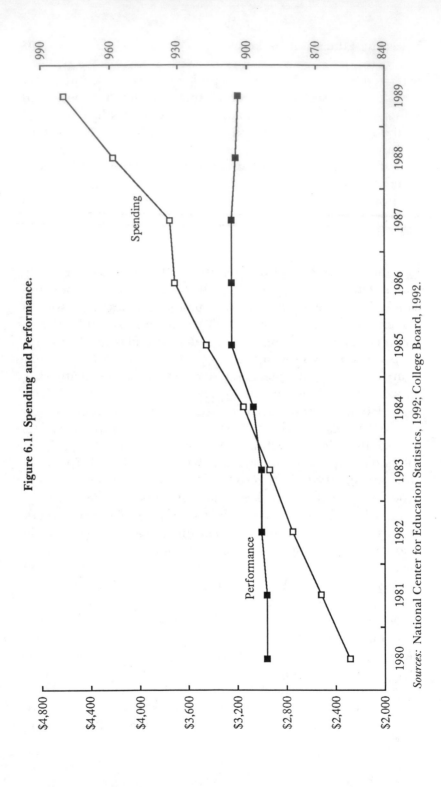

Figure 6.1. Spending and Performance.

Sources: National Center for Education Statistics, 1992; College Board, 1992.

distorted as to constitute something close to fraud. The graph depends exclusively upon the Scholastic Aptitude Test (SAT) as an indicator of pupil performance. The SAT, a widely accepted indicator of student achievement among the media, is an examination developed by the Educational Testing Service (ETS) under contract to the College Entrance Examination Board (CEEB). The latter is a chartered consortium of higher education institutions that collaborate regarding the design and conduct of college admissions procedures.

Despite repeated disclaimers by ETS, CEEB, and almost every testing expert in the Western world, the public and the press continue to accept the SAT as a measure of what schools teach or students learn. In fact, the examination is designed only to predict freshman success in college. It is analogous to a test of physical agility. Such an examination might measure one's prospective success as a basketball player, which is quite different than actually assessing whether someone can currently play basketball. Aptitude and achievement are related, but they are not the same thing.

SAT questions are not now, and never have been, designed to measure what secondary schools teach. They are not linked systematically to the curriculum offerings of secondary schools. Rather, the examination is carefully honed by a cadre of extraordinarily talented testing technicians to have predictive validity. Test questions that are easily answered are generally eliminated. Similarly, only a few exceedingly difficult questions are included. The remaining test items are included because of their ability to predict freshman-year college performance. No effort is made to link the tests to what is contained in high school curriculum or textbooks or to what teachers or school boards believe is significant. There is not even an effort to link test questions to what colleges and universities believe is important to have learned in secondary school. In short, the SAT does not measure student achievement.

There are substantial additional difficulties with Figure 6.1, aside from the inappropriate measure of student achievement. For example, only some high school students interested in attending college typically take the SAT. We have no measure in the SAT of non-college-bound students who do not take the examination or community college students who do take the examination. What are we to assume regarding their achievement? Do they know more or less than was the case in the past?

Furthermore, not every state uses the SAT to measure college aptitude. Approximately half the states rely upon a different examination—the ACT, published by the American Council on Testing. Now, what are we to suppose—that states where SAT scores are stable or declining are the ones in which school spending has been increasing? Or is it perhaps the case that SAT-using states have actually had stable or declining school spending and ACT states have experienced increased school spending?

Answers to questions such as these might or might not make a big difference for the thesis being portrayed by Figure 6.1. However, because the media, and thus the public, are accustomed to an oversimplified and inaccurate achievement measure, we cannot tell. Measurement is not automatically accurate.

Flaws in Figure 6.1 raise larger questions. If not SAT scores, then what should be taken by policy makers and the general public as an appropriate measure of educational productivity? Dropout rates? However important school persistence may be, surely it is not by itself a sufficient indicator of the education system's success.

Then what about college admission? This indicator would capture both secondary school persistence and academic achievement. Or would it? Is admission as a freshman to a community college the same thing as being admitted to Stanford University or the California Institute of Technology? What about the large percentage of youngsters who graduate from secondary school and immediately enter the workforce or join the military? Would they then show up in a college admissions indicator scheme as a negative mark against a high school?

The National Assessment of Educational Progress (NAEP)—initiated for the nation as a whole in 1966 and currently being retooled to permit appraisals of student achievement on a state-by-state basis—will eventually provide at least a partial solution to the productivity measurement problem. NAEP will produce national and individual state student achievement scores for subject dimensions such as reading, writing, mathematics, and science. However, this measure alone is also likely to prove insufficient. It will not, for example, specify how many youngsters drop out of school, perform well at work, or return to college later in life.

In short, it is difficult to imagine a single indicator that captures school complexities well enough by itself to measure education "productivity." Similarly, measurement of other schooling dimensions, for example, resource inputs, student characteristics, and schooling processes, entails equally complicated issues. Single indicators are seldom, by themselves, sufficiently sophisticated to capture the complexity of schooling. Advocates of sophisticated school measurement propose the use of what can be called *composite indicators*.

Composite Indicators

The consumer price index (CPI), gross national product (GNP), air quality index, and National Football League quarterback performance index are all examples of composite indicators. They rely upon information gleaned from separate status or performance dimensions and combined into a single number. The number may be large (the Dow Jones index now approximates 3,000). It may even be artificial (the quarterback index enables quarterbacks to perform at higher than 1,000). The number may be the result of substantial mathematical manipulation in order to assign appropriate weighting to subcomponents or to convert varying subindices to a common and understandable metric (Norwood, 1990).

Whatever the underlying statistical procedures, the final number is technically justified, professionally defended, analytically employed, widely displayed, and generally accepted. However, it is not necessarily publicly understood.

It would be a rare layperson, selected at random on a city sidewalk, who could even remotely specify the names of the corporations used to form the Dow Jones industrial average

(DJIA).[1] Similarly, not many individuals, other than the technicians intimately involved, are familiar with the components of
the market basket of goods and services regularly used in compiling the consumer price index (CPI). The same could be said
of air quality indices, which are issued for cities and regions.
Probably not even many economists, not to mention laypersons,
could clearly explain the manner in which the U.S. Department
of Commerce produces quarterly estimates of the gross national
product (GNP).

   The list could continue, but the point would be the same.
The fact that the general citizenry is uninformed regarding the
technical bases of these sophisticated composite indicators is no
apparent barrier to the indicators' professional use or widespread public acceptance.

   There is hardly a significant component of Americans'
lives for which there is not an applicable, regularly issued composite performance measurement or status metric. The national
economy, collective health, physical environment, personal relationships, and leisure and recreational activities are all re-
lentlessly recorded, compiled, and portrayed by batteries of
composite indicators.

What About a Composite School Finance Indicator?

Education appears to be the only major societal activity that
does not have a publicly accepted composite performance or
process indicator. But what might composite education indicators look like? What would they indicate? What areas or education activities or resource availability might they reflect? Four
major topical areas have been suggested (Guthrie, 1989):
(1) student performance, (2) overall conditions of children, (3)
education service quality, and (4) public support for education.
These are all candidates for inclusion as education mega-
indicators. Each of these would be an unusually large aggregate
of information on an important education-related dimension.

   In a larger framework, school finance measures might be
a component of a "public support for education" indicator.
Professional educators contend that if an index of school or

student performance is a good idea, then an index of public support is only fair in return.[2] Here could be included data items such as the results of annual public opinion polling regarding school performance (such as the annual *Phi Delta Kappan* poll), expenditures for schooling as a percentage of personal income, school board election turnout results, mean teacher salaries as a percentage of national mean personal income, and college freshman views of teaching as an occupation.

The purpose of this chapter, however, is to explore a smaller, albeit quite important, component of one of these suggested megaeducation indicators: a composite indicator for school finance. The components of a school finance composite indicator ought eventually to be the outcome of substantial professional and technical discussion, and the initial practical product should not be regarded as the final version. It could well take five years to a decade to hone a set of components to the point where a school finance composite indicator was publicly understandable and technically acceptable. Moreover, the debate should proceed on at least three dimensions: (1) values important to include in a composite school finance measure, (2) appropriate weightings, and (3) statistical data to be employed in representing the value dimensions.

Values to Be Represented

A school finance composite indicator should reflect four fundamental conditions or values related to public school finance policy (Guthrie & Reed, 1991): (1) adequacy, (2) equality, (3) efficiency, and (4) liberty. These are conditions viewed as just, right, desirable, and important for public policy to maximize. A problem, of course, is that these values are themselves difficult to define. It is also possible that exclusive pursuit of one may preclude fulfillment of one or more of the others. Nevertheless, all of these dimensions are held by American culture to be important, and a composite school finance indicator ought to represent them.

Adequacy. This value dimension has a long school finance history. It is represented in the majority of state school finance arrangements by the provision of a resource foundation to ensure at least a minimally necessary level of school services for each student. In addition to education significance for the polity as a whole, most societies also depend upon formal education to assist individuals in fulfilling their personal preferences. Consequently, for both societal and personal reasons, public policy typically guarantees provision of a fundamental level of education.

Today's complex world continually elevates this minimum to increasingly higher levels. Thus, the minimum foundation is a dynamic concept. What is adequate is always subject to interpretation and change given society's shifting conditions. In short, adequacy is relative, and measures of adequacy for a school finance composite indicator will almost assuredly also have to be relative.

Establishing and measuring this foundation are almost always controversial. Education cuts close to the heart of a society's core values, and it is altogether possible for reasonable persons to disagree about what is important to teach and how much students should learn. However, one of the few means by which agreement can be reached, or at least compromises struck, is to accept a dollar amount per pupil as a proxy for adequacy.

Equality. Another long-standing and deeply held value undergirding American public policy is "equality." Opportunity is important in a society that aspires to be open, democratic, and free of permanent social class conditions; hence, a large body of statutes, judicial decisions, practical operations, and professional efforts is directed at ensuring that school finance resources are equitably distributed. It is important for a composite finance indicator system to appraise the extent to which this value is met.

Efficiency. Important resources are limited. Money, time, prestige, and talent allocated for one endeavor are generally unavailable for another; hence, the long-standing public policy preference to use scarce resources in an efficient manner. School revenues are no exception, and a school finance composite index should strive to capture the degree to which a local, state, or national system is efficient in its use of tax revenues.

Liberty. This value generally is expressed in education policy in terms of the range of choices available to households and students. School electives, attendance policies, extracurricular activities, teacher assignments for students, and instructional philosophies are all schooling dimensions on which it is possible to offer choices. The degree to which a nation's or state's school system empowers local jurisdictions or schools to tailor education programs to the preferences of clients is another dimension that might well be expressed in a school finance composite indicator.

Weighting

There is no technical or scientific means for determining the significance of each of the preceding four values. The larger political system is always assessing and reassessing their relative significance, and the constantly changing nature of school finance arrangements testifies to the dynamic interplay among all four value dimensions. Thus, the easy answer is to assign to each an equal weight and regard composite statistics for each component as of equal importance. However, even if politically expedient, this solution may be inappropriate.

The extent to which a minimal education foundation is provided appears logically more important than any other value dimension. Regardless of how equal, efficient, or diversified a polity's education system, if students are not provided with a minimally adequate education foundation, other value dimensions pale. Hence, adequacy should be the sine qua non of indicator components and weighted more heavily. Therefore, for the proposed school finance indicator, adequacy is arbitrarily accorded a weight of 40 percent. Each of the other three value dimensions is weighted equally at 20 percent each.

These are arbitrary assignments of weights. They will suffice for illustration. However, a serious effort to apply these notions would necessitate a far more intense deliberation among parties directly involved.

Statistical Measures

There are literally hundreds of different means by which the four suggested value dimensions could be appraised and the results calibrated into a composite indicator. Thus, what follows is only illustrative. The suggested scheme assumes a scale in which a state school finance system, if rated top on each of the four proposed measurement dimensions, could accumulate 1,000 points.[3]

Adequacy. The ideal manner in which to measure this dimension would be to develop a comprehensive set of national education goals that each state was expected to accomplish and to determine the cost of providing services necessary to meet these goals. The cost for each state could be adjusted for state-wide or regional economic conditions. Then, the extent to which a state's school finance system ensured full provision of this minimum amount would constitute its score on the adequacy scale.

In the absence of a uniform set of national goals it is possible to permit the political system to define adequacy through the appropriations process. A state would receive 8 basis points for each upward position in the overall national distribution. The highest-per-pupil-spending state, perhaps adjusted for regional cost-of-living differences, might be accorded an initial score of 400. The lowest ranking of the fifty states would be accorded an initial score of 8. It would be possible to measure the extent to which any particular state system was staying abreast of inflation by weighting its distributive rank by the percentage to which the latest annual increment (or decrement) in per-pupil spending matched consumer price index (CPI) increases.

Current spending per pupil is, obviously, only one component of schooling adequacy. There are other considerations, such as the quality and quantity of teachers, textbooks, and curricular offerings. In effect, this suggested approach assumes, some would assert heroically, that dollars translate to quality. Obviously, resources are expressed in many ways, and this is not the forum for debating the extent to which financial resources equate to instructional effectiveness. However, this relative dollars-per-pupil measure appears to be better than the alternatives.

Current per-pupil spending, however, is deficient on at least one dimension. It fails to adequately take into account the quality of school facilities. Buildings are frequently financed through capital outlay measures, separate from current operating costs. Thus, an adequacy component might productively be adjusted for the percentage of students in a state housed in inadequate facilities. This would have to result from a statewide survey that ranked school buildings in terms such as their enrollment capacity, degree of deferred maintenance, and modernity of equipment. (States frequently survey facilities on these variables. This is particularly true where state systems are responsible for funding school construction, such as in Maryland and California.) A state's adequacy ranking would be adjusted downward by the percentage of pupils housed in inadequate (that is, crowded, outdated, or poorly maintained) schools.

Equality. The first impression for many individuals concerned with this dimension is the degree of absolute per-pupil spending difference in a state. To measure equality, the coefficient of variation, McLoone index, or some other measure of spending dispersion might suffice (see Berne & Stiefel, 1984). But if the minimum spending level met an adequacy standard, spending above the base might be viewed as acceptable. The problem with allowing spending above the base is that some districts have a larger property tax base to tap for these funds than do others; overall spending often is related to property wealth or household income. To measure this dimension of the inequality, it would be necessary to calculate a correlation coefficient or simple wealth elasticity between measures of wealth and school spending for school district jurisdictions in a state and

then multiply the resulting figures by whatever arbitrary weighting was being employed for this value dimension.

However, equality must be balanced against other values
that argue for differences in spending, for example, need for
compensatory or special education services, local preferences
for schooling, or concerns for efficiency. Thus, equality could also
be defined as "per-pupil school spending unrelated to other measures of wealth, such as property wealth or household income."

Appraising equity would depend upon a stepwise multiple regression analysis in which the dependent variable was
"current operating spending per weighted pupil" and the ex-
planatory variables included items such as school district assessed valuation per pupil and household income. The percentage of a state's school spending that could be explained by
measures of wealth would be deducted from the highest possible
score on this value dimension, 200 points. A state completely
free of wealth-determined school spending would be accorded a
score of 200. Conversely, a state in which district property value
was highly associated with per-pupil spending would have an
equivalent percentage deducted from 200 points.

Efficiency. This too is a controversial dimension. One approach, again contingent upon having a comprehensive set of
national education goals, would be to measure the ratio of
students achieving at an adequate level and compare it to the
percentage of adequate base funding provided by the state. For
example, a state that provided 75 percent of base revenue funding and in which 75 percent of students were scoring at the
adequate level relative to goals would be rated 100 percent
efficient. This percentage could then be multiplied by 200, the
weighting for this value dimension.

An alternative approach would be to measure the percentage of total per-pupil spending allocated to purposes
closely related to instruction and take that dollar amount as a
percentage of total per-pupil spending. The higher the percentage, presumably, the more efficient the state. The difficulty here
is taking into account differences among states in the amount of
money they spend on activities such as transportation. Such

expenditures might appear inefficient when, in fact, students could not be instructed unless they were transported to school.

Liberty. Quantifying choice on an overall education composite index might be done by using the percentage of school-age students who possibly could attend schools outside their assigned geographical area or school district. The assumption is that those who could attend school outside their area represented the extent to which a state accommodated different household preferences for education.

Under this arrangement, a state such as Minnesota, which permits household choice of any public school, would score 100 percent. Presumably, in Minnesota every student can attend a school outside his or her geographically defined school district or attendance zone. In California, parents can select their assigned school or a school near their place of employment. If the latter is outside their regular school district, if the parents receive permission, they can transfer their child. This is a far more limited choice plan. Perhaps as many as 20 percent of California students would fall into such an eligibility category. California would rank lower than Minnesota on this dimension.

An allowance might well be made in such a scheme for the degree to which the choice plan permitted selection of private, or nonpublic, schools. Perhaps for a state to be rated 100 percent on this dimension, school-age children would have to be eligible to attend any accredited school and have their tuition publicly paid.

Another approach would be to assume that the greater the amount of money districts spend above the state-specified minimum foundation level (exclusive of state and federal categorical aid funds), the more districts are trying to satisfy client preferences. A maximum 200 basis points could be accorded the top-rated state on this dimension. If a state permitted or encouraged spending in high amounts above the specified foundation but such spending was heavily wealth related, the state would be penalized on the equality dimension (described earlier). However, if the added per-pupil spending was wealth neutral, then the state would be rewarded on this liberty or choice dimension.

A Practical (Hypothetical) Illustration

It would be possible to construct a composite education finance indicator for the entire nation. However, data for the issues just discussed simply are not available nationwide. The financing of schools is a remarkably decentralized phenomenon. The federal government, to be sure, plays a role. However, the overwhelming responsibility resides with state governments, and it is state data that currently are most available and lend themselves most readily to illustrations. Hence, this section provides a state-level hypothetical example. However, leaving aside for a moment the costs of information collection, there is no logical impediment to creating these indices for the nation or, for that matter, for a local school district or another jurisdiction.

In order to have meaning, a composite index needs a baseline against which to compare existing conditions. Two kinds of comparisons are possible: longitudinal and cross-sectional. Specifically, a state or another jurisdiction can be compared with itself over time, with other states, or both. In this instance, the hypothetical states are compared with each other.

Table 6.1 and Figures 6.2 and 6.3 display hypothetical data for four states and are intended to show how a mega-indicator might work. The megaindicator uses the following measures (see Table 6.1):

- Adequacy: percentage of adequate program funded
- Equity: percentage of education spending that is wealth neutral
- Efficiency: ratio of student achievement relative to base funding
- Liberty: percentage of students eligible to attend a school outside their local attendance boundary

Adequacy is weighted 40 percent; the other three factors are each weighted 20 percent.

Figure 6.2 shows the number of points each measure contributes to the composite indicator, and Figure 6.3 shows the composite indicator for each hypothetical state. The results

Table 6.1. Composite Education Finance Indicator:
Statistical Data for Four Hypothetical States.

State	Adequacy (400 points)		Equity (200 points)	Efficiency (200 points)	Liberty (200 points)
	Percentage of Adequate Programs Funded	Percentage of Students Inadequately Housed	Percentage of Education Spending Wealth Neutral	Ratio of Achievement to Base Revenues	Percentage of Pupils Eligible to Attend Alternative School
1	50	5	50	70	30
2	30	15	100	75	35
3	15	20	90	85	20
4	1	30	60	80	20

show that the adequacy component is a major determinant of the size of the composite indicator and that no state ranks at a full 1,000 points.

But Who Needs Them?

So what? Is there more to be gained than lost from having a school finance composite indicator? Even if philosophical and technical impediments were overcome, what would be the policy-level advantages and disadvantages of having a national or statewide school finance composite indicator?

Composite Education Finance Indicator Advantages

There are five reasons for developing such school finance indicators. The indicators could be used to measure progress, foster accountability, facilitate communication, promote awareness, and enhance support.

Measure Progress. If appropriately constructed, one (or more) composite education finance indicator could provide a useful baseline against which to judge U.S. resource allocation progress or lack thereof. Such an indicator could simultane-

Figure 6.2. Points for Each Component of a Composite
Education Finance Indicator for Four Hypothetical States.

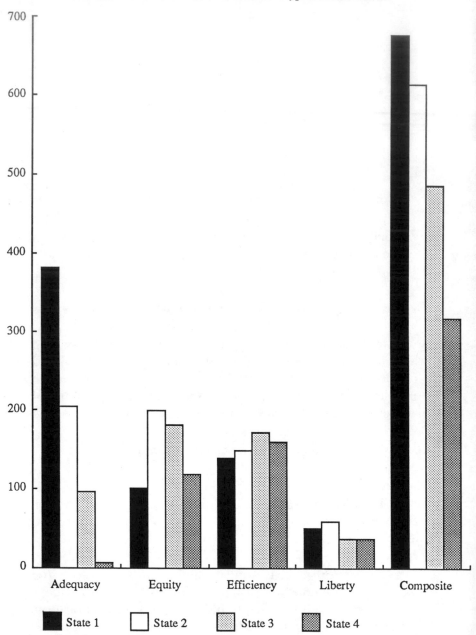

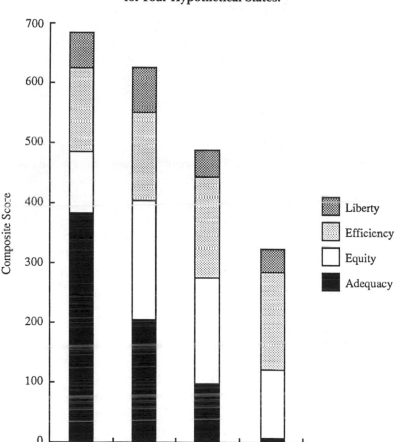

**Figure 6.3. Composite School Finance Indicators
for Four Hypothetical States.**

ously serve as a target for the future and a thermometer to measure the present.

Foster Accountability. If what is measured is important, then a composite finance indicator could heighten educator sensitivity to the need to be productive. This is particularly the case if the indicator is developed so that state, local district, and

school resource measures can be constructed and compared to
national measures.

Facilitate Communication. A properly constructed composite finance indicator need not be completely understood by
the general public to be useful. It does have to have sufficient
technical validity to gain the endorsement of experts. Assuming
such a threshold condition occurred, then public awareness and
reliance could be fostered. The indicator would serve to com-
press complicated school finance information, currently misun-
derstood by the public, into an easily digested format for ready
public consumption.

Promote Awareness. An indicator's visibility would promote greater public awareness of school finance. If, for example,
the indicators were issued yearly, they could be used by the
media and the public to develop a heightened consciousness of
the status of financial resources for American education.

Enhance Support. Supporters contend that the public believes education is important for the nation's long-run well-being
and would be willing to allocate more resources if there were
means for easily conveying the education finance system's relative status. This need not always justify more money. Presumably, low efficiency measures might also dampen requests for
added resources. Regardless of the direction of results, however,
a convenient and credible communication mechanism would
enhance the prospect of added resources by engaging the public more effectively in the debate.

Composite Education Finance Indicator Disadvantages

Critics and skeptics contend that widespread reliance upon a
select few composite education finance indicators would vastly
oversimplify the education policy development and resource
allocation process. They argue that such indicators might be
inappropriate, distorting, costly, and misleading.

Inappropriate. At its roots, this is a philosophical objection. Composite finance indicator critics sometimes claim that education resource allocation debates, indeed almost everything connected with education, are too important to be reduced to a single number. The ultimate objective of schooling is to instill in students a desire to learn. If this is accomplished, then students will assume a larger responsibility for their own education. The entire indicator movement seems philosophically inimical to the humane and spiritual essence of true education. To subject schooling to an excessive amount of measurement and appraisal is to squeeze the vitality from the process and intervene inappropriately in a number of complicated and delicate political and personal processes.

Distorting. Measurement can drive a harmful wedge between teacher and learner, policy makers and profesionals, and the public and its representatives. In addition, heavy reliance upon indicators, particularly upon composite finance indicators, can distort the purposes and processes of education institutions.

The assumption, at least among those employed in the institutions subjected to measurement, is that if a dimension or an activity justifies measurement, then it must somehow be important. Given this assumption, then it is also important to determine how to enhance the agent's or agency's score on whatever is being measured. Activity is then directed, perhaps disproportionately, toward what is to be measured and deflected away from other, perhaps more important activities. The higher the consequences of measurement are thought to be, the greater the likelihood that the measurement process will occupy the minds of those engaged in the activity.

The distortion may be of several types. For example, the measured activity may replace other activities, even more significant activities. This is known among organizational sociologists as goal displacement. Also, those believing themselves to be judged or rated by the measure may attempt to elevate scores by illegitimate means, for example, by manipulating measured results. Any system that encourages dishonest or unprofessional behavior should be carefully considered.

Costly. The direct cost involved in collecting, compiling, and distributing the information connected with a composite finance indicator would redirect resources from other, presumably more important information activity.

Misleading. Critics assert that numbers simply do not convey a sufficient amount of the truth. Unemployment figures do not capture the discomfort and loss of dignity among unemployed individuals and poverty-stricken families. The consumer price index (CPI) may display relatively low inflation for the entire nation, but if any component of the index is particularly important to a region, such as energy prices, then the index does not accurately reflect that region's economic circumstances.

Such could be the case with school finance. While an overall index might reflect increasing resources, resources allocated to Hispanic or black students might be stable or declining. The nation's total resource commitment could be rising but falling in certain regions or local districts. Critics contend that a composite finance indicator could not begin to capture and reflect this kind of complexity and thus runs the risk of misleading the public and education policy makers.

Conclusion

A composite indicator for education finance could assist the public, policy makers, and professional educators in assessing the range of complex issues connected with resource allocation. However, the components of such a composite need careful deliberation and debate because they will not only reflect reality; in time, they will influence reality.

Notes

1. Ironically, the Dow Jones industrial average (DJIA) does not measure what many people think it does. The DJIA is widely

perceived to measure the spectrum of financial market activity. In fact, it is intended only to measure industrial stock activities. It consciously omits bonds, commodity futures, metals, currencies, services, and a host of other financial market activities.

2. This position also is justified in light of America's cultural ambivalence about the intellect and academic matters. The United States has long had mixed feelings about education. On one hand, high school graduation and college degrees are viewed as something of a pathway to secular salvation and economic security. School persistence is encouraged, and dropping out is bad. On the other hand, "ivory tower" and "egghead" are disparaging descriptors; "Yankee ingenuity" and the experience of meeting a payroll are often thought to be more useful than book learning, and the popular media are frequently playing up stories of success in the face of academic adversity.

3. An alternative is to use a similar weighting scheme but array the points on a percentage scale, that is, 0 to 100 percent. The outcome is not significantly different from what is employed here for illustrative purposes. Some contend that the smaller number might possibly be more understandable to the public. However, the percentage approach strongly implies that 100 percent is somehow perfect, and there is little about the proposed measurements, at this preliminary point, that is perfect.

References

Bacon, K. (1990, November 5). Use of free enterprise philosophy is urged for reform of public schools. *Wall Street Journal.*

Berne, R., & Stiefel, L. (1984). *The measurement of equity in school finance: Conceptual, methodological, and empirical dimensions.* Baltimore, MD: Johns Hopkins University Press.

College Board. (1992). Telephone interview.

Guthrie, J. W. (1989). *Mega educational indicators.* Paper prepared for the National Center for Education Statistics, Washington, DC.

Guthrie, J. W., & Reed, R. J. (1991). *Educational administration and policy: Effective leadership for American education*. Needham Heights, MA: Allyn & Bacon.

Kirst, M. W. (Ed.). (1989). *Conditions of children in California*. Berkeley: University of California, School of Education.

National Center for Education Statistics. (1992). *Digest of Education Statistics: 1991*. Washington, DC: U.S. Department of Education.

Norwood, J. L. (1990). Distinguished lecture on economics and government: Data quality and public policy. *Journal of Economic Perspectives, 4*, 3–12.

Weiss, J. A., & Gruber, J. E. (1987). The managed irrelevance of federal education statistics. In W. Alonzo & P. Starr (Eds.), *The politics of numbers* (pp. 363–391). New York: Russell Sage Foundation.

7

Financing Public School Choice:
Policy Issues and Options

Allan R. Odden
Nancy Kotowski

While education choice, as tuition tax credits and vouchers, seemed to be a dead issue a few years ago, it currently is a critical policy issue in the form of public school choice. Public school choice plans have been enacted by legislatures in several states, public school choice policies are supported by the National Governors' Association, and even President Bush now supports school choice. Policy makers seem to support a variety of public school choice plans, from interdistrict to intradistrict policies.

Much has been written on education choice, but little has been written on the finance dimensions of these policies. As long as school choice was contained within school district boundaries, finance issues were not paramount. But with choice plans that cross district boundaries, finance issues become more critical.

This chapter addresses several of the finance dimensions related to public-sector choice programs and suggests a new school financing structure that addresses them. The first section provides a short overview of public school choice by describing different types of policies that can be included under the rubric

Note: We would like to thank Joe Nathan, Ted Kolderie, and James Guthrie for several good suggestions on an earlier version of this chapter.

of "school choice" and discusses several issues that must be addressed to make school choice policies work. Section two describes various state approaches to public school choice, emphasizing the finance arrangements. The third section identifies a variety of school financing issues that have been overlooked in the design of most public school choice programs. Section four then outlines a new school finance structure that accommodates both the traditional property tax, district-based finance mechanism and a new income tax, school-based structure appropriate for school choice programs.

An Overview of Public School Choice Issues

Today, public school choice, while rooted in more conservative economic voucher proposals (Friedman, 1962), is increasingly supported by a broad range of political and education leaders (although there is still widespread suspicion of choice proposals, especially the 1991 public and private choice proposals offered by President Bush). The resurgence of school choice as a mainstream education policy issue is somewhat surprising. The late 1970s and early 1980s versions of choice—vouchers and tuition tax credits—were firmly defeated just a few years ago. Yet, the governors in their first report on education reform— *Time for Results* (National Governors' Association, 1986)—catapulted education choice onto their reform agenda.

The major change between earlier and most present choice versions is the limitation of choice proposals to the public sector. The bulk of current political support for education choice excludes public aid to private schools. Once that exclusion was widespread, the choice issue began to gain bipartisan political support. Minnesota's open enrollment program—the nation's first statewide school choice program—was proposed by a Democratic governor and enacted by a Democratic Senate and Republican House, with support from the business community and several education organizations, including the Parent-Teacher Association (PTA) and the League of Women Voters. Across the country, both Democratic and Republican governors have proposed various public school choice policies. The next section describes the finance mechanisms for these programs.

This section briefly describes the variety of public-sector choice programs that can be created and factors related to their success. This section does not analyze in depth the arguments for or against choice nor the factors associated with each choice mechanism. Bridge and Blackman (1978), Boyd and Kerschner (1988), Boyd and Walberg (1990), the Education Commission of the States (1989), Elmore (1986), Finn (1987), Levin (1989), Murnane (1986), Nathan (1989), Raywid (1985), and Thomas (1978) provide extensive discussion of the various issues related to education choice, including their potential impact on education productivity. The purpose of this section is to provide a brief description of various choice alternatives and what is needed to make them work.

Public School Choice Alternatives

The Education Commission of the States (1989) and Levin (1989) identify eight different, though related, public school choice programs:

1. *Interdistrict open enrollment.* This program allows parents to send their children to their neighborhood school, another public school in their district, or another public school in a different school district. This structure is the most grandiose public-sector choice policy since it potentially involves all schools in a state. This policy effectively gives parents and students the option to attend any public school in any district for any reason. While such a policy would have to address issues of selection, transportation, information dissemination, and so on, the general idea is to open up public school choice across the entire state. Limitations to such a completely open program would allow cross-district choice but only in contiguous districts, that is, districts that border the resident district. The key distinguishing feature of interdistrict open enrollment programs, however, is the ability of the student to choose to attend a school in a district outside of the district in which the student resides.

2. *Intradistrict open enrollment.* This approach is similar to interdistrict open enrollment in trying to provide an alternative to the neighborhood school, but school choice is limited to public schools within the district. For small districts, this approach does not provide much choice. In large urban districts, this program potentially provides a wide range of school choices. By limiting choice to public schools within a district, most of the tricky issues of finance are avoided (assuming comparability of school funds within a district).

3. *Minischools or schools within schools.* These programs provide education alternatives within a particular school site. One objective is to overcome the impersonal nature of large schools at all levels. Schools within a school have been developed for compensatory education programs. The Coalition of Essential Schools has developed "houses" within several high schools across the country that group several teachers with about eighty students, emphasize thinking and problem solving, and teach mathematics/science and English/history in multidisciplinary ways. The American Federation of Teachers has suggested creating teacher-initiated "charter schools," and the National Education Association has sponsored a different version called "mastery learning schools." These approaches obviously do not entail a transfer of funds across school district boundaries; each school is restricted to the base revenues the district provides.

4. *Magnet schools.* Magnet schools are limited versions of intradistrict open enrollment programs. Magnet schools typically have unique characteristics or themes designed to make them attractive school options, to serve as a "magnet" to attract a broad range of students from throughout the district. Magnet schools have been used in several urban districts as mechanisms for integration; the theory is that the magnet characteristic will attract students from all ethnic groups interested in the particular school emphasis. Magnet themes include an emphasis on the performing arts, mathematics and science, the health professions, an open school environment, a basic and fundamental school approach, theater, financial services, and so on. Often

(but not always) magnet schools receive additional funds to create their program attraction. Increasingly, magnet schools receive the same dollar allocations as other schools but use them to create their distinctiveness. About a dozen states have created special, statewide magnet schools for top students, such as the North Carolina School for Mathematics and Science.

5. *Postsecondary options.* This program allows students to take courses at neighboring postsecondary institutions, often instead of attending the last years of high school. Participation in this type of option is usually limited to secondary students, most often high school juniors and seniors. Such a program necessitates coordinating high school graduation requirements with allowable postsecondary courses. Like an interdistrict choice option, this alternative has students attending an education institution that is not part of the resident district, though in this instance choice is limited to postsecondary institutions. Both alternatives usually require some transfer of funds from the district to an institution not part of the resident district. Note that postsecondary institutions might be geographically within a school district.

6. *Minivouchers.* This program, while using the "v" word, is limited in scope but again involves a flow of funds outside of the resident district. Minivouchers would be available to students who are allowed to purchase specific and limited services outside of the resident school system. The most common proposals allow attendance at public (or private) vocational schools, special programs of compensatory education, or special education programs not available in the resident district. Minivouchers tend to be provided only after students have had the common school experience through grade 10.

7. *Second-chance or continuation schools.* Second-chance programs are usually available to students who have dropped out of high school or are likely to drop out. These programs tend to be provided in nontraditional school settings and are usually publicly funded (often federally funded). Since the student already

has dropped out of the resident district, funding for second-chance programs usually is not connected to the regular, K–12 funding structure, although in theory it could be. Continuation high school programs are variations of alternative schools but are usually intradistrict alternative schools. California has a long history of continuation high schools. These schools usually are small (less than 300 students), are flexible in their organization and management, provide a more personal environment in both their scale and style of operation, are attended by choice by many students, provide a more individualized curriculum to students at risk of dropping out of high school, and are funded through the regular K–12 funding structure.

8. *Private contractors.* This option would entail public schools contracting out to private firms to provide certain services, for example, foreign language training from the Berlitz schools. In the early 1970s, a few school districts hired private contractors to provide reading instruction and help boost reading performance. Under the private contracting option, the initiative to invoke the choice option is taken by the local school district or school. Under all of the other seven options just reviewed, the initiative to invoke a choice alternative is taken by the student or parent.

While most discussions of public school choice list the above types of options (or some variation of them), a more conceptual approach to public school choice helps identify the critical dimensions of the discussion. To begin, public school choice simply transfers the school attendance decision from the education system to the student (or the family). This transfer is the key policy shift. Viewed in this light, public school choice does not seem such a dramatic shift as it often is portrayed to be.

Next, to implement this new policy, states need to make regulations in each of three areas: school eligibility, student eligibility, and scope of choice program. School eligibility determines whether only public schools can be selected (usually called public school choice), whether both public and private schools can be selected (commonly called vouchers), or whether choice is available only for a particular school level, such as the middle school choice program in Cambridge, Massachusetts.

Student eligibility includes the issue of whether all students are eligible (as in most interdistrict open enrollment programs), only students at certain age levels (such as high school students for postsecondary option programs), or only students who have not succeeded (such as Colorado's second-chance program discussed below).

Scope pertains to the geographical area over which school choice is provided: only schools within a school (such as the Coalition of Essential School's houses approach), only sections of a city (such as the District 4 program in New York City), citywide (such as most magnet programs or the choice programs provided by many Minnesota metropolitan districts before that state's open enrollment program), or statewide (such as a state interdistrict open enrollment program).

Decisions on these three critical variables determine the major characteristics and dimensions of most choice programs. Different decisions affect finance in different ways. Some entail a revenue flow outside the district; others do not. Revenue flows are driven by family and student choice in some alternatives and by school and district choice in others. Each option, moreover, has advantages and disadvantages, provides various forms of family choice, and makes different assumptions about school improvement — which is the prime goal underlying the political support for choice. Table 7.1 summarizes the issues for the first seven of these alternatives.

Conditions That Help Choice Programs Work

However categorized or conceptualized, there are four other major conditions critical to making choice programs work. The first is a *school-based information system*. If families are to make informed decisions about which school their children attend, they need information about specific aspects of the school. They need information on the academic program in the school, knowledge about the philosophy of teachers, and extensive data on school performance. Few states have a robust and compre-

Table 7.1. Priorities Addressed by Various Public School Choice Programs.

Type of Choice Plan	Family Freedom	Equity	School Improvement
Interdistrict open enrollment	Emphasizes right to choose a public school in any district.	Must be protected by providing parent information, transportation for poor families, and nonselective admissions.	Assumed to result from competition. Can be enhanced by providing technical assistance, planning, grants, staff development, and waivers.
Intradistrict open enrollment or controlled choice	Allows all families to choose among all district schools, subject to racial balance guidelines.	Strives to ensure that all elements of the plan are fair so that voluntary desegregation will have wide support.	Must provide support to help schools develop capacity to attract and retain families.
Teacher-initiated minischools	Attracts families to diverse schools whose goals they share and style of teaching they prefer for their child(ren).	Must be protected by providing nonselective admissions, parent information, and transportation.	Implemented by allowing teachers to create and manage diverse schools and by supporting school-based improvement in all schools.
Magnet schools	Allows a small number of families to attend a handful of special schools within a district.	Power to attract based on assumed difference in quality between magnet and all other schools.	Magnet schools often receive special resources and have ability to create a distinctive program. Other schools do not receive extra resources.
Second-chance, continuation schools, and minivouchers	Allows poorly performing students and dropouts to choose other educational settings.	No special provisions. Can isolate and label at-risk students in marginal alternative programs if program standards are low.	Does not address causes of schools initially not meeting student needs.
Postsecondary options	Allows high school students to choose between high schools and postsecondary institutions.	Protected by ensuring nondiscriminatory admissions and extending options to at-risk youth.	Follows from competition. Can be enhanced by providing technical assistance, planning, grants, staff development, and waivers.

Source: Compiled from Education Commission of the States, 1989.

hensive *school-based* information system since most education data have been collected on a *district*, not school, basis. Thus, most states will need to devote new resources to develop and maintain a comprehensive *school-based* information system in order to implement a school choice program. Further, districts will need to expand schoolwide information systems to include similar data on the minischool or school-within-a-school options.

Second, states will need to develop *equitable selection and transfer systems*. Policies will need to be developed for selecting students in oversubscribed schools and will need to ensure fair treatment along income, ethnic, and gender lines. If the income tax surcharge financing option proposed in the last section is adopted, a modified price mechanism—one that treats poor families fairly—might help resolve this selection dilemma. Currently, most states have opted for a lottery approach to selecting students for oversubscribed schools.

Third, states, especially those with diverse student bodies, will need to more creatively address the issue of *racial diversity and integration* when designing and implementing choice programs. The dominant policy now is to restrict choice if family decisions would diminish racial balance in a school. In an interdistrict choice program, this could have the unintended consequence of restricting choice to homogeneous communities. For example, minorities now bused across town for integration purposes might choose to attend their neighborhood schools, thus increasing racial isolation in both schools. These same minorities might rather choose to attend a school in another district, again decreasing integration in the school to which they had been bused. The same is possible for majority students. Most states have added a clause to choice options that prohibits choice if it would reduce integration in a school. These clauses need to be written more creatively in order to allow a wider use of choice options.

A fourth condition is *full access to a school of choice through expanded school district transportation policies*. Transportation arrangements are needed to make school choice a feasible option. Transportation to and from a school of choice in a reasonable

length of time and without undue extra financial burden is a
minimum requirement.

Finance Issues

There are numerous finance factors associated with public
school choice programs, especially those programs that allow
choice across district boundaries. Five finance issues, discussed
in the next section, are prominent:

- Adequate and fair funding in terms of state and local revenue flows, that is, the revenues that follow the student. State
  aid alone is insufficient.
- Existence of interdistrict fiscal disparities, which can reach
  ratios of more than two to one in base spending per pupil.
  Thus, even if base spending per pupil follows the child,
  students moving from low- to high-spending districts do not
  carry sufficient funds with them, and vice versa.
- Categorical aid flows. Even when base revenue issues are
  resolved, there are various categorical programs for special
  student needs, such as compensatory, special, and bilingual
  education programs, that also are affected when a student
  attends school in another district or even in a school across
  town in the resident's district.
- Existence of discretionary funds to create "attractive" alternatives. Additional pots of dollars, or discretion over some
  pool of money, may be needed by schools in order to create
  features that might attract different students.
- Transportation. If students are to invoke a choice option,
  they need transportation from their residence to their
  school of choice. Do the districts provide that transportation? Do parents? Do they work together? This dilemma is
  both an operational and a finance issue, one not easy to
  resolve.

Finally, this chapter assumes that resources are distributed comparably across school sites within districts, and
thus intradistrict fiscal disparities can be ignored. On the one

hand, this is a reasonable assumption because several years of Title I (now Chapter 1) comparability have induced most dis-tricts to provide equitable school-by-school resource allocations. But Title I comparability ignored fiscal differences caused by teacher salary increments for education and experience on the salary schedule, and thus there are absolute differences in dol-lars per child that are allowed. It could be reasonably argued that this is a problem with intradistrict choice programs. Fur-ther, Title I (now Chapter 1) comparability requirements have been eliminated; practices could have changed, even though recent studies showed that most large districts have retained the procedures required by the old comparability requirements (Farrar & Milsap, 1986). While this issue needs to be monitored by all states, this chapter assumes intradistrict comparable re-source allocation and focuses on financing problems associated with interdistrict public school choice programs.

Current State Approaches to Financing Public School Choice Programs

By the end of 1990, several states had enacted some form of school choice program. States adopted a variety of approaches to financing these newly developed public school choice programs.

Table 7.2 displays the dimensions of state financing for interdistrict open enrollment choice programs enacted by the end of 1990 in ten states: Arkansas, California, Colorado, Idaho, Iowa, Minnesota, Nebraska, Ohio, Utah, and Washington. Cal-ifornia limited choice to the district in which the parent either lives or works. Ohio limited choice to schools in contiguous school districts. There were no limitations in the other states: students could select any school in the state.

State aid follows the child to the receiving district in just one state—Arkansas. Nebraska made a special appropriation for choice students. Each receiving district receives an amount equal to the total appropriation divided by the number of choice children (an amount that decreases as the number of choice students increases). In California, Idaho, Iowa, Min-

Table 7.2. State Approaches to Funding Interdistrict Open Enrollment Choice Programs: 1990.

State	Total State/Local Base Funding Follows Child to Receiving District	Only State Aid Base Funding Follows Child to Receiving District	State Aid Base Funding Also Remains in Sending District	Funding Adjusted to Accommodate Interdistrict Spending Differences	Categorical Dollars
Arkansas: interdistrict open enrollment	No	Yes. Student counted as a pupil in resident district.	No	No	Generally, student counted as pupil in attending district. Not addressed specifically in law.
California: interdistrict open enrollment	Yes	No	No	Most districts spending at same level.	Generally, student counted as pupil in attending district.
Colorado: second chance	Yes	No	No	Yes, according to the basic Colorado school finance formula.	Generally, student counted as pupil in attending district. Categorical aids follow child to receiving district.
Idaho: interdistrict open enrollment	Yes, generally. Student counted as pupil in attending district.	No	No	Yes, since student counted as pupil in district attended.	Student counted as pupil in attending district for all categorical aids.
Iowa: interdistrict open enrollment	Yes. Sending district provides lower of either the sending or receiving district's average instructional costs per pupil.	No	No. Except for excess aid when sending district's base cost is less than receiving district's.	Yes, in a way. The *lower* of the sending or receiving district's average instructional costs per pupil follows the child.	Special education funds follow child to receiving district.

Minnesota: interdistrict open enrollment	Yes. About $3,600 per child.	No	No	For special education, student counted in attending district. Compensatory education funds follow the student.
Nebraska: interdistrict open enrollment	Yes, to a degree. A special state appropriation for choice students (equaled $1,850/child for 1990–91).	No	No	Categorical aids follow the child to receiving district.
Ohio: interdistrict open enrollment	Yes. Foundation expenditure adjusted by a district cost-of-doing-business factor.	No	No	Yes, for excess cost of special education. No, for compensatory education and transportation.
Utah: interdistrict open enrollment	Yes. Sending district provides receiving district current operating expenses per pupil (less transportation) of sending district.	No	No. Sending district receives aid but remits more than aid amount to receiving district.	No. Sending district sends its operating expenditures per pupil (less transportation) to receiving district.	Follows the child to the receiving district.
Washington: interdistrict open enrollment	Yes, generally. Student counted as pupil in attending district.[a]	No	No	Yes, since student counted as pupil in district attended.	Student counted as pupil in attending district for all categorical aids.

[a] Receiving district can charge parents a tuition fee equal to the average local property tax dollars per student in district attended. Most districts do not charge this fee, but some do. Parents charged a fee effectively pay property taxes in both their resident district and the district their child attends.

nesota, Ohio, Utah, and Washington, the total base funding
follows the child. Since base funding is about the same in all
California districts, the same dollar amount follows each child.
In Colorado, the law initially allowed only 85 percent of the
district's base revenues per pupil to follow the child; as a result,
districts initially declined to participate in the program. Subsequently, changes were made so that all of the per-pupil base
revenue follows the child.

In Idaho and Washington, the student is counted as a
pupil in the district attended, and the district is provided the full
level of base per-pupil revenues. In Iowa, the lower of the sending
or the receiving district's base instructional per-pupil funding
follows the child. In Ohio, the foundation amount times the
sending district's cost-of-doing-business index is sent to the receiving district. In Utah, the sending district provides to the
receiving district an amount equal to the sending district's current operating expenditures (minus transportation) per pupil.

In short, the tendency is for total base funding—not just
state aid—to follow the child. Indeed, recently states have begun
simply to count the student as a pupil in the district attended. As
is discussed below, this procedure streamlines the process and
produces all the appropriate revenue flows.

The major new twist to these finance mechanisms is the
Washington option that allows the receiving district to charge a
tuition fee to the parents (not the sending district) equal to the
local property tax per pupil. While not many districts have
invoked this option, some have, and the option creates equity
problems of access to choice for poor families.

Categorical dollars (last column in Table 7.2) are treated
differently from state to state. In many cases, categorical aid
allocations were not explicitly mentioned in the law. In Arkansas, California, Colorado, Idaho, and Washington, the individual student is counted as a pupil in the district attended for
the purposes of categorical aid calculations. In Iowa and Ohio,
special education aid follows the child, but compensatory education aid does not. In Minnesota, the student is counted as a
pupil in the attending district for calculating special education
aid, and compensatory education funds follow the child to the

attending district. In both Nebraska and Utah, categorical aids follow the child.

At least four states—Colorado, Florida, Minnesota, and Ohio—have adopted postsecondary options programs (see Table 7.3). Colorado's program covers only tuition, which the district remits to the postsecondary institution. The Minnesota and Ohio programs pay for tuition, books, materials, and fees and reduce the resident district's state aid by a similar amount. In Florida, no funds are transferred; students simply are able to maintain dual enrollment in their resident high school and a community college and take a restricted number of postsecondary courses.

Table 7.3. State Approaches to Funding Postsecondary Options Choice Programs.

State	Total State/Local Base Funding Follows Child to Receiving Institution	Only State Aid Base Funding Follows Child to Receiving Institution	State Aid Base Funding Also Remains in Sending District
Colorado: postsecondary option	District pays college tuition charges.	No	Yes
Florida: postsecondary option	Dual enrollment in both high school and community college: no charge and no dollar transfers.	—	—
Minnesota: postsecondary option	Not applicable	State pays tuition, books, materials, and fees.	Yes, but reduced by payments made to postsecondary institutions.
Ohio: postsecondary option	Lesser of foundation amount times district cost-of-doing-business factor or tuition, books, materials, and fees.	No	State aid reduced by postsecondary costs.

Table 7.4 displays information on how transportation is funded and whether discretionary funds are provided to create quality choice programs for the interdistrict open enrollment plans. Transportation poses a difficult dilemma for states. All states recognize that choice is a vacuous option if students cannot get from their home to a school of choice, especially in a district outside their resident district. But if transportation were provided for all students to any schools, logistics would be enormous and costs quite high. Thus, most states have parents transport students either to the boundary of the receiving district or to the nearest bus stop in the receiving district; then the receiving districts transport students to schools.

For the interdistrict open enrollment programs, this strategy was adopted in Arkansas, Iowa, Minnesota, Nebraska, Ohio, and Utah. Further, Iowa, Minnesota, and Ohio reimburse poor parents — usually defined as parents with an income below poverty level or with students eligible for free or reduced lunch — for their transportation costs. Neither the California, Idaho, nor Washington laws address the issue of transportation for those invoking the choice option. Colorado reimburses districts for transportation the same as it reimburses for regular transportation. It is a district option to transport choice students.

States generally do not provide discretionary funds to improve or expand the supply of attractive options (although there are usually targeted funds for desegregation magnets or for dropout prevention programs). This can restrict the creation of quality options. For example, magnet programs often cost from 10 to 12 percent more than traditional schools. The acclaimed Los Angeles County High School for the Arts annually must raise almost $1,000 more per student than the state currently provides. Many alternative school designs likely would cost more than traditional schools. Specialty schools are more expensive than traditional programs. For example, the Illinois Mathematics and Science Academy's instructional expenses in 1989–90 were about $9,600 per year, far higher than spending in most school districts in the country; moreover, the state pays an additional $8,400 for students' room and board. But no state currently provides additional funds to schools to develop any of these more costly alternatives.

In the four postsecondary option programs (see Table 7.5), two states—Minnesota and Ohio—have parents provide the transportation and reimburse poor parents for the costs. In Florida, the local district provides transportation, and costs are shared by the district and local community college according to local agreements. Colorado did not provide a transportation appropriation for its postsecondary option program. Districts may provide transportation or pay students/parents to provide it. State reimbursement is made to the district.

In sum, the general trend is to support choice students with the full amount of state and local general revenues for the base program, as well as with the full complement of categorical aids. Indeed, the recent practice is to count the student as a pupil in the district attended for calculating both general and categorical revenues. Further, the trend is to have the parent provide transportation to the school or to a bus stop in the new district, with the state reimbursing low-income parents for transportation costs.

The Finance Problems Related to Public School Choice Programs

As the previous section shows, current state approaches to financing public school choice programs treat several finance issues differently. But state choice financing mechanisms also leave several problems unaddressed. This section outlines several of these problems, which point to the structural mismatch between a property tax, district-based school finance system and an interdistrict, school-based attendance system. The next section proposes a new type of school finance structure to remedy these problems.

The most obvious problem unaddressed by most public school choice programs is interdistrict expenditure-per-pupil disparities, a characteristic of nearly all state school finance systems. The issue here is that students who leave low-spending

Table 7.4. State Approaches to Funding Transportation and Discretionary Funds in Interdistrict Open Enrollment Choice Programs.

State	Transportation Provided	Transportation Funded by the State	Transportation Funded by the District	Discretionary Funds Provided to Create Quality Choices – State Funded	Discretionary Funds Provided to Create Quality Choices – District Funded
Arkansas: interdistrict open enrollment	Partially: parent transports from home to attending district boundary. District transports to school from there.	Aid provided to attending district.		No	No
California: interdistrict open enrollment	No			No	No
Colorado: second chance	At district option.	Yes. On same basis as regular transportation.	Yes. On same basis as regular transportation.	No	No
Idaho: interdistrict open enrollment	No. Not specifically addressed in law.			No	No
Iowa: interdistrict open enrollment	Partially: parent transports from home to attending district boundary. District transports to school from there.	Aid provided to attending district.	Sending district reimburses poor parents for transportation costs.	No	No

Minnesota: interdistrict open enrollment	Partially: parent transports from home to attending district boundary. District transports to school from there.	Aid provided to attending district.	Attended district reimburses poor parents for transporation costs.	No	No
Nebraska: interdistrict open enrollment	Partially: parent transports from home to attending district boundary. District transports to school from there.	—	—	No	No
Ohio: interdistrict open enrollment	Partially: parent transports from home to attending district boundary. District transports to school from there.	Receiving district reimbursed for an average of 42 percent of all transportation costs.	Receiving district reimburses poor parents for transportation costs.	No	No
Utah: interdistrict open enrollment	Partially: parent transports from home to attending district boundary. District transports to school from there.	Aid provided to attending district.	Bus transportation within district boundaries provided by attended district.	Yes, under phase 3 of a school improvement program. These funds follow the child.	No
Washington: interdistrict open enrollment	No. Not specifically addressed in law.			No	No

Table 7.5. State Approaches to Funding Transportation
in Postsecondary Options Choice Programs.

State	Transportation Provided	Transportation Funded by the State	Transportation Funded by the District
Colorado: postsecondary option	At district option.	Yes. On the same basis as regular transportation.	Yes. On the same basis as regular transportation.
Florida: postsecondary option	Yes	No	District or college pays according to local agreement.
Minnesota: postsecondary option	Parents provide transportation.	Reimburses district for reimbursements to poor parents.	Attended district reimburses poor parents for transportation costs.
Ohio: postsecondary option	Provided by parents.		District reimburses poor parents for transportation costs.

districts for schools in high-spending districts clearly benefit, but at the expense of the high-spending district. If only general state aid follows the child, the receiving district does not receive enough funding to fully finance the new student's total education program.

But having just state aid follow the child creates problems even for parents with equal base spending but different wealth. If one district receives $1,000 in per-pupil state aid and another $500, what happens when a student transfers from one district to another? If the student transfers from the $500 district to the $1,000 district, does the recipient district receive the $500 previously paid by the state to the old district or the $1,000 it gets for its other children? Does the sending district have its state aid reduced? If so, by which amount: the amount it receives ($500) or the amount the state pays to the receiving district (perhaps $1,000)? Similarly, is state aid both retained by the sending district and received by the recipient district, the practice now in some states (for example, the desegregation interdistrict open enrollment program in St. Louis, Missouri, and its surrounding suburban districts)?

In short, the concept of "state aid follows the child" is simple, but putting it into practice is not. As Table 7.2 indicates, moreover, this dictum, while surrounding choice proposals initially, has been dropped, and the trend seems to be to have the entire base funding follow the child.

The concept of how state and local base revenues are viewed could be altered somewhat to accommodate some of these obvious financial problems (T. Kolderie, personal communication, 1990). Rather than split local and state base revenues across all students in a district, one could argue that local revenues cover a certain number of students for the full base perpupil spending level and that state aid covers the remaining students at that level. In property wealthy districts, local revenues cover more students, while in property poor districts, state aid covers more students. Students who decide to attend school in another district could be considered state aid students and carry the total base revenue amount with them. If this were the case, the sending district might lose an amount much larger than just its average per-pupil state aid. Indeed, algebraically this is what happens when the choice student is counted for state aid purposes as a pupil in the district attended. The sending district loses the full amount of total base funding, and the receiving district gains that full amount. Of course, this concept gets more problematic if a large number of students leave the district and require revenues beyond the total amount of state aid. The new funding mechanism proposed in the next section, however, accommodates this potential problem.

But even if the higher-spending receiving district collects, under some rationale or other, an amount that equals the sending district's total per-pupil base revenues, it still would be less than the receiving district's base revenues per pupil. In order for the receiving district to receive an amount equal to its base spending per child, either the sending district would have to send an amount higher than it actually spent for students who did not leave or the state would have to make up the difference, thus allocating even higher revenue amounts to higher-spending districts, which obviously would conflict with general school finance equalization objectives.

Several states (for example, Iowa and Ohio) have resolved this issue by simply accepting the inequities: when a student attends school in another district, the smaller of the base revenues per pupil in the two districts follows the child. This policy works reasonably well when only a small number of students invoke the choice option and attend school in another district. If large numbers of students chose to attend school in a different district, then the marginal differences on a per-pupil basis could add up to a large total amount, thus making this policy more problematic. Indeed, no district participated in Colorado's original program, which initially guaranteed just 85 percent of a district's base revenues per pupil to students selecting to attend school in another district.

A way to resolve this dilemma is simply to count the student as a pupil in the school/district attended. In states with foundation programs, the sending district would lose an amount equal to the foundation expenditure level and the receiving district would gain that amount. In states with guaranteed tax base or district power-equalizing programs, the sending district would lose an amount equal to its total base spending per pupil and the receiving district would gain an amount equal to its total base spending per pupil. In foundation states, local revenue for the foundation program equals the foundation tax rate times the local tax base; this amount is unaffected by the number of students. State aid is the difference between this amount and the product of the foundation expenditure level and the number of students. Thus, if the number of students declines by one, the revenue lost is the amount of the foundation expenditure level. Likewise, in a receiving district, the amount of revenue gained with one more student also is the total of the foundation expenditure level. The same is true for guaranteed tax base states, but the foundation level is simply replaced by the district's operating tax rate times the per-pupil tax base. (James Phelps, of the Michigan State Department of Education, pointed out this operational feature of school finance programs.)

Even with this adjustment, there are still problems when a student decides to attend a school in another district that spends more per child. Suppose that the state had a perfect equalization system and that extra per-pupil expenditures were caused only by higher tax effort. All the problems discussed above would remain. Suppose further that the receiving district decided it wanted to spend even more and needed a local vote to increase its school tax rate. The parents of the child in the sending district could neither participate in that vote nor incur the extra costs that a positive vote would require of all taxpayers in the receiving district.

In other words, a district-based school funding structure that allows voters to increase taxes to spend above some base level essentially disenfranchises parents of students who participate in an interdistrict choice program and send their children to a school in another district. These problems raise a fundamental structural issue of the mismatch between a district-based school funding system and a school-based attendance system in states that have differences in base expenditures per pupil across district boundaries, which is the case for the majority of the states in the United States. This underlying structural problem has essentially been ignored in all state public school choice programs. But should interdistrict public school choice programs expand in popularity and use, these fundamental issues must be recognized and addressed.

On the positive side, the above fiscal anomalies could actually reduce the typical school finance inequities in most states. Assume that the general pattern is that students leave low-spending districts to attend schools in high-spending districts and only the sending district's state aid or its base revenue per pupil follows the child, as is current practice in many proposals. Since new students would bring with them a revenue amount below the receiving district's base revenue per child, average base revenues per pupil would drop in the higher-spending districts. The remaining revenues in the sending district would be spread across fewer students, thus slightly increasing the district's average expenditures. The overall effect is to reduce interdistrict expenditure-per-pupil disparities. While this impact is somewhat salutary, the mechanism for getting there is at best indirect; in this instance, the means might not justify the ends.

States with full state funding systems, such as Hawaii and California, avoid many of the above finance problems related to school choice programs. In California, for example, base state and local revenues per child are nearly equal across all school districts (Guthrie, Kirst, & Odden, 1990), and when a student chooses to attend a school in another district, the base amount is both lost by the sending district and gained by the receiving district. Since California districts are not allowed to raise their property tax rates above the statewide uniform 1 percent rate for all local services, the problems related to spending above the base with an extra tax effort also do not arise. The same would be true in Hawaii.

But in these states, choice still remains a constrained policy option. Parents and students are able to choose schools but are unable to choose how good those schools can be or how much they think those schools ought to spend. Some in California would argue that a public school choice program simply provides choice among a set of mediocre schools. If school choice is arguably better than no school choice, school and quality-level choice arguably are even better options. The following section outlines a proposal that addresses the quality issue and the problems of what money should follow the child.

A New School Finance Structure for Interdistrict Public School Choice Programs

Three issues need to be addressed in designing a finance structure that equitably accommodates an interdistrict public school choice program. The first concerns the funding mechanism for the base program. The second concerns the funding mechanism for spending above the base program. The third concerns categorical program dollars and other revenues, such as discretionary funds, to help create attractive choice options.

Funding the Base Program for Interdistrict Public School Choice Programs. Several points need to be made about finance policy for the base program in public school choice policies. First, more than state aid must follow the child. The previous section shows that a student who attends school in another district must carry more than state aid alone; no matter how large state aid is, it will always be below the amount that the receiving district spends for the base program. Admittedly, the marginal per-pupil costs for the first few students are small (less than the average per-pupil costs), and most schools could accommodate one or two additional students in many classes with little extra cost. But over time, if enough students participate, the receiving district will need to add classes and teachers, thus bringing marginal costs closer to average costs.

If the student carries with him or her an amount that is more than just state aid, an obvious candidate is base spending per pupil. That would exclude categorical funds; categorical aids are important, and categorical aid flows in public school choice plans are discussed separately below. But even having base revenues per pupil follow all children in choice programs still leaves some dilemmas.

As the previous section outlined, the existence of dramatic differences in base per-pupil spending makes even the full base per-pupil amount insufficient for students who move from low- to higher-spending districts (and more than sufficient if students move from high- to lower-spending districts). When there are large differences in base spending per pupil, there simply is no way to allocate funds in a manner that both treats schools equitably and supports overall school finance equity goals.

If base spending per pupil were the same across school districts, however, this conundrum would be remedied. The base amount could be available to the district/school wherever the student happened to attend, which is the policy in California. Thus, in order to make choice programs function on an equitable fiscal foundation, the state needs to ensure that base revenues per pupil are close to the same across all districts and that this base amount "follows the child."

This conclusion suggests that an appropriate school finance system for a public school choice program would be a

high-level foundation program across all school districts. Given
national and many state student performance goals, it could be
argued that the base should be set at a level that would allow all
students, on average, to meet those performance goals. There
are several programmatic and technical issues that would need
to be addressed to determine the actual amount of the base level
of funding. This chapter cannot address these issues. The conceptual point is to ensure a high base level of resources sufficient
to fund programs that would produce high levels of student
achievement related to state student performance goals. Whatever yardstick is used to determine the base, a common base
program as the first fiscal tier seems to be a prerequisite to
making a public school choice program work financially. Technically this strategy can be implemented by counting the student as a pupil in the school/district attended.

   *Funding Above the Base Program for Interdistrict Public
School Choice Programs.* What then should be done for spending
above the base? First, what about district decisions to spend
above the base? The problem with this option has been outlined
above. Parents of students outside the district neither can vote to
spend more (or less) nor can their property taxes be increased
(decreased) if a school tax rate increase vote passes (fails). In
other words, *district* options to spend above the base program
through increasing local property taxes do not work with a
school-based attendance policy. The policy implication of this
conclusion is that *districts* should not be allowed to spend above
the base! This also, then, means that the first tier of the state
school finance program is a high-level foundation program for
all schools in all districts, with the base dollar figure allocated to
the school the child attends, and a requirement that districts not
be allowed to spend above the base.

   But what about schools? Could they be allowed to spend
above the base? Many would argue that spending per pupil (with
adjustments for needs and prices) should be the same across
all schools (or districts in the current education governance
structure).

   If the answer is that schools could be allowed to spend

above the base, the question is, what finance structure would be appropriate? First, it would be difficult to link such an option to the property tax. Since students attending any one school could live in a variety of local property taxing jurisdictions, there is no easy — perhaps even feasible or legal — way selectively to increase the property tax rates. Most states require uniformity of tax rates within a property tax jurisdiction, thus obviating the possibility of differential individual rates for whatever purpose. When property tax rates are increased, they are increased for all property owners within a jurisdiction. There are no examples of property tax increases on a selective, or parcel-by-parcel, basis within jurisdictions and certainly not across jurisdictions.

But there are examples of *individually based* modifications in the income tax structure. Property tax circuit breaker programs provide individual property tax relief through the income tax structure in many states. Individual tax credits of a variety of sorts are provided through the income tax. Over the years, states also have enacted various forms of individual income tax surcharges. Further, several states have taxpayers identify their local school district on their income tax returns and use the data in the school finance formula.

The income tax, then, could be used to give parents in local schools the choice to spend above the base level. Parents of students in a school could be given the option to increase spending by a vote, similar to what is now done on a district basis for the property tax. The vote would be for an income tax surcharge for all parents at the school. How large a majority vote is a design issue. It could be a simple majority; it could be a larger majority. California could adopt this proposal today by requiring a two thirds majority vote, the tax increase requirement of Proposition 13.

If the parents voted for a surcharge, the school would send an official form to the state listing all parents and their social security numbers. The state then would send a notice to all parents informing them of their income tax surcharge. When parents completed their state income tax form, there would be an additional line where they would indicate their surcharge and compute the additional amount for local school spending.

The system would be monitored by computers, just as miscellaneous and interest income is now monitored through Form
1099 notices and taxpayer social security numbers. (Technically,
this system could also work through the federal income tax!)

Second, the state would have a schedule that would indicate the additional dollars per pupil that would be provided for
different levels of income tax surcharges. The per-pupil yield
could be related to the statewide average taxable income per
pupil, for example, $50,000, or a figure above the average. Thus,
a 1 percent additional income tax would produce an extra $500
per pupil. The state would send this amount to the school as
additional resources. Just as in current district power-equalizing
or guaranteed tax base (GTB) programs, the state would create a
schedule that would indicate the per-pupil yields for different
surcharge levels. But unlike most current GTB programs, which
allow districts with a property wealth above the GTB to raise
more with a given tax rate, the proposed income tax surcharge
schedule would stipulate the yield for all schools, regardless of
the school's level of income per student. Table 7.6 is an example
of such a schedule. The state also could cap the surcharge at
some level, for example, 2 percent. For parents with children
at more than one school, the total surcharge could be capped at
the maximum on the schedule.

Just as for current GTB programs or district power-
equalizing systems, there are several constraints on this type of

Table 7.6. Schedule of Per-Pupil Yield for a School Site
Income Tax Surcharge.

Income Tax Surcharge	Per-Pupil Yield
0.25%	$ 125
0.50	250
0.75	375
1.00	500
1.25	625
1.50	750
1.75	875
2.00	1,000

structure. First, the yield schedule would be subject to legislative appropriations; if the legislature did not appropriate funds to provide the per-pupil yields (which in nearly all instances would be higher than the amount of money raised by the income tax surcharge at any one school), the yields would not be available. Second, the schedule likely would have some type of surcharge cap built into it, just as is the case with most GTB programs or district power-equalizing systems. Third, parents voting on a site surcharge proposal would face a price for their actions; if they approved a proposal, they would increase their income tax payments. In other words, even though the per-pupil yield is greater than what is raised at the school, each parent would pay higher state income taxes. Michigan is one of the few states with a full GTB program in effect. It has not experienced runaway local tax increases; the local price component acts, as an econo-mist would predict, as a deterrent to irresponsible behavior.

The overall proposal is similar to the school finance struc-ture originally suggested by Garms, Guthrie, and Pierce (1978); the school-based income tax surcharge option here replaces their voucher proposal. There are several intriguing features of this proposal. First, the poor would be protected from paying additional taxes to the degree that the poor do not pay state income taxes. The system could include a small fee for families that pay no income tax (they too would face a price in voting a school-site surcharge); but a fee might be at odds with broader income tax equity issues. Second, all taxpayers in the state would help pay for this school finance increment. By using the state average income per pupil, the yield is much larger than would be raised just by the parents in any school. School parents, just like district taxpayers in a traditional GTB program, would trigger the additional statewide aid. But also, again as in a traditional GTB program, no state funds would flow unless local funds also increased; there would be a price for each site to trigger extra state aid flows. Third, this program would allow spending-per-pupil differences across schools, but these differ-ences would be caused by greater income tax effort and not differences in income-per-pupil levels. Fourth, to use school finance terminology, this plan has total recapture. If any school actually raised more than the statewide yield, it would retain only the state-guaranteed yield. Very rich schools might try to raise the funds through a local, nonprofit school foundation, but the amounts school foundations have raised so far are much below the yield that an income tax surcharge could produce. Further, the income tax surcharge would ensure that every tax-paying parent in the school contributed, which cannot be guaranteed by fundraising through a local school foundation mechanism. Fifth, all these funds would be discretionary at the site level; they would come with no strings attached, just as extra general aid funds now flow to the district. Thus, fiscal freedom would be increased at each site. Finally, this second tier, which allows for school spending above the base, would provide full-fledged choice at the site level, both on which school to attend and on the level of quality in the school.

The income tax surcharge approach also could work with intradistrict choice programs. Parents at each school in the district could be given the same option of voting an income tax surcharge, and the state could send the discretionary funds directly to the school. Thus, for magnet programs, districtwide open enrollment, and minischool programs within districts or even within schools, parents could be given the option to exert a larger fiscal effort for their child's school program. The simplicity of the income tax surcharge proposal is that once the structure is put into place, it can work with just about any of the public-sector choice options described in the first section of this chapter.

In an economic sense, the income tax surcharge functions as a type of user fee. Any family that sends a child to the school would have to pay the income tax surcharge. In this sense, the income tax surcharge injects a price mechanism into public-sector school choice plans, a feature that would increase the seriousness of decisions about which school a child would attend. Further, this price feature could be greater or lower depending on the adequacy of the base program and the level of the income tax surcharge cap. While this chapter suggests a high base program (sufficient for students on average to meet national performance goals) and a relatively low income tax surcharge cap, state policy makers reasonably could reach different conclusions. The lower the base and the higher the level of allowable surcharge, the more the system takes on private school characteristics.

Finally, site-based budgeting would need to be a larger component of local district management than it is today. With all schools provided a base program and with potentially large amounts of discretionary (as well as categorical) funds available at the site level, more budgeting and decision making about resource allocation and use would need to be done at the site and by site personnel.

The proposal could not work in states without an income tax. But the program could be a federal initiative and operate through the *federal* income tax structure.

Categorical Program and Discretionary Program Funds. The second section of this chapter showed that many states inadvertently overlooked the issue of categorical funding in designing public school choice fiscal policy. Categorical funds rarely follow the child. Remedying this situation is not straight-forward. Take compensatory education dollars, for example, such as federal Chapter 1 funds. These dollars are allocated to districts on the basis of the number of resident poor children. Within districts, however, the funds are allocated on the basis of student education need. If students leave the district to attend schools in another district, they probably would lose eligibility to participate in their resident district's program. One could argue that they should retain this eligibility and carry the dollars with them to their new schools. An equally reasonable argument is that they would not be eligible for intradistrict allocations for their resident district and thus would not carry compensatory education aid with them. They could, however, be eligible for categorical program support in the district where they attended.

But what about categorical dollar flows to the district? Should the pupil be considered a student in the resident or attending district? Again, arguments can be made for both positions. To simplify matters, this chapter suggests counting the student in the district she or he attends, as is the policy in

Arkansas, California, Colorado, Idaho, and Washington. Thus, district and school attendance becomes the consistent criterion for determining eligibility for categorical aid—and all other state and federal aids. Characteristics of students actually attending schools within a district would be used to determine federal as well as state allocations to districts and intradistrict allocations to sites.

This would mean that a student who leaves a poorer district to attend a school in a more affluent community might give up eligibility for certain categorical funds. The environment and program of the more affluent school, however, might more than compensate for the loss of program eligibility, and the funds in the resident district could then be concentrated in larger amounts on the students who remained and attended neighborhood schools.

This policy of counting the individual as a pupil in the district attended would affect categorical as well as general aid programs, as mentioned above. Since there is a service requirement for special education regardless of what school the student attends, this policy would not likely affect special education funding for any individual student.

Further, with the income tax surcharge option, separate state discretionary pots of dollars would not have to be created. Discretionary money would be raised and earned by each site to the degree that it passed income tax surcharges. Since use of the state (or federal) income tax would shield low-income families from higher-income tax burden, this option is not onerous for low-income families. Indeed, since most families with students enrolled in low-income neighborhood schools might be completely protected from increased income tax burdens, this proposal actually could make it easier for such schools to raise additional funds. The state also could provide an up-front discretionary amount of, for example, $50–$100 per child to ensure that all schools have some discretionary funds above the base. But the value of the proposed plan is that it provides opportunities for school sites to raise discretionary money, even large amounts of discretionary money.

Finally, what about transportation? There is no easy solution, either operationally or fiscally. Current state practice that makes it the parent's responsibility to transport students either to the school or to a bus stop in the school's district—with reimbursement of costs to poor parents—seems to be a reasonable, albeit imperfect, solution. Transportation arrangements need to be based on the transportation systems available and creative options that can be developed. Transportation in large urban areas, such as New York City, with elaborate subway and bus systems becomes easier, especially compared to Los Angeles, which has no subway system and a less elaborate bus system. High-quality, sophisticated metropolitan public transportation systems that cross several school district boundaries are the best hope for resolving the transportation dilemmas for public school choice programs in the metropolitan centers. In these situations, students would simply need a transportation pass, and the system would let them get from their home to the schools of their choice.

Summary and Conclusions

There are several finance dimensions to public school choice proposals, most of which were ignored in initial state designs of interdistrict school choice programs. Two are critical. The first is the mind set that if a student lives in one district and attends school in another, an elaborate system of revenue transfers needs to be created. The easy solution to the problems that result from transferring funds is simpy to treat the child as a pupil in the school/district attended for all state aid purposes. This straightforward approach eliminates the necessity for complicated revenue transfers and provides a simple structure for addressing finance issues.

The second major problem is the mismatch between a district-based property tax finance structure and a school-based attendance structure. This chapter suggests that the way to resolve the problems inherent in this two-structure system is to adopt a new, two-tiered school finance structure. In the first tier, a high-level base program would be provided to all schools and districts in the state; a base program sufficient to allow all students on average to meet national student performance goals is a reasonable goal for determining the size of the base. This tier would be financed with a combination of state funds and local property tax dollars. The base amount would be ensured for each student in each school. For the second tier, each school site would be allowed to enact an income tax surcharge, which would be administered through the state (or federal) income tax structure. The yield for the surcharge would be determined according to a state-set schedule; the per-pupil yield would be far above the amount raised by the school's surcharge. The yield schedule would be determined and funded by the state, as is true for current guaranteed tax base (GTB) and district power-equalizing systems. All families with students attending a school with a surcharge and who pay state income taxes would face an added price for attending that school.

The second tier component of the proposed new school finance structure, of course, could be dropped. Indeed, Chubb and Moe (1990) did not include a second tier in their public and private school choice proposal. But the second tier adds to the dimensions of choice — of both school choice and quality choice — and makes both dimensions equally available to high- and low-income households.

References

Boyd, W. L., & Kerschner, C. T. (Eds.). (1988). *The politics of excellence and choice in education*. Philadelphia: Falmer.

Boyd, W. L., & Walberg, H. J. (1990). *Choice in education: Potential and problems*. Berkeley, CA: McCutchan.

Bridge, G. J., & Blackman, J. (1978). *A study of alternatives in American education: Vol. 4. Family choice in education*. Santa Monica, CA: RAND Corporation.

Chubb, J., & Moe, T. (1990). *Politics, markets and America's schools*. Washington, DC: Brookings Institution.

Education Commission of the States. (1989). *Policy guide: A state policy maker's guide to public school choice*. Denver, CO: Author.

Elmore, R. (1986). *Choice in public education*. Santa Monica, CA: RAND Corporation.

Farrar, E., & Milsap, M. A. (1986). *State and local implementation of Chapter I.* Cambridge, MA: Abt Associates.

Finn, C. E., Jr. (1987). Education that works: Make the schools compete. *Harvard Business Review, 65,* 63–68.

Friedman, M. (1962). *Capitalism and freedom.* Chicago: University of Chicago Press.

Garms, W. I., Guthrie, J. W., & Pierce, L. C. (1978). *School finance: The economics and politics of public education.* Englewood Cliffs, NJ: Prentice-Hall.

Guthrie, J. W., Kirst, M. W., & Odden, A. R. (1990). *Conditions of education in California, 1989.* Berkeley: University of California, School of Education.

Levin, H. M. (1989). *The theory of choice applied to education.* Stanford, CA: Stanford University, Center for Educational Research at Stanford.

Murnane, R. J. (1986). Family choice in public education: The roles of students, teachers and system designers. *Teachers College Record, 88,* 169–189.

Nathan, J. (1989). *Public schools by choice: Expanding opportunities for parents, students and teachers.* Minneapolis, MN: Institute for Learning and Teaching.

National Governors' Association. (1986). *Time for results.* Washington, DC: Author.

Raywid, M. A. (1985). Family choice arrangements in public schools: A review of the literature. *Review of Educational Research, 55,* 435–467.

Thomas, M. A. (1978). *A study of alternatives in American education: Vol. 1. The role of the principal.* Santa Monica, CA: RAND Corporation.

8

Reducing Disparities Across the States: A New Federal Role in School Finance

Allan R. Odden
Lori Kim

The federal role in education policy and school finance has always been small. In 1990, the federal government provided just 6 percent of public school revenues (see Chapter One of this book). Most federal dollars traditionally have supported modest research and data-gathering activities; programs for low-achieving poor students, handicapped students, limited-English-proficient students, and students in vocational education programs; and a variety of offices that helped to prohibit discrimination. The federal role was considered ancillary to that of the states; the states defined curriculum and instruction, certified teachers, accredited schools, funded district operations, and governed the overall public education system. There were no national education goals. A common school curriculum was viewed as violating local control. National testing of individual students was simply something done by other countries, but not by the United States.

When President Bush and the fifty state governors met for an education summit in the fall of 1989, these traditions were broken and a new era was inaugurated. Today the country has national education goals (White House, 1990), there is widespread talk of a national curriculum (Smith, O'Day, & Cohen, 1990), and work is proceeding to develop a national student testing system (National Council on Education Standards and Testing, 1992). Further, the governors have issued a blueprint for how states can accomplish the national education goals (National Governors' Association, 1990), and the president and governors created a National Education Goals Panel, which is deciding how to measure progress toward the goals (National Education Goals Panel, 1991), even though movement to implement the goals has been slow.

This chapter raises the issue of whether the existence of national education goals implies a new federal role in school finance. It first assesses in greater detail general implications of nationwide education goals for a country that currently has fifty different education systems. It then analyzes disparities across states in terms of fiscal capacity and effort, education spending, and several measures of education outcomes. The next section summarizes a study of variables that predict states with high and low scores for student mathematics achievement. The last section identifies new federal roles that logically follow from national education goals and disparities across the states, including a federal role in providing general education aid.

National Goals and Current State Education Policy

After the historic October 1989 education summit, the president and the nation's governors met again in early 1990 and formally adopted a set of national education goals (White House, 1990), which state that by the year 2000:

1. All children in America will start school ready to learn.
2. The high school graduation rate will increase to at least 90 percent.
3. American students will leave grades 4, 8, and 12 having demonstrated competency in challenging subject matter including English, mathematics, science, history, and geography. Every school in America will ensure that all students learn to use their minds well, so they may be prepared for responsible citizenship, further learning, and productive employment in our modern economy.

4. U.S. students will be first in the world in science and mathe-
    matics achievement.
5. Every adult in America will be literate and will possess the
    knowledge and skills necessary to compete in a global
    economy and to exercise the rights and responsibilities of
    citizenship.
6. Every school in America will be free of drugs and violence
    and will offer a disciplined environment conducive to
    learning.

The president and governors developed these goals for all
students, not just the best and the brightest. All students need to
start school ready to learn, and all students need to show proficiency in the core areas of mathematics, science, writing, language arts, history, and geography. "All of our people, not just a
few, must be able to think for a living, adapt to changing
environments, and to understand the world around them"
(White House, 1990, p. 1). Never before in the history of the
country have such education goals been set for everyone.

Moreover, the goals are bold and ambitious. They are
education goals for achievement far above what is accomplished
in America's schools today. The Nation's Report Card (Mullis,
Owen, & Phillips, 1990) shows that only 5–7 percent of today's
students show proficiency in these core areas sufficient for doing
regular college study, while the percentage is much higher in
other countries, especially Germany and Japan. Even the performance of our top students is below that of many other countries
(Policy Information Center, 1991). Thus, not only are the goals a
stretch for the country's top students, but they also constitute a
major leap for students in the middle and at the bottom.

Finally, it is hoped that all states will adopt these national
goals as state goals and possibly even define a broader set of
goals. States could add proficiency in the arts, music, and physical fitness. States could explicitly add competency in thinking,
problem solving, communication, and working in collegial
groups, all skills increasingly needed in the workforce (Commission on the Skills of the American Workforce, 1990). Thus, while
the nation's education goals entail difficult-to-achieve outcomes

(with progress toward the goals measured and reported to the nation annually), state goals are likely to be even more ambitious.

Today, however, states are at very different places with respect to these education goals. Poverty is a good indicator of the degree to which students, at the age of five, are able to come to school ready to learn. On average from 1983 to 1987, about 21 percent of children lived in a home with an income below the poverty level (Children's Defense Fund, 1991). This figure is higher than it was ten years ago and continues to grow. States varied greatly about the average. In Mississippi, 34.3 percent of students lived in poverty, while in New Hampshire, only 6.2 percent of children lived in poverty. The high-poverty states have a bigger challenge in ensuring that students at the age of five are ready to learn. Accomplishment of the first goal, in short, affects states very differently, with the toughest challenges for the states with the highest poverty rates and the lowest ability to raise funds to fight poverty.

Likewise, the high school graduation rate varied dramatically across the states, according to the U.S. Department of Education's 1990 Wall Chart. While the nationwide average figure was 71.2 percent in 1989, it ranged from a low of 58.0 percent in Florida to a high of 90.2 percent in Minnesota. The differences are quite dramatic. States with the highest graduation rates appear to be graduating 50 percent more of their students from high school than do states with the lowest graduation rates. In other words, goal 2 poses a much greater education challenge for some states than for others.

Similarly, with the June 1991 release of the first valid student outcome data on a state-by-state basis, the nation discovered that student achievement also varied by state (Mullis, Dossey, Owen, & Phillips, 1991). While results are provided only for eighth-grade mathematics achievement, they are ominous and suggest that accomplishing the nation's goals on a state-by-state basis will be difficult. No state had a large number of students showing proficiency in mathematics. The results showed that what eighth-grade students know and can do in mathematics is far below what the nation desires.

In short, there is variation in current state position with respect to the nation's education goals. Although federal and state education and political leaders have stated that the nation should not compare states as the country moves toward accomplishing the national goals, the differences between the states can hardly be ignored. No state governor could (or should) easily set his or her state's education goals below those of the nation. The fact is that states farther behind on any goal simply have a greater distance to travel because of the pressure on all states to meet the nation's education goals by the year 2000.

In order to make substantial progress toward meeting the goals, all states will need to create and implement a comprehensive and cohesive set of education reforms. At the state level, the systemic reforms needed will include a unifying education vision with explicit goals stated in measurable student achievement terms, curriculum frameworks linked to those goals, substantial professional staff development, new forms of accountability assessment to measure current status and progress over time in attaining the goals, revised instructional materials, and restructured education governance (Smith & O'Day, 1991).

These general strategies will need to be formulated into cohesive school programs at each local site. Examples of such comprehensive programs include, for example, Success for All Schools (Madden, Slavin, Karweit, Dolan, & Wasik, 1991) and Accelerated Schools (Levin, 1988) at the elementary level, restructured middle schools such as those envisioned in *Turning Points* (Carnegie Task Force, 1989), and changes in high school organization and programs (see Sizer, 1990). Not all of these programs cost substantially more than is spent today (see Chapter Three of this book). But Success for All Schools, which has been called the "Cadillac" of new school programs and produces large increases in student performance, is costly (Madden et al., 1991). To fund this program would require fully financing the federal Chapter 1 program and adding an extra $1,000 per pupil (Madden et al., 1991).

Indeed, the types of programs and services needed to bring *all* students to proficiency levels on national student achievement goals will likely take substantial new resources.

Further, such programs will require highly skilled teachers with the level of knowledge and skills outlined by the National Board for Professional Teaching Standards (1991), but this level of professional expertise seems to be in short supply (Cohen, 1991). While the nation has been putting significant new funds into the schools each decade (see Chapter One), there have been wide differences across regions and states in school funding changes (Odden, 1990). In low-funding-increase states, putting these expensive new programs in place to meet national and state education goals will be difficult.

The fact is that states differ widely in fiscal capacity, the ability to raise funds for school (or any governmentally provided) services. As a consequence, education revenues per pupil are quite different from state to state. More importantly, as will be shown below, the states with the farthest to go in accomplishing the nation's education goals are now spending at the lowest levels and generally have the least fiscal capacity with which to raise more money in order to increase education spending. These differences among the states, which are discussed at more length in the next sections, form a major obstacle to accomplishing the country's education aspirations. Remedying these differences could very likely imply a new federal role in school finance beyond just fully funding current programs for special needs students, such as Head Start, Chapter 1, and programs for the handicapped.

Interstate Fiscal and Education Outcome Disparities

About 13.3 percent of total government expenditures were spent on education in 1988 (Advisory Commission on Intergovernmental Relations [ACIR], 1990). Education is the third largest governmental (federal, state, and local) spending function, behind national defense/international relations and Social Security/Medicare. But the federal government alone allocated only 1.6 percent of its expenditures to education, whereas state and local governments allocated 29 percent of their expenditures to education. Further, states and local governments allocated an even larger portion (35 percent) of direct general expenditures for education. General expenditures include all government expenditures other than the specifically enumerated expenditures such as liquor store expenditures, insurance trust expenditures, and utility expenditures. General expenditures include state and local government expenditures for education services, social services and income maintenance, transportation, public safety, environment and housing, governmental administration, interest on general debt, and other general expenditures.

A policy question for national goals—pertinent for any goal but especially for those that must be accomplished by all of the states—is the degree to which states have relatively equal fiscal capacity and dollars for education from which to fund programs to meet the goals. The fact is that, *within* most states, the ability to raise funds for education purposes varies considerably across local districts; partly as a result, per-pupil spending—and resultant programs, services, and student achievement—also differs, sometimes dramatically. Further, there is a pattern to the intrastate differences: districts high in property wealth per child (the local tax base) usually enjoy higher-spending and better-quality programs than districts low in property wealth, which usually have below-average spending per pupil even with above-average tax rates. The policy question for national goals is whether these intrastate fiscal disparities are mirrored by cross-state disparities.

For the past twenty years, states have been vigorously addressing their intrastate disparities. Indeed, state school finance structures that make the level of spending a function of local property wealth have been the subject of court litigation based on both state equal protection and education clauses (Odden & Picus, 1992, chap. 2). By the end of 1990, courts had overturned about fifteen state school finance structures. The number is likely to rise in the 1990s since there were active cases in nearly half the states by mid 1991. Both in response to a court decision overturning a school finance system and as part of an eighty-year tradition to reduce school finance fiscal disparities, states became more active in funding school finance, increasing the state role from 40 percent in 1970 (just before the modern era of school finance) to 49 percent in 1990, while reducing the local role from 52 percent in 1970 to 45 percent in 1990. Indeed, only the state could intervene and redress the fiscal differences across local districts.

When the early legal challenges to intrastate school finance inequities were taken to the U.S. Supreme Court, it ruled that such disparities did not violate the Equal Protection Clause of the 14th Amendment to the U.S. Constitution. There has been no court case challenging interstate school finance disparities although, as the next section shows, such disparities exist in about the same magnitude as many intrastate disparities. Interstate disparities could be addressed by the federal government in the 1990s.

A renewed federal interest in school finance inequities emerged during the 1990 congressional session. A bill was introduced that would have conditioned receipt of federal education aid on the degree of intrastate inequality in per-pupil spending across districts. That was not the first time the issue of school finance fiscal disparities was debated in Congress and the issue of a federal role in general school finance raised. In the 1970s, after the initial rash of school finance court cases, a federal role of general aid was proposed. The Congress responded by enacting a program for states to conduct research studies of intrastate school finance equalization. A federal role in general school finance was then an idea whose time had not yet arrived.

In the 1960s, the National Education Association proposed that education funding be split among the three levels of government: one-third local, one-third state, and one-third federal. But this idea, too, was ahead of its time.

National education goals thus raise the issue of a federal role in a brand-new light. If school finance fiscal disparities similar to those within states exist across the states and especially if the disparities are related to student performance, the federal government is the only level of government that can intervene to remedy them. This section explores the degree to which such disparities exist and their linkage to outcomes.

Although no two states in America have the same educa-

tion or taxing system, indicators of interstate fiscal and education disparities are discussed below using six general variables:
personal income per capita, tax effort as reflected by the ACIR
representative tax system (RTS), expenditures per average daily
attendance, percentage of population completing high school
by age twenty-five, and percentage of graduating high school
seniors taking the Scholastic Aptitude Test (SAT). The newly
acquired data on eighth-grade mathematics scores are included
for the thirty-seven states that chose to participate in the 1990
National Assessment of Educational Progress (NAEP) trial state
assessment (Mullis, Dossey, Owen, & Phillips, 1991).

   State average personal income per capita roughly indicates state tax capacity, that is, the relative ability of states to raise
tax revenues. There are many potential measures of tax capacity:
the property, sales, and income tax base; the ACIR's representative tax base; gross state product; and total taxable resources.
But per capita income is highly correlated with all of them, is
relatively well understood by the public, and is used in many
intergovernmental aid programs as an indicator of tax capacity.
The measure used is for 1988.

   The willingness to raise revenues in a state is represented
by the 1988 ACIR index of tax effort relative to its representative
tax system (RTS). The relative tax effort is determined by taking
each state's tax revenues and expressing them as a rate applied to
the state's ACIR relative tax capacity measure. The result is then
standardized to an index by dividing each state's tax effort by the
average for all states. The index for the U.S. average is 100.

   Expenditures per pupil is used as the indicator of how
much each state spends on public education for current operating purposes. The figure used was an estimated figure provided
by the National Education Association for the 1989–90 school
year.

   Since there are no comprehensive education achievement
indicators that have been developed for interstate comparison,
three single indicators were selected: percentage of population
completing high school by age twenty-five, percentage of high
school seniors taking the SAT examination, and (for thirty-seven

states) the average score of eighth graders on the 1990 NAEP Trial State Assessment.

Determining the high school graduation rate is complicated. There is a big difference between a measure that indicates the proportion of a ninth-grade cohort that graduates from high school four years later and one that measures the proportion of the population that earns a high school diploma by age twenty-five. The analysis uses the latter measure, which is the measure more closely related to national education goal number 2. However, the most recent state-level data available for determining percentage of population completing high school by age twenty-five derive from the 1980 census. High transient rates during the last decade, along with other economic and social factors, may produce a different picture from the 1990 census, but these more recent data are not yet available. Our analysis uses the 1980 data.

The analysis uses the percentage of graduating high school seniors taking the SAT examination simply because the SAT is a figure often used in public debates about education. The measure probably says more about the nature of college admissions in a state than about student achievement; the SAT is not a valid indicator of student achievement. However, percentage taking the SAT at least points up differences among the states in college-bound high school seniors.

In June 1991, the first valid comparison of student achievement across the states was made public (Mullis et al., 1991). NAEP provides information on mathematics achievement among eighth-grade students in thirty-seven states. These data are the most direct indicators of student achievement in the following analysis, even though limited to one subject at one grade level.

Table 8.1 shows the actual data for the six variables mentioned above for all fifty states. Table 8.2 provides descriptive statistics for these variables, such as maximum, minimum, mean, standard deviation, and coefficient of variation, all of which indicate the degree to which the variables differ across the states.

Table 8.1. Selected Characteristics of Interstate Disparities in the United States.

State	Personal Income per Capita (1988)	Representative Tax System (RTS) Tax Effort Index (1988)	Expenditure per Average Daily Attendance (1989–90)	Percentage of Population Completing High School by Age Twenty-Five (1980)	Percentage of Graduating High School Seniors Taking the SAT (1990)	NAEP Eighth-Grade Mathematics Exam Score (1990)
Alabama	$12,851	84	$3,319	56.5%	8%	252
Alaska	19,079	127	7,252	82.5	42	—
Arizona	14,970	96	3,858	72.4	25	259
Arkansas	12,219	84	3,272	55.5	6	256
California	18,753	94	4,620	73.5	45	256
Colorado	16,463	89	4,878	78.6	28	267
Connecticut	23,059	90	7,930	70.3	74	270
Delaware	17,661	84	5,848	68.6	58	261
Florida	16,603	82	5,051	66.7	44	255
Georgia	15,260	89	4,456	56.4	57	258
Hawaii	16,753	112	4,504	73.8	52	251
Idaho	12,665	93	3,016	73.7	17	272
Illinois	17,575	102	4,853	66.5	16	260
Indiana	14,924	93	4,126	66.4	54	267
Iowa	14,662	113	4,590	71.5	5	278
Kansas	15,759	104	4,706	73.3	10	—
Kentucky	12,822	88	3,824	53.1	10	256
Louisiana	12,292	90	3,313	57.7	9	246
Maine	15,106	105	5,577	68.7	60	—
Maryland	19,487	108	5,887	67.4	59	260
Massachusetts	20,816	94	6,740	72.2	72	—
Michigan	16,552	112	5,073	68.0	12	264

State					
Minnesota	16,674	112	4,935	79.1	14	276
Mississippi	11,116	94	3,220	54.8	4	—
Missouri	15,452	86	4,226	63.5	12	280
Montana	12,866	102	4,254	74.4	20	276
Nebraska	14,774	98	3,874	73.4	10	—
Nevada	17,511	69	4,260	75.5	24	273
New Hampshire	19,434	66	4,833	79.3	67	269
New Jersey	21,094	101	8,439	67.4	69	256
New Mexico	12,488	99	4,180	63.9	12	261
New York	19,305	152	8,165	63.3	70	250
North Carolina	14,304	93	4,164	54.8	55	281
North Dakota	12,833	91	3,581	66.4	6	264
Ohio	15,536	97	4,394	67.0	22	263
Oklahoma	13,323	89	3,484	66.0	9	271
Oregon	14,885	99	5,085	75.6	49	266
Pennsylvania	16,233	97	5,728	64.7	64	260
Rhode Island	16,892	104	6,523	61.1	62	—
South Carolina	12,926	96	3,692	53.7	54	—
South Dakota	12,755	95	3,312	67.9	5	258
Tennessee	13,873	83	3,506	56.2	12	—
Texas	14,586	88	4,011	62.6	42	264
Utah	12,193	106	2,733	80.0	5	—
Vermont	15,302	100	5,418	71.0	62	—
Virginia	17,675	91	4,986	62.4	58	264
Washington	16,473	102	4,639	77.6	44	—
West Virginia	11,735	88	4,094	56.0	15	256
Wisconsin	15,524	119	5,763	69.6	11	274
Wyoming	13,609	94	5,391	77.9	13	272

Sources: Data from National Center for Education Statistics, 1991; Advisory Commission on Intergovernmental Relations, 1990; College Board, 1991; Mullis, Dossey, Owen, & Phillips, 1991.

A brief glance at the figures reveals wide differences across states for all variables. Personal income per capita in 1988 varied widely; the average for the United States was $15,719. But the difference of $11,943 between the lowest state, Mississippi, and the highest state, Connecticut, was almost as large as the average itself. Personal income per capita in Connecticut ($23,059) was more than twice that in Mississippi ($11,116). The coefficient of variation, 0.19, also indicates a wide variation in per capita income. Two-thirds of the states have a per capita income between 19 percent below to 19 percent above the mean, that is, between $12,732 and $18,705.

All tax revenues are derived from personal income; families spend what money they have left after paying taxes. As a fiscal capacity indicator for education, the per capita income measure suggests that Connecticut has more than twice the ability to support education as Mississippi. In short, the ability of states to raise revenues for education (or other governmental activities) is dramatically different.

There is also a wide variation in tax effort, even though smaller than the differences in fiscal capacity. Using the ACIR index of tax effort, about two-thirds of the states (thirty-three) scored below the average while the other third (seventeen states) scored above the average. This skewed distribution is a result of New York's extremely high index. The tax effort index for New York, the highest-tax-effort state (index = 157), is about 2.5 times as high as New Hampshire's, the lowest-tax-effort state (index = 66). High effort in a high-fiscal-capacity state, such as New York, can produce large revenues, but high effort in a low-fiscal-capacity state, such as Utah, usually produces below-average revenues. The striking conclusion of the data is that higher effort seems to be associated with higher fiscal capacity.

Education expenditures per average daily attendance is shown in column four of Table 8.1, and this measure also exhibits variation across the states. The national average expenditures per pupil in 1989–90 was $4,824, about the 58th percentile. The data indicate that the highest-spending state—New Jersey—spent $8,439 per student, which is more than three times the expenditure of the lowest-spending state—Utah, which spent

Table 8.2. Descriptive Statistics for Selected Variables of Interstate Disparities.

Descriptive Statistics	Personal Income per Capita (1988)	Representative Tax Effort Index (1988)	Expenditure per Average Daily Attendance (1989–90)	Percentage of Population Completing High School by Age Twenty-Five (1980)	Percentage of Graduating High School Seniors Taking the SAT (1990)	NAEP Eighth-Grade Mathematics Exam Score[a] (1990)
Maximum	$23,059	152	$8,439	82.5%	74%	281
Minimum	11,116	66	2,733	53.1	4	246
Mean	15,719	98	4,824	67.8	34	264
Standard deviation	2,910	16	1,399	7.9	24	9
Coefficient of variation	0.19	0.16	0.29	0.12	0.71	0.04

[a] Thirty-seven states only. Scores not available for Alaska, Kansas, Maine, Massachusetts, Mississippi, Missouri, Nevada, South Carolina, South Dakota, Tennessee, Utah, Vermont, and Washington.

Sources: Data from National Center for Education Statistics, 1991; Advisory Commission on Intergovernmental Relations, 1990; College Board, 1991; Mullis, Dossey, Owen, & Phillips, 1991.

just $2,733. These differences would not be eliminated even if the expenditures were adjusted for cost-of-living differences across the states.

The coefficient of variation indicates that two-thirds of the states spend within 30 percent of the mean. This indicates that disparity among states within the range of just one standard deviation of the mean is still high; the difference in spending between the highest- and the lowest-spending states within this restricted band is still about $2,800 per pupil. Compared to the average of $4,824, this difference should be a matter of both analytical and policy interest now that all states are striving to raise the level of education achievement to meet national achievement goals.

While these measures suggest that there are wide differences in state fiscal capacity, tax effort, and education spending, the first outcome measure — the percentage of the population completing high school by age twenty-five — indicates that differences among states, while less than for the fiscal variables, were also quite large. In 1980, the average percentage of the population that earned a high school diploma by age twenty-five in the United States was 67.8 percent. Alaska had the highest percentage of high school graduates (82.5 percent), whereas Kentucky had the lowest (53.1 percent). The coefficient of variation indicates that two-thirds of the states had 60 to 76 percent of the population completing a high school education by age twenty-five.

As expected, the percentage of high school seniors taking the SAT (the second outcome variable) varied greatly, ranging from 4 percent in Mississippi to 74 percent in Connecticut. On the average, 24 percent of graduating high school seniors in the United States took the SAT in 1990. Variation among the states is so great that in a range of just one standard deviation above and below the mean, which captures two-thirds of the states, the range is from 10 percent to almost 60 percent.

NAEP eighth-grade mathematics scores, the most direct student outcome measure, exhibit the least variation among the thirty-seven states that participated. The average score of all states was 264, out of a possible score of 500. On the average, the eighth-grade students answered 53 percent of the questions correctly. North Dakota scored the highest—a score of 281 (56 percent correct)—while Louisiana had the lowest score—246 (49 percent correct). Between the highest and the lowest scores, the difference in correct responses is only 35 points (7 percent). This small variation is also indicated by the value of the coefficient of variation, 0.04. Two-thirds of the thirty-seven states scored within 10 points of the mean. Nevertheless, very few states had an average score at a high level of mathematics proficiency (Mullis et al., 1991).

While variation across the states for these data is not unexpected, the more interesting analytical and policy questions are whether there are relationships among these data. Table 8.3 presents these data sorted by personal income per capita and grouped into deciles with about equal numbers of students. Several findings are suggested by the figures in this table. Column 3 shows that per capita income increased by about $1,000 across each decile. The increase is expected because that is how the data are sorted; the size of the increase is large, with the top decile having almost twice the per capita income of the bottom decile. Column 4 indicates that there is no clear pattern for tax effort, although the effort of the top five deciles seems to be a bit higher than the effort of the bottom five deciles.

Column 5 shows that education expenditures per pupil increase over each decile except for the eighth decile, which is represented by California alone. The data show quite clearly that states with higher personal income per capita spend more money per pupil on education than do states with lower per capita income. California is the major exception to this rule. It used to spend at a high level (Picus, 1991), and its lower spending in 1990 is largely explained by its twin tax and spending limitation measures—Proposition 13, which limits raising local property tax revenues, and the Gann limit, which restricts spending of state revenues (Guthrie, Kirst, & Odden, 1991).

Just as is the case within most states (Odden & Picus, 1992), education spending is linked to fiscal capacity: the higher the state's per capita income, the higher its current operating expenditures per pupil. Indeed, as shown in Table 8.4, the

Table 8.3. Decile Means of Selected Characteristics of Interstate Disparities in the United States, Sorted by Personal Income per Capita.

Decile	Number of States Included in Each Decile	Personal Income per Capita (1988)	Representative Tax Effort Index (1988)	Expenditures per Average Daily Attendance (1989–90)	Percentage of Population Completing High School by Age Twenty-Five (1980)	Percentage of Graduating High School Seniors Taking the SAT (1990)
1	10	$12,312	93	$3,455	63.4%	8.9%
2	7	13,393	92	3,973	62.8	24.4
3	4	14,727	100	4,390	70.8	26.5
4	7	15,220	98	4,775	66.9	40.1
5	4	15,998	97	4,927	70.9	31.0
6	3	16,543	99	4,921	70.8	33.3
7	7	17,249	96	5,130	68.7	40.6
8	1	18,753	94	4,620	74.0	45.0
9	3	19,273	115	6,750	73.7	59.7
10	4	21,339	98	7,249	69.3	68.5

Sources: Data from National Center for Education Statistics, 1990; Advisory Commission on Intergovernmental Relations, 1990; College Board, 1991.

correlation between per capita income and expenditures per pupil is 0.83, which is quite high. This is higher than the correlation between spending and local district fiscal capacity within most states. In short, the intrastate fiscal inequities that have dominated school finance policy and research for this century are mirrored even more strongly by disparities across the fifty states. In an era of national education goals, these differences might impede attainment of those goals.

More sophisticated regression analysis also supports the above conclusions (see Table 8.5). The model analyzed postulated that education expenditures were a linear function of (1) fiscal capacity (per capita income), (2) tax effort, (3) education need (percentage in poverty, percentage minority, and percentage handicapped), (4) price, and (5) education preference (percentage of parents who are college graduates). The model explained 86 percent of the variation in education spending across the states. The statistically significant variables were fiscal capacity, tax effort, percentage handicapped, and price. Except for a portion of state tax effort, changes in these variables are dependent on intervention by a higher level of government.

Although the pattern is less consistent, Table 8.3 also shows that the percentage of the population that earns a high school diploma by the age of twenty-five also tends to increase with state personal income per capita. The percentage is in the low 60s for the first two deciles, rises to about 70 percent for the

Table 8.4. Correlation Coefficients with Personal Income per Capita.

Expenditures per Average Daily Attendance (1989–90)	Representative Tax Effort Index (1988)	Percentage of Population Completing High School by Age Twenty-Five (1980)	Percentage of Graduating High School Seniors Taking the SAT (1990)	NAEP Eighth-Grade Mathematics Exam Score[a] (1990)
.834	.188	.361	.697	.116

[a] Thirty-seven states only. Scores not available for Alaska, Kansas, Maine, Massachusetts, Mississippi, Missouri, Nevada, South Carolina, South Dakota, Tennessee, Utah, Vermont, and Washington.

Table 8.5. Regression Results for Determinants of
State Education Expenditures per Pupil.

Variable	Coefficient	T Value
Per capita income	0.23	3.31[a]
Tax effort	27.94	3.91[a]
Percentage in poverty	0.43	0.17
Percentage minority	– 10.86	1.31
Percentage handicapped	162.04	2.77[a]
Price factor	3264.71	1.89[a]
Percentage parents who are college graduates	– 9.22	0.45
Intercept	– 5861	
R squared	0.86	

[a] Statistically significant at 0.10 level.

middle deciles, and is above 70 percent for deciles nine and ten. As shown in Table 8.4, the correlation between completing a high school education and per capita income is a positive 0.36, statistically significant but at a modest level.

A stronger relationship is shown between state per capita income and the percentage of high school seniors taking the SAT examination. With the exception of the fourth decile, the percentage increases consistently over each decile of income. The correlation coefficient for the relationship between these two variables is 0.70, a strong positive relationship.

States with higher personal income per capita appear to have greater percentages of high school seniors taking the SAT. This indicates that high-income families tend to reside in states where a greater portion of high school seniors intend to go on to colleges that require the SAT for admission. While this requirement is not a quality indicator in and of itself, most of the country's prestigious colleges and universities require an SAT score.

Table 8.6 compares the states that participated in the NAEP eighth-grade mathematics examination. Personal income per capita was found to be only slightly related to mathematics achievement, with a correlation coefficient of 0.12 (see Table 8.4). Because the NAEP scores show little variation across the states, it is difficult statistically to run correlations with other

Table 8.6. Decile Means of Selected Characteristics of Interstate Disparities in Thirty-Seven States of the United States, Sorted by Personal Income per Capita.

Decile	Number of States Included in Each Decile	Personal Income per Capita (1988)	Representative Tax Effort Index (1988)	Expenditures per Average Daily Attendance (1989–90)	Percentage of Population Completing High School by Age Twenty-Five (1980)	Percentage of Graduating High School Seniors Taking the SAT (1990)	NAEP Eighth-Grade Mathematics Exam Scores (1990)
1	7	$12,436	90	$3,611	61.6%	11%	260
2	5	13,391	92	4,122	65.9	21	263
3	4	14,727	100	4,390	70.8	27	271
4	4	15,170	99	4,551	66.2	37	265
5	3	16,077	94	5,000	70.1	38	266
6	3	16,610	102	5,020	69.3	23	265
7	5	17,311	99	5,343	66.5	49	259
8	1	18,753	94	4,620	73.5	45	256
9	2	19,570	109	6,499	69.0	69	267
10	3	21,513	100	7,419	68.4	67	266

Note: Scores not available for Alaska, Kansas, Maine, Massachusetts, Mississippi, Missouri, Nevada, South Carolina, South Dakota, Tennessee, Utah, Vermont, and Washington.

Sources: Data from National Center for Education Statistics, 1990; Advisory Commission on Intergovernmental Relations, 1990; College Board, 1991; Mullis, Dossey, Owen, & Phillips, 1991.

variables that do vary, such as personal income per capita. Although the results show that eighth-grade students in some states with high income per capita seem to know more mathematics than some students in states with low income per capita, the pattern is inconsistent. Several states in the upper Midwest with below-average per capita income but relatively homogeneous populations have students who scored quite well on the mathematics test. California, on the other hand, had high per capita income but a diverse population and scored in the bottom third.

Student achievement and family income generally seem to be related, but other variables, such as spending level, types of programs and services, and diversity of the student population, also play a role. The modest, and inconsistent, relationship between these state-level data suggests that state education systems have not, to date, been able to overcome the disadvantages of low family income or poverty. The relationship between state fiscal capacity and achievement also suggests that the states that need to make the largest student achievement improvements have the lowest incomes to tap for revenues to finance new education initiatives.

In short, personal income per capita is strongly related to both expenditures per pupil and the percentage of high school seniors taking the SAT; it is moderately related to the percentage of population completing high school by age twenty-five and eighth-grade student achievement in mathematics. These findings demonstrate how difficult it will be for all states to achieve the nation's education goals and suggest that the federal government may need to intervene; only a level of government above the states can adjust for differences in state fiscal capacity, which in turn affects education spending and student performance.

To underscore these points, Table 8.7 exhibits the correlation coefficient between expenditures per pupil, state fiscal capacity and effort, and student outcomes. The high correlation with personal income per capita was discussed above. The correlation between tax effort and expenditures per pupil is also high—0.46—higher than the correlation with personal income per capita (0.19). States with higher tax efforts seem to have higher education expenditures per pupil, even though the rela-

Table 8.7. Correlation Coefficients with Expenditures per Pupil.

Personal Income Per Capita (1988)	Representative Tax Effort Index (1988)	Percentage of Population Completing High School by Age Twenty-Five (1980)	Percentage of Graduating High School Seniors Taking the SAT (1990)	NAEP Eighth-Grade Mathematics Exam Scores (1990)
.834	.458	.274	.681	.175[a]

[a] Thirty-seven states only. Scores not available for Alaska, Kansas, Maine, Massachusetts, Mississippi, Missouri, Nevada, South Carolina, South Dakota, Tennessee, Utah, Vermont, and Washington.

tionship is moderate. The correlation between expenditures per pupil and the percentage of population completing high school by age twenty-five again is positive, but just 0.27, while the correlation between expenditures and the percentage of graduating high school seniors taking the SAT examination is higher at 0.68.

Finally, states spending more on education appear also to produce somewhat better eighth-grade mathematics achievement, with the correlation at 0.18. In other words, the higher the state's per capita income and tax effort, the higher is its per-pupil education spending; the greater the number of students earning a high school diploma, the greater is the percentage of students who take the SAT, and the higher is the mathematics achievement. In short, higher fiscal capacity leads to higher education spending, which seems to produce higher student outcomes. Likewise, lower fiscal capacity seems to produce lower education spending and, unfortunately for national education goals, lower student outcomes. Again, only a higher level of government can intervene and reduce these cross-state differences. If all students are to achieve the nation's bold education goals, the links among personal income per capita, education spending, and achievement must be broken.

Differences Between High- and Low-Scoring States

While the variation in eighth-grade NAEP scores for the middle group of the thirty-seven states was quite small, the differences between the top twelve and bottom twelve states were more dramatic. Using a model proposed by Centra and Potter (1980) that identified groups of variables that influence student achievement (see Figure 8.1), a discriminant function analysis was conducted for the top twelve and bottom twelve states. The model contains six factors that influence student learning outcomes: (1) outside-school conditions, (2) within-school conditions, (3) teacher characteristics, (4) teacher performances, (5) student characteristics, and (6) student behaviors. Outside-school conditions could include school size, fiscal resources, and racial composition; within-school conditions could include the reward system, instructional organization (for example, tracking), enacted curriculum, student peer group influences, and quantity of schooling. Teacher characteristics include such variables as teaching experience, knowledge of subjects and of teaching, values and attitudes, and social class. Teacher performances could include such variables as reinforcement, questioning technique, time on task, and instructional strategies. The model does not specify variables for student behaviors except that they are classroom behaviors in interaction with teachers. Finally, student characteristics are social class, race, parental influence, aptitudes and prior learning, values and attitudes, and learning styles.

Drawing upon the data base in the NAEP report, ten variables were chosen for the discriminant analysis:

**Figure 8.1. Structural Model of Variables Influencing
Student Learning Outcomes.**

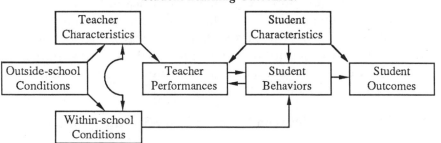

Source: Compiled from Centra & Potter, 1980.

Factor 1: Outside-school conditions
- Operating expenditures per pupil in 1987–88
- Percentage of students living in a disadvantaged urban community

Factor 2: Within-school conditions
- Percentage of students whose teachers placed heavy instructional emphasis on numbers and operation, that is, basic skills, as a measure of the enacted curriculum

Factor 3: Teacher characteristics
- Percentage of students whose teachers had more than ten years of teaching experience
- Percentage of students whose teachers had taken four or more math courses

Factor 4: Teacher performance
- Percentage of students whose teachers had mathematics instructional time that equaled or exceeded four hours per week
- Percentage of students whose teachers had students work in small groups one or more times per week
- Percentage of students whose teachers had students take class tests one or more times per week

Factor 5: Student behavior
- Percentage of students who read more than five pages a day for schoolwork and homework (all subjects)

Factor 6: Student characteristics
- Percentage of students whose parents did not graduate from high school

Multivariate analysis of variance showed that the top twelve and the bottom twelve states were significantly different on these ten variables (Kim, 1991).

As a follow-up analysis, a discriminant analysis was done to identify the variables on which high- and low-scoring states differed the most and to verify how well these variables could distinguish between these two groups of states. The result again confirmed that the two groups were significantly different in the independent variables combined (see Kim, 1991).

Next, the contributions of the individual variables in dif-

ferentiating high- from low-scoring states was determined, and
the weights of the variables were evaluated to assess how important each variable was in discrimination. Table 8.8 also summarizes the results of univariate tests for each independent variable. The results show that means of the two groups were significantly different on all variables except the percentage of students whose teachers have taken four or more mathematics
courses. The other nine variables made significant contributions to distinguishing the high- from the low-performing states.

In order to determine the degrees of importance of the

Table 8.8. Discriminant Function Analysis of the Variables
Related to NAEP Performance Level.

| | Means of the Groups[a] | | | | |
Predictor Variable	High-Scoring States	Low-Scoring States	Wilks's Lambda	F Scores	p
Expenditures per pupil	$5,140	$3,985	.807	5.25	.032
Urban disadvantaged	5.3	11.6	.796	5.64	.027
High numbers and operations emphasis	41.8	53.7	.491	22.81	.000
Teachers with more than ten years of experience	70.7	59.8	.568	16.72	.001
Teachers who have taken four or more math courses	81.6	74.2	.841	4.17	.053
Instructional time four or more hours per week	26.6	41.5	.677	10.51	.004
Small group work one or more times per week	52.1	43.8	.830	4.51	.045
Testing one or more times per week	59.0	75.7	.421	30.24	.000
Reading more than five pages per day	71.3	64.6	.456	26.20	.000
Parents not graduated from high school	5.2	11.7	.307	49.65	.000

[a] The unit of the means of the groups for all variables except expenditures is percentage of students.

nine significant variables, the score of the discriminant variable (composite synthetic variable) was analyzed. This step determined how much contribution to the score was made by each individual variable. The discriminant function was found to be statistically significant (Kim, 1991), meaning that there were significant differences between the group means in the predictors combined. The canonical correlation, R_c, a measure of the degree of association between the discriminant score and the groups, was 0.933, indicating that the percentage of variance accounted for by the function was 0.933^2, or 87 percent.

In order to determine the importance of individual variables, both standardized coefficients and structural coefficients can be used. Standardized coefficients in discriminant function analysis can be interpreted in a manner analogous to beta coefficients in multiple regression analysis; the relative magnitudes of the standardized coefficients can be used to indicate the relative contribution of the predictor variables to the discrimination between the groups. Structure coefficients are correlations between discriminant scores (computed from the discriminant function) and each of the original variables. But standardized coefficients are unstable when variables are correlated. Since some of the predictor variables were correlated in this study, structure coefficients were used instead. The square of a structure coefficient indicates that proportion of variance that is accounted for by the given discriminant function.

The structure matrix (Table 8.9) shows the proportions of variance that are associated with the ten independent variables. The results indicate that percentage of students with parents who did not finish high school appears to make the largest contribution. Testing frequency, high emphasis on numbers and operations (basic skills), and urban disadvantage all, interestingly, negatively contribute to student achievement. By contrast, student reading, teacher experience, and expenditures per pupil positively contribute to achievement.

Kim (1991) also used the results of the discriminant analysis to classify states into high- and low-scoring categories. Membership of all twelve states in the high-performing group and of all twelve states in the low-performing group was predicted

Table 8.9. Discriminant Structure Matrix of Variables
Related to State Performance.

Variable	Structure Coefficient	Percentage of Variance Explained
Percentage parents not graduated from high school	− .579	33.5%
Testing one or more times per week	− .452	20.4
Reading more than five pages per day	.421	17.7
High numbers and operations emphasis	− .392	15.4
Teachers with more than ten years of experience	.336	11.3
Instructional time four or more hours per week	− .266	7.1
Percentage urban disadvantaged	− .195	3.8
Expenditures per pupil	.188	3.5
Small group work one or more times per week	.174	3.0
Teachers who have taken four or more math courses	.167	2.8

correctly. The overall percentage of cases classified correctly by
the discriminant analysis was 100 percent, indicating that the
ten predictor variables were robustly able to identify states that
scored high or low on the NAEP eighth-grade mathematics
achievement test.

In short, the ten variables used in the discriminant analysis were strongly able to distinguish high- from low-scoring
states on the mathematics performance of eighth-grade students. All of the ten variables used were found to be statistically
significant. Low-performing states tend to have greater percentages of students whose parents did not finish high school
than high-performing states. They appear to have a greater
portion of students taking tests at least once a week. In lower-
performing states, students tend to have been exposed to very
limited mathematics *content*, as teachers had emphasized basic
skills such as numbers and operations. Lower-performing states
also seem to have greater percentages of students living in
disadvantaged urban areas. Finally, these states spent less per
pupil for education. By contrast, students in higher-performing
states have greater percentages of parents who graduated from
high school, take fewer tests, are exposed to a broader curricu-

lum, read more, and attend school where spending per pupil is higher.

Kim (1991) also showed that instructional time was positively related to heavy teaching emphasis on numbers and operations (which is negatively related to achievement) and negatively related to heavy teaching emphasis on geometry and algebra (which is positively linked to achievement). This finding suggests that when more instructional time is spent on teaching basic concepts and skills than on teaching higher-level mathematical skills, the result is lower student performance on the NAEP mathematics assessment.

The above findings on factors related to differences in student achievement across states represent only the beginning of what needs to be analyzed in more depth as additional data become available during the 1990s. Given the relatively small variation in interstate scores, the number of significant relationships found in the above analysis is surprising. Clearly, the curriculum is the major determinant of interstate differences in student achievement in mathematics. While expenditures per pupil is a statistically significant variable in the analysis, its specific role in accounting for variations in achievement was small. How expenditures per pupil are related to curriculum quality and depth and how well teachers are able to teach the curriculum are matters for future study.

Just as it required state intervention to reduce differences in education spending caused by variations in the local tax base across local school districts, so also it will require federal government or nationwide intervention to reduce differences in education spending caused by variations in state fiscal capacity across the states. In addition, the federal government could implement categorical programs that also would help all states meet national education goals.

The results from the discriminant analysis reviewed above underscore the importance of creating a nationwide consensus on expectations for student achievement and on a core curriculum that should be taught to all children. The analysis suggests that a primary emphasis on basic skills is a detriment to student learning in mathematics. The reason is that a focus on numbers and operations fills the curriculum with arithmetic, and little attention is given to probability, statistics, measurement, geometry, and algebra. As a result, students tend not to learn these topics well and score low on the type of mathematics assessment that NAEP now administers. Further, there is an emerging consensus that students should be appropriately proficient in these broader mathematics areas. These content areas are more in tune with the national goals, and they are materials mastered by eighth-grade students in other countries.

It is to be hoped that the emerging professional consensus on appropriate school curriculum in mathematics, science, language arts, history, and social studies (described in Chapter One) will influence what is taught in classrooms and thus bolster student achievement in these content areas. Further, these professional agreements do not require a federal role or a new congressionally enacted program. If there is agreement that this new curriculum should be taught in all public schools, any type of national testing or assessment system should be tightly linked to its substantive concepts and topics. As the next section argues, moreover, there are also possibilities for new federal initiatives.

New Federal Roles in Education Funding

Traditionally, education efforts of the federal government have been directed toward two major objectives: enhancement of education productivity and equalization of education opportunity (Guthrie, Garms, & Pierce, 1988). Table 8.10 shows that federal education revenues were low until the 1960s, when Chapter 1 (then Title I of the 1965 Elementary and Secondary Act) was begun, and then increased to a high point in 1980. The federal fiscal role declined during the 1980s; federal revenues were 6.4 percent in 1990.

National goals potentially imply a new federal role in the regular education program to reduce the disparities in fiscal capacity, education spending, and student outcomes discussed in the previous sections. The preceding analyses show that there are substantial differences in fiscal capacity and student achieve-

Table 8.10. Percentage of U.S. Federal Revenues Allotted for
K–12 Public Education: 1919–1990, Selected Years.

Year	Percentage	Year	Percentage
1920	0.3	1983	7.1
1930	0.4	1984	6.8
1940	1.8	1985	6.6
1950	2.9	1986	6.7
1960	4.4	1987	6.4
1970	8.0	1988	6.3
1980	9.8	1989	6.4
1982	7.4	1990	6.4

Sources: Data from National Center for Education Statistics, 1991; National Education Association, 1990, 1991.

ment across the states. Some will think those differences are significant enough to propose a new federal role to reduce them. Others will argue that until fiscal capacity is more directly and strongly linked with differences in student achievement, a large and expensive new federal role is unwarranted. Clearly, more analysis on the determinants of achievement differences across all schools in the nation is needed in order to clarify the variables that contribute to achievement differences and thus allow for potential policy interventions.

Nevertheless, the above analyses suggest the need for a broader federal role in school finance. Perhaps the most costly federal intervention—a new federal role in general revenue sharing—could be targeted to reduce differences in state fiscal capacity. While the design of such a program would be technically complex, the general idea would be for the federal government to ensure a per capita tax yield across the states for similar tax efforts, similar to an intrastate guaranteed tax base program of school financing (Odden & Picus, 1992, chap. 7). But the country had a general revenue-sharing program during the 1970s and 1980s. It was recently eliminated by the Congress as part of a budget-balancing program and is unlikely to be resurrected. On the other hand, in 1991 there were emerging proposals for a new federal role in strengthening state tax revenue systems. Rivlin (1991) suggested a series of tax-sharing strategies, including a uniform corporate income tax and replacement of varying state sales tax rates with a uniform value-added tax, with the proceeds shared with the states.

A more targeted, and less federal, role could focus more narrowly on education. One could argue that national education goals suggest that there should be a nationwide base funding program across all states and local school districts. This base could be adjusted by state and regional cost-of-living differences to produce equal purchasing power. The level of the base would need to be sufficient to allow states, districts, and schools to mount the types of programs and services that would produce student outcomes in line with the national goals.

The current patchwork quilt of school financing across 50 states and 16,000 local districts produces results far from this conceptual target. In 1991, base education spending ranged from about $2,000 per pupil in the lowest-foundation-program states to over $10,000 per pupil in the highest-spending states, a difference of five to one. This is hardly a fiscal foundation that allows all states to meet the country's education goals. While the distribution of current federal dollars modestly helps to offset these fiscal differences, a much larger role would be needed to produce a common per-pupil fiscal base across the country. The bulk of federal aid is for the Chapter 1 program and thus flows in larger amounts to states with high poverty and low per capita income. The amount of federal education aid, however, is not sufficient to dramatically affect differences in either state per capita income or education spending per pupil.

There are several ways such a federal role could be structured. One way would be for the federal government to bring base education spending up to some minimum level, such as the national average expenditure per pupil or the median expenditure-per-pupil level. If this were fully funded by the federal government, it would require a large boost in federal education revenues but would leave intact current differences in state education tax effort.

A second alternative would be to make federal revenue for such a program contingent upon a state's exerting a minimum general tax effort, using measures such as an amount of own source tax revenues per capita or a tax rate index at or above 100 on the ACIR tax effort index.

A third, more direct alternative would be for the federal government to implement a nationwide district- or school-based foundation expenditure-per-pupil program. This program would function just like a state foundation program (Odden & Picus, 1992, chap. 7). First, the federal government would set a base spending level, or a foundation per-pupil expenditure level, for all districts or schools. The amount could be adjusted using a state-by-state cost-of-education index (see, for example, American Federation of Teachers, 1990). The federal government would make up the difference between this per-pupil amount and an amount that would have to be raised by the state. The latter amount could be the yield from a statewide property tax or it could be the yield from a statewide property tax and an amount of state general fund revenues. Note that such a program would address both inter- and intrastate spending differences.

In order to implement such a program, there would need to be a policy decision on the proportion of the base that would be supported by federal funds and the proportion supported by state and local funds. A 20 percent federal/80 percent state and local division does not seem to be unreasonable. The specific proportion would be determined *analytically* by the size of the base spending figure and the yield from state and local tax rates and *politically* by congressional deliberation and federal government ability to increase education funding.

The bottom line, though, is that some type of nationwide base per-pupil spending level is the logical school finance policy for the implementation of national education goals, especially since spending differs across states and spending differences are correlated with a variety of student outcomes. While the particular design of a new federal role in school finance could take many forms, it seems that a federal role in supporting the core education program is a policy whose time has arrived.

This policy suggestion would be consistent with the current district and school attendance area approach taken by nearly all state education systems today. It would work with a system of public school choice or a system of charter schools. As noted in Chapter Seven of this book, public school choice programs require the state to provide a base per-pupil spending fiscal foundation for every school. A nationwide focus on this same policy is consistent with the type of state school finance system needed to undergird a school choice program. Further, such a federal program is also supportive of states' allowing professionals to create charter schools, as Minnesota provided in a new 1991 law. In short, such a new federal role in school finance would make the current education structure fairer fiscally and would also support systems that provided for student choice of public school.

Fully funding the current array of federal categorical programs is also consistent with the federal role in supporting state attainment of national education goals. First, Chapter 1 could be fully funded. Created in 1965, Chapter 1 is the federal program designed to improve the performance of low-achieving students in schools with students from low-income family backgrounds. And the new state NAEP eighth-grade mathematics scores show that several of these states need to considerably boost student achievement. For the 1991 school year, Chapter 1 is funded at $6 billion, which provides enough money to serve 60 percent of eligible students. Fully funding this program would require an additional $4 billion.

P.L. 94–142 is the federal program designed to help states provide adequate programs for handicapped students. The law authorizes the federal government to support up to 40 percent of special education expenditures, but current funding of $2.6 billion supports only 13 percent of state special education costs. Increasing the federal role to its fully authorized level would require approximately $5.4 billion.

Research shows that preschool and extended-day kindergarten produce student learning gains and are highly cost effective (Barnett, 1985, 1990). Even though only twenty-seven states have enacted prekindergarten legislation, almost all states provide some type of early childhood education for either all or just at-risk children. Table 8.11 shows that the number of children receiving preprimary education increased dramatically over the

Table 8.11. Enrollment of Three- and Four-Year-Old Children in
Preprimary Programs, October 1965–October 1989.

Year	Enrollment (in thousands)	Percentage Enrolled of Total Population of Three- and Four-Year-Old Children	Percentage Enrolled in Public Nursery Schools	Percentage Enrolled in Full-Day Programs[a]
1965	886	10.6%	22.9%	—
1970	1,461	20.5	28.5	12.3%
1980	2,280	36.7	30.9	29.4
1989	2,887	99.0	31.3	40.0

[a] Kindergarten is included.
Source: Data from National Center for Education Statistics, 1990.

last thirty-five years. In 1989, almost two-thirds of three- and four-year-old children were enrolled in either public or private nursery programs, compared to just a little more than one-tenth in 1965. Table 8.11 also shows that public schools have not been quick to respond to the increasing demands for nursery education, even though they served more three- and four-year-old children over each of the last three decades. In 1989, a very large portion of these children, about 70 percent, continued to be educated through private schools. In addition, only 40 percent of five-year-old children receive full-day instruction.

Since 1965, the federal Head Start program has provided comprehensive services to poor children and their families. Head Start served more than 548,000 children in 1990, about 27 percent of eligible children (Children's Defense Fund, 1991). In late 1990, the Congress authorized a series of funding increases that, if appropriated, would allow all eligible three- and four-year olds and 30 percent of eligible five-year-olds to participate by 1994. The Head Start appropriation for fiscal year 1991 is $1.95 billion. Appropriations could climb to $7.66 billion by 1994 if the authorized level is fully funded. Head Start generally provides a half-day program; Barnett (1985) showed that more long-term benefits are derived from full-day, full-year programs.

In short, fully funding the federal Chapter 1 program for low-achieving–low-income students, P.L. 94–142 for handicapped students, and Head Start would also contribute substantially to all states' ability to accomplish the national education goals for all their students. The extra costs would be just $15 billion.

Conclusion

There are substantial differences in fiscal capacity, education spending, and student outcomes across the fifty states. These differences make it difficult for all states to meet the national education goals by the year 2000. Several of the states with the lowest per capita income have the lowest education expenditures per pupil and the lowest level of student outcomes. These states will have a hard time "pulling themselves up by their own bootstraps."

The time may have arrived for a federal role in reducing these interstate disparities. A logical implication of federal goals is some type of nationwide base education spending, adjusted by state and regional cost-of-education differences, that would allow each district and school to meet the nation's bold and ambitious education goals. This type of new fiscal role may be required because the president and the nation's governors are explicit that the goals are for *all* students in all states. Fully funding key federal categorical programs, such as Head Start, Chapter 1, and P.L. 94–142, also would contribute toward all states meeting the nation's education goals.

Although such new federal initiatives might be expensive, the federal government is the only level of government that can intervene to reduce wide interstate disparities. While states and local districts are likely to infuse education with new money during the 1990s (see Chapter One), they cannot reduce wide interstate differences in fiscal capacity and education spending. It may be time for a federal role in general education aid, although that aid should be restricted to programs and services likely to improve student achievement relative to the national education goals.

References

Advisory Commission on Intergovernmental Relations. (1990). *Significant features of fiscal federalism: 1990.* (Vol. 1). Washington, DC: Author.

American Federation of Teachers. (1990). *Survey and analysis of salary trends.* Washington, DC: Author.

Barnett, S. W. (1985). Benefit-cost analysis of the Perry Preschool Program and its policy implications. *Educational Evaluation and Policy Analysis, 7,* 333–342.

Barnett, S. W. (1990). Developing preschool education policy: An economic perspective. *Education Policy, 4,* 245–265.

Carnegie Task Force. (1989). *Turning points: Preparing American youth for the 21st century.* New York: Carnegie Corporation.

Centra, J. A., & Potter, D. A. (1980). School and teacher effects: An interrelational model. *Review of Educational Research, 50,* 273–291.

Children's Defense Fund. (1991). *The state of America's children.* Washington, DC: Author.

Cohen, D. (1991). Revolution in one classroom. In S. Fuhrman & B. Malen (Eds.), *The politics of curriculum and testing* (pp. 103–123). Philadelphia: Falmer.

College Board, The. (1991). *Average SAT scores by state, 1980, 1985–90.* New York: Author.

Commission on the Skills of the American Workforce. (1990). *America's choice: High skills or low wages.* Rochester, NY: National Center on Education and the Economy.

Guthrie, J. W., Garms, W. I., & Pierce, L. C. (1988). *School finance and education policy.* Englewood Cliffs, NJ: Prentice-Hall.

Guthrie, J. W., Kirst, M. W., & Odden, A. R. (1991). *Conditions of education in California: 1990.* Berkeley: University of California, School of Education.

Kim, L. (1991). *The state of mathematics achievement: How do high-performing states differ from low-performing states.* Los Angeles: University of Southern California, Center for Research in Education Finance.

Levin, H. (1988). *Accelerated schools for at-risk students.* New

Brunswick, NJ: Rutgers University, Consortium for Policy Research in Education.

Madden, N. A., Slavin, R., Karweit, N., Dolan, L., & Wasik, B. (1991, April). *Multi-year effects of a schoolwide elementary restructuring program*. Paper presented at the annual meeting of the American Educational Research Association, Chicago.

Mullis, I.V.S., Dossey, J. A., Owen, E. H., & Phillips, G. W. (1991). *The state of mathematics achievement*. Washington, DC: U.S. Department of Education, Office of Educational Research and Improvement.

Mullis, I.V.S., Owen, E. H., & Phillips, G. W. (1990). *Accelerating academic achievement: A summary of findings from 20 years of NAEP*. Princeton, NJ: Educational Testing Service.

National Board for Professional Teaching Standards. (1991). *Towards rigorous and high standards*. Detroit, MI: Author.

National Center for Education Statistics. (1991). *Digest of education statistics: 1990*. Washington, DC: U.S. Department of Education.

National Council on Education Standards and Testing. (1992). *Raising standards for American education*. Washington, DC: U.S. Department of Education.

National Education Association. (1990). *Estimates of school statistics*. Washington, DC: Author.

National Education Association. (1991). *Estimates of school statistics*. Washington, DC: Author.

National Education Goals Panel. (1991). *Measuring progress toward the national education goals: Potential indicators and measurement strategies*. Washington, DC: Author.

National Governors' Association. (1990). *Educating America: State strategies for achieving the national educational goals*. Washington, DC: Author.

Odden, A. R. (1990). School funding changes in the 1980s. *Educational Policy, 4*, 33–47.

Odden, A. R., & Picus, L. O. (1992). *School finance: A policy perspective*. New York: McGraw-Hill.

Picus, L. O. (1991). *Cadillacs or Chevrolets: The effects of state control on school finance in California*. Los Angeles: University of Southern California, Center for Research in Education Finance.

Policy Information Center. (1991). *Performance at the top: From elementary through graduate school*. Princeton, NJ: Educational Testing Service.

Rivlin, A. (1991, September 1). Uniform state taxes offer shared relief. *Los Angeles Times*, p. D2.

Sizer, T. (1990). Educational policy and the essential school. *Horace*, 6(2), 1–3.

Smith, M. S., & O'Day, J. (1991). Systemic school reform. In S. Fuhrman & B. Malen (Eds.), *The politics of curriculum and testing* (pp. 233–267). Philadelphia: Falmer.

Smith, M. S., O'Day, J., & Cohen, D. K. (1990). National curriculum American style: What might it look like? *American Educator*, 14(4), 10–17, 40–47.

White House, The. (1990). *National goals for education*. Washington, DC: Author.

9

Supporting School-Linked Children's Services

Michael W. Kirst

Children's education outcomes are influenced by the overall conditions and family circumstances of the children. Consequently, there have been many attempts to enlarge the responsibilities of schools to include more and better-coordinated health and social services; the history of health and social services in schools dates back to the major initiative era around the turn of the century (Tyack, 1979). School leaders, however, understandably are wary of new social service responsibilities that may be accompanied by insufficient funding. But in the 1990s there are different concepts, for example, school-linked services, that are gaining increasing acceptance and may overcome most problems of the past.

School-linked services have become a major component of the discussion surrounding school restructuring. So far, such services exist primarily as scattered demonstration projects. The momentum for this concept, however, is gaining, as evidenced by its inclusion in President Bush's Education 2000 program and in similar proposals by Governor Wilson of Cal-

Note: Some of the material in this chapter was prepared for: Jehl, J., & Kirst, M. W. Getting ready to provide school-linked services: What schools must do. *The Future of Children*, 2, 95–106. Published by the Packard Foundation.

ifornia and Governor Chiles of Florida. There is a growing realization that conditions of children, crucial for success in school, are deteriorating. Schools, however, cannot finance and provide a complete array of noneducation services. What schools can do is *collaborate* with other public and private providers of children's services to encourage a more comprehensive array of integrated services at or near the school site.

A definition of *school-linked services* starts with the proposal that schools be linked to at least four or more children's services agencies in an ongoing, collaborative relationship. A more complete definition of school-linked services is a system that enables parents to better consume and tailor public and private services to their special needs. Such a system would link schools and local public and private agencies to meet interrelated children's needs. Service providers must develop attitudes conducive to collaboration. All levels of government must change their fiscal requirements and incentives to enhance school linkages. The scope of school linkage may vary with the local context, but all districts should adopt a common client intake and management information system.

The concept of school-linked services does not necessarily entail that the school be the sole site for the delivery of services. Think of a school linkage system as providing one-stop shopping for children's services in an era of multiple and interrelated family problems. Unlike a large supermarket that offers food, engine oil, and floor cleaner under one roof, the typical situation for the consumer of children's services is the division of about five agencies (welfare, children's protection, health, job training, nutrition) in five separate offices — a supermarket split into five places all over a large county — that forces the consumer to take many bus rides for one shopping trip. Further, each service agency has a different set of elaborate eligibility requirements. The proposed one-stop place would not necessarily be located in the school, simply because there is not enough room on some school grounds and, in some areas, the school is not the ideal site. For example, some inner-city parents are hostile to the idea of going to a school for children's services because of negative experiences or associations.

The second school-linked concept is *collaboration*. Collaboration is different from *coordination*, which usually means that agencies agree to coordinate and refer to each other but do not really join together to help solve the problems of individual children. Collaboration is a joint venture between schools and other agencies to deal specifically with a set of families and their children. There must be a commitment from many types of line workers around the school, such as social workers and juvenile justice workers, as well as top school leadership.

The third concept—how to fund this collaboration— merges children's policy, *children's finance*, and traditional school finance. One solution is *not* to fund school-linked services over the long haul with "soft money" or through separate project grants. The way to fund school-linked services is to divert exist-ing funding streams like Medicaid and drug prevention money to schools or nearby facilities, that is, to the one-stop shopping location. This configuration is discussed in detail later in this chapter.

The Need for a New Children's Services Strategy

Obviously, children's fiscal issues move far beyond traditional school finance. But then children's conditions have evolved in ways that require more interventions than can be provided by traditional school finance. Today over 20 percent of children in the nation live in poverty, up from 14 percent in 1969. Race and ethnicity, gender, and family structure are strongly associated with the likelihood of poverty. In California, for example, 27 percent of Asian, 32 percent of black, and 34 percent of His-panic children were poor in 1985–86, in contrast to 10 percent of all white children. In 1990, half of single women with children lived in poverty, compared to 11.4 percent of two-parent families (Kirst, 1989).

Most institutions that serve children and youth are struc-tured on the assumption that children live with two biological parents, one working in the home and the other in the formal labor market. This traditional type of family now comprises only a small proportion of families, less than one-fourth. Forty-six percent of children live in homes where both parents — or the only parent — work. Because of an increase in divorce and a rise in the number of births to single mothers, about one-half of all children and youth will live in a single-parent family for some period of their lives. As of 1990, over half of all mothers with children under six and nearly 70 percent of mothers with children aged six to seventeen were seeking employment or worked in the formal labor market outside the home (Children's Defense Fund, 1990).

The risks add up. Johnny cannot read because he needs glasses and breakfast and encouragement from his absent father. Maria does not pay attention in class because she cannot understand English very well, she is worried about her mother's drinking, and she is tired from trying to sleep in the car. Dick is flunking because he is frequently absent. His mother does not get him to school; she is depressed because she lost her job. She missed too much work because she was sick and could not afford medical care.

The solution to these types of problems is not as simple as expanding existing programs like Head Start. What is needed is a complete overhaul of children's services, bringing together public and private organizations to meet the comprehensive needs of children, adolescents, and parents. Schools should constitute one of the centers of a coordinated network of total children's services.

Even at a time when funding for social services is down, some children receive redundant services for various overlapping problems; others receive no help at all. Children with multiple problems are typically given a single label — substance abuser, delinquent, dropout, teen parent — that oversimplifies the nature of the trouble and obstructs a real evaluation of what is going on and what needs to be done. As these children move from one level of care to another — from home to juvenile hall or from inpatient psychiatric hospitalization to residential treatment — they move in and out of different departmental jurisdictions and encounter different groups of service providers who tend their own turf.

Not all the ills of childhood can be solved by better-integrated services. There are at least several contending views on the major line of attack, including vouchers and improving the morality and responsibility of parents. However, the coordinated-services approach is a crucial component of any solution.

Further, the coordinated-services approach also assumes that the current problem with children's services is both service fragmentation and underservice. When about 25 percent of children are not covered by health insurance, better linkage among existing suppliers is insufficient. There must be an increase in the supply of low-cost health services as well as more effective delivery. But this chapter focuses on linkage and leaves to others solutions for underservice.

The concept of school-linked services requires a fundamental reorientation of how school finance scholars and state and local directors of special programs think about their jobs and their essential knowledge base. The first step is to move the conceptual focus from schooling policy to children's policy. State and local school administrators, who know the existing array of federal and state education programs, must also master the children's programs within the federal Departments of Health and Human Services and Labor (see, for example, U.S. House of Representatives, 1989). For example, the question "How can I get a federal waiver to make my school Medicaid eligible?" involves expertise in a different categorical domain than special education. Part of the slow growth of the school-linked services policy concept is due to lack of knowledge and vision about the potential of integrated children's policy by people working in scattered children's service agencies. This chapter attempts to fill in some gaps by focusing on the financial aspects of some specific approaches.

Financing School-Linked Services

To implement a school-linked services approach, schools must use existing financing sources for programs in health, social services, juvenile justice, and so on, rather than adding social workers and nurses to the school payroll. A school-linked-services fiscal strategy is to divert these funding and program streams and aim them all at one location at or near the school. The school stays open from 6 A.M. to 6 P.M. to provide city-funded day care, recreation, and adult education. School health clinics are subsidiaries of a local hospital, which provides the necessary medical licenses, eligibility to receive federal Medicaid funds, and liability insurance. The bills for health services are handled by the accounting department of the local hospital, and the health employees at the school site are technically employees of the hospital. Federal Title IV E provides funds for children's protective services, and the federal maternal and child health grant is used for mental health counseling. State categorical funds for children's services provide some "glue money" for planning and administration of this complex through federal and state drug abuse prevention funds. United Way fills in the cracks where none of the federal or state categorical programs provide any coverage, for example, emergency needs like clothing and rent payment. City funds are used for after-school recreation and before-school child care. Community colleges provide programs to help parents become wage earners and improve their parenting skills.

Line workers — teachers, social workers, law enforcement personnel, and parent educators — should discuss collaboration techniques at the start. This process can be reinforced by certain fiscal strategies, including hooks, glue, and joint ventures that let workers know that no one agency can solve all the problems (Gardner, 1989). Hooks formally link a child's participation in one program with participation in another. For example, a foster child automatically qualifies to move from school to a local job-training program when the student leaves high school. Glue money allows one agency to subcontract with other agencies and ensures that children can get services in one place. The lead agency becomes the "broker" for the child; for example, a school could subcontract with health, social service, and job-training agencies. Glue money would allow each child to be assigned a case manager who could procure resources from other agencies. In joint ventures, several agencies create partnerships to raise funds for jointly operated programs. This type of collaboration makes it less likely that agencies will put out tentacles into other domains. For example, drug prevention would not be grafted onto schools, but the school system, along with several other agencies, would apply for federal and state funds to conduct an integrated reinforcing program. A crucial element in all these financial arrangements is the credibility of the initial community planning by administrators, line workers, and parents (Kirst, 1991).

Funding Principles for School-Linked Services

Fiscal strategies need to be revamped to support the arrangements just discussed (Farrow, 1990). A first principle is that school-linked services primarily should use dollars already being spent on children's services. For example, existing state and local expenditures can be used as matching funds to increase federal financial participation by making schools Medicaid eligible or using the federal JOBS program to provide school-based child care.

The consolidation of money from several physical locations to one, such as a school, is another crucial theme. Often, funds will be shifted from more restrictive to more inclusive school-linked services. For example, specialized funds to combat drugs and smoking should be combined into a broad children's health prevention approach. In general, back-end treatment funds should be shifted to increase preventive interventions (Center for the Study of Social Policy, 1991).

Further, if collaboration among agencies is more effective than the current fragmentation, then funding mechanisms should create incentives for collaboration. If service interventions are more effective at an early age, then financing mechanisms should be redirected to front-end priorities. If flexibility between frontline service providers of many agencies (teachers, social workers, public health nurses, and so on) achieves better outcomes, then financial formulas should provide such flexibility.

Federal and state funding sources should be designed to meld multiple funding sources together and cut across historically separate children's service domains. This includes hooks, glue money, and blending entitlement dollars with discretionary funds. Funding formulas should not encourage adding functions to schools if other agencies' funds can be used instead.

Lastly, school-linked financing strategies, by themselves, are not likely to change service systems enough to create better children's outcomes. Finance changes must be accompanied by related transformations in the governance, technology, and attitudes and capacities of employees up and down the system. There must be combined intake, referral, and evaluation systems. For example, in Ventura County, California, all family preservation services have uniform eligibility standards. New relationships among frontline workers must be based on trust and satisfying informal working relationships. One way to capitalize on federal funding is to claim more federal reimbursements and thereby free up more state and local funds. For example, federal Title IV E could be used for many types of family preservation services funded by state and local children's protective services.

Federal Sources

More creative and flexible use of federal program dollars is a recurrent theme in financial strategies for school-linked services. The bulk of federal revenues derives from major programs: Medicaid; Early Period Screening, Diagnosis, and Training Service (EPSDT); the Maternal and Child Health Block Grant; Title IV E of the Social Security Act; and the Family Support Act of 1988 (FSA). Each is discussed below. Medicaid, EPSDT, and Title IV E require state matching funds that may be difficult to obtain in states experiencing recession.

Medicaid. Medicaid was created in 1965 through Title XIX of the Social Security Act and is a state-administered program to provide health services to the poor. Medicaid coverage and eligibility vary widely among the states (Halfon & Klee, 1991). States choosing to offer a Medicaid program must provide particular mandated services and may provide up to thirty-one optional services. One optional service is to expand a category known as "rehabilitation services," which are defined as "any medical or remedial services recommended by a physician or other licensed practitioner of the healing arts for maximum reduction of physical or mental disability and restoration of any individual to his best functioning level" (section 4719 of the U.S. Omnibus Budget Reconciliation Act of 1990). States could develop a new category of rehabilitation services to be furnished by local school districts for Medicaid-eligible, low-income children. The recommended services by a medical practitioner could be based upon a handicapped child's individualized education plan (IEP). Under this optional rehabilitation services classification, local school districts could become eligible Medicaid providers. A variety of services not currently reimbursable could be reimbursed, including paraprofessional health providers (who are supervised by professional staff). Medicaid could pay for IEP assessments and related services under a law passed in July 1989. The school district could bill the state, which in turn bills the federal government.

Another alternative is used in San Jose, California, where the school health clinics are subsidiaries of a local hospital. The hospital has authority to utilize Medicaid funds, and all billing is done by the hospital. In 1985, Medicaid added "targeted case management" to help low-income children gain access to needed medical services. The Center for the Study of Social Policy (1991, p. 12) points out that

> Unlike traditional Medicaid benefits which must be provided in the same amount, duration and scope statewide, case management services can be targeted to high-risk population groups and substate geographic areas. The only restrictions on the provision of case management services are that states must define: 1) case management services; 2) the target groups and geographic areas where services will be provided; and 3) the educational and professional qualifications of the providers.
>
> Targeted case management can be used to

pay for the cost of case management services for any high-risk special population. These services could include case planning, assessment, referral and collateral services. Several states are currently using Targeted Case Management in creative ways: most target the mentally ill and mentally retarded/developmentally disabled population; Utah and Alabama target child welfare populations; Washington targets a number of groups, including pregnant and parenting teens and all Medicaid recipients under 21 whose family needs assistance obtaining services for children.

Early Period Screening, Diagnosis, and Treatment Service (EPSDT). All states participating in Medicaid must provide Early Period Screening, Diagnosis, and Treatment Service (EPSDT), which targets children and stresses prevention. EPSDT is designed to detect, diagnose, and fully treat children's health needs. States must provide outreach and case management services and may target services to particular high-risk populations. EPSDT could be used to finance special education-related services, case management services, and outreach, screening, and health prevention. Services provided under EPSDT are not required for Medicaid-eligible adults so that costs can be limited to children.

There are problems with state matching, however. For example, California must put up 50 percent and Kentucky 28 percent for each EPSDT dollar. This may mean that EPSDT is cut when state revenue declines. Moreover, pediatricians have been reluctant to offer EPSDT because of paperwork and low reimbursement levels.

But EPSDT is very flexible and can reimburse for administrative costs as well as specific medical treatments. In San Jose, California, school-based health clinics utilize the San Jose Medical Center (a private hospital) to do all billing for Medicaid and EPSDT. The hospital is more familiar with the billing procedures and also provides billing to private health insurers for those pupils covered by private health insurance. The hospital is

obtaining more clients in return for providing its experience
with federal health billing procedures.

Maternal and Child Health Block Grant (MCH). Another
potential source for school site health funds is the Maternal and
Child Health Block Grant (MCH). MCH was established in 1981
as a consolidation of seven programs operating since 1935
designed to serve children and pregnant women. Eligibility for
MCH is set by individual states and federal appropriations are
over one-half billion dollars. MCH Block Grant funds go to local
health departments that could become part of the school-linked
services operation. Schools could also apply directly for MCH
funds.

Title IV E of the Social Security Act. This federal program
primarily reimburses states for foster care maintenance but was
expanded in 1980 to include efforts to prevent placement and
restore families. It includes very complex paperwork and
federal requirements and is best used for children already involved with the child protective services system. For such children, IV E can be used for preschool, after school, and summer
school, as well as case management. Title IV E requires state
matching of between 50 percent and 75 percent, depending on
the state's wealth. Eligible services could be provided on school
grounds.

The Family Support Act of 1988 (FSA). The FSA is designed
to help Aid to Families with Dependent Children (AFDC) parents obtain skills and training needed to avoid long-term welfare
support. Adult education programs on school grounds could be
federally reimbursed and offer child care at the school. AFDC-
eligible teen parents could be covered for case management and
other school-based supportive services. FSA funds have a matching rate of between 50 and 72 percent.

    In short, there are several current federal social services
programs that could be used to provide the bulk of funding for
school-linked social services. To tap these sources requires understanding their program requirements, creative design of

school-linked services to meet those requirements, and new school planning, record keeping, and documentation to comply with federal billing and accountability standards.

It is now useful to see how the above school-linked funding principles and creative new uses of federal program resources can work in specific localities. The New Beginnings Schools in San Diego, the school-based services program in forty-one New Jersey locations, and the Kentucky school-based family support and youth centers provide examples not only of these funding principles and federal programs but also of creative use of other state and local programs and resources as well.

Planning School-Linked Services in San Diego

One of the best-documented examples of planning and starting school-linked services is the New Beginnings project at Hamilton Elementary School in San Diego, California. A discussion of this finance plan may prove instructive for other localities. San Diego has some distinctive features, such as earthquake retrofitting for school buildings, but most costs probably are similar to other locations. The San Diego effort took eighteen months of planning before any services were provided. San Diego began with a $45,000 planning grant from the Stuart Foundations in San Francisco in 1989 to

- Identify significant health, social, and economic problems facing families
- Identify services families need and want
- Identify areas of duplication of effort among agencies
- Identify barriers to receiving services, both within families and within agencies providing services (San Diego Unified School District, 1991)

The planning for New Beginnings had five distinct components:

- An action research component that would place a social worker at the school to investigate families' needs for services and barriers to receiving services

- Interviews with students and families to understand their perspective and needs for services
- Focus groups of agency and school line workers to assess issues concerning collaboration
- A data match to determine the extent of agency involvement and the number of multiple-program families
- A migration study to determine which schools students attended before their enrollment at Hamilton

Over 63 percent of the school's households were involved with one service provider in addition to the schools; 20 percent were known at some point during the last seven years to Child Protective Services. The County Department of Social Services alone provided an annual expenditure of $5,700,474 to the families of children attending Hamilton. Service priority is given to students whose families are involved with three or more agencies based on the match of school and participating institution data.

The major costs of the New Beginnings Center, which is located in a site near Hamilton School, include salary funds for the family services advocates, the center director, and clerical support and revenues for office space and operating costs. The staffing funds include a mixture of job redefinitions and entitlement funds redirected to the school center. For the family services advocates, sources required redefining the role of school counselors, Department of Social Services workers, United Way, and city community-based agency staff. Entitlement programs that provide personnel include federal Medicaid Title XIX reimbursements for case management, federal Title IV E reimbursements for prevention of foster care, and increased state average daily attendance funds generated by the site-based family services advocates. Waivers were needed from the federal agencies for Medicaid Title XIX and IV E in order to fund case management systems, and the waivers were granted. Office space is funded by the overhead funds from positions that were redirected to the center.

Unlike education agencies, the federal Health and Human Services Department has extensive authority to grant waivers for the type of revenue use just described. The key waivers are:

- *Funding:* ability to use existing funding sources more flexibly
- *Confidentiality:* ability to designate the center team as a full interdisciplinary team for case information exchange
- *Title XIX and IV E changes:* ability to receive reimbursement for case management staffing
- *Unified eligibility:* ability to establish a unified program eligibility system
- *Cross-training:* ability to cross-train the center team from the best funding source
- *Waiting list priority:* ability to give priority to the center's families for service/treatment (particularly substance abuse treatment)

Note that the entire San Diego plan is based on existing regular funding sources and not new project funds that are provided for a brief period. For example, the health component includes school nurse practitioners paid for by the county and district health agency, with medical supervision provided so that they can treat common childhood conditions. Unlike a school nurse, the nurse practitioner license enables the school-based provision of a wider array of health services. San Diego was concerned that reliance on too much "soft money" would become a problem because after the foundation grants terminate, the district could not sustain the funding base. Moreover, a large foundation project would raise expectations about scale that cannot be fulfilled over the long run. A list of in-kind contributions, which total over $200,000, for the planning phase of the San Diego project is presented in Table 9.1. Table 9.2 includes funds for the first phase of operations in San Diego, which does not yet include child care.

Evaluation of the San Diego effort, which began in the fall of 1991, will include the issue of cost effectiveness because some of the case loads will be low by normal local agency standards. One question is whether benefits such as prevention of family

Table 9.1. New Beginnings: In-Kind Contributions
During Planning Phase.

City of San Diego	
Community Programs Division and Deputy City Manager's Office	$3,908.00
Police Department	100.00
San Diego City Schools	
Office of Deputy Superintendent	$15,000.000
Planning, Research, and Evaluation Division project research components	8,553.27
Planning, Resource, and Evaluation Division project team	11,200.00
Information Systems: Data Match project	6,660.00
Data processing	500.00
Materials, fax, copying, and so on	450.00
Legislative Office	300.00
Executive Committee	3,160.00
San Diego Community College District	
Instructional Services Department	$15,000.00
San Diego County Department of Social Services	
Director	$24,000.00
Assistant Deputy Director/Support	72,268.20
Training and Development Center	720.00
Various staff for focus groups	545.40
Children's Services Bureau: family services advocate	17,001.00
Electronic data processing	22,213.94
Hamilton Elementary School	
Principal's Office, focus group members	$6,600.00
San Diego County Department of Health	
Director, Assistant Health Director, Mental Health Department	$3,514.00
San Diego County Housing Department	
Housing Management Department	$1,740.86
San Diego County Probation Department	
Director, Assistant Director, staff	$4,000.00
Total	$217,434.67

Source: San Diego Unified School District, 1991.

breakup make the added low case load costs worthwhile. A crucial evaluation question is the cost of moving New Beginnings up to scale for the entire school district. Can the in-kind contributions and regular funding sources be redefined for a

Table 9.2. New Beginnings: Staffing, Services, and Funding Sources for Hamilton Elementary School, San Diego.

Institutional Collaboration:

Feasibility study	Stuart Foundations, County Department of Social Services (DSS)
Confidentiality research	DSS
Common eligibility research	Danforth Foundation, United Way
Funding streams research	DSS
Health component/ licensing and reimbursement	U.S. Department of Health and Human Services
MIS development	Stuart Foundations
Evaluation	Pew Charitable Trusts
MIS equipment	Stuart Foundations
Administrative assistant	Danforth Foundation

Center Start-Up

Portable classrooms and installation	San Diego City Schools (SDCS)
Classroom remodeling	Stuart and Danforth Foundations
Utilities installation and hookup	City of San Diego
Health classroom remodeling	Department of Health Services (DHS) (state tobacco tax funds)
Touchscreen video	IBM Corporation

Center Staffing:

Coordinator	Stuart Foundations
Receptionist/clerk	Danforth Foundation
Family services advocates	DSS (2), SDCS (1), Home Start (.5)
Adult counselor (.2)	San Diego Community College District
Mental health workers (2)	DHS (County level)
Nurse practitioner	SDCS

Future:

Supervising physician	University of California, San Diego/ Alliance Health Foundation
Nurse practitioner	Alliance Health Foundation
Outreach workers	Alliance Health Foundation, Pacific Telesis Foundation

Notes:
— Numbers in parentheses refer to number of full-time positions.
— Will be applying for Medicaid provider status.
— Other potential resources: federal Title IV E, Maternal and Child Health Block Grant, state child care categorical funds.

Source: Jehl, 1992.

large-scale effort? Funding at scale requires both horizontal alliances (public and private) and vertical alliances (federal, state, and local).

New Jersey's High School Program

While San Diego focused on elementary schools, New Jersey oriented its school-linked services to youth ages thirteen–nineteen, with $250,000 grants from the New Jersey Department of Human Services. Each high school in the program must provide job training and employment and mental and physical health services. Additional services include day care and nutrition counseling. Each high school applicant must explain how school activities will be coordinated and integrated with the broader services. Overall, these projects have been judged successful by New Jersey state officials and are now being expanded by the New Jersey legislature.

New Jersey specifies that there must be a site project manager, who can come from a variety of agencies. State funds can be used for the site manager. The New Jersey projects also have an employment specialist, a nurse or part-time physician, and a human services coordinator for case management. These personnel are usually funded by nonschool agencies from their regular budgets and located at the school site. Moreover, each project must demonstrate the availability of a certified alcohol and drug abuse specialist.

Budgets are disaggregated by state project funding, local matching funds, and other funding sources. Matching funds may be in-kind services such as facilities, staff, or other agency sources. There are careful requirements to prevent supplanting, and only 10 percent of the state grant can be used for facility renovation.

Family Resource and Youth Service Centers in Kentucky

The Kentucky Education Reform Act appropriated $9.5 million to support school-based family support and youth centers. The Center for the Study of Social Policy (1991) analyzed the potential of a refinancing strategy that would supplement the $75,000 per school state grant with other existing services. The center's plan specifies four criteria for refinancing:

1. No expenditure of any new state funds.
2. No additional risk of federal audit exceptions.
3. Benefits outweigh any increased administrative difficulties.
4. Refinancing strategies must support and be subordinate to agency program goals.

The center identified $16 million in potential new federal revenue for Kentucky, primarily from the five programs discussed above, but cautioned schools to have a perspective viewing service goals and funding programs in ways that are broader, less categorical, and more interactive.

The Politics of Financing School-Linked Services

School leaders are wary of new responsibilities without adequate and stable funding. They are increasingly wary of projects funded by soft money. In hard times the health and social services often are the first to be eliminated, as cuts are made as far away from the classroom as possible.

School-linked services is another in a long wave of changes in the school role, and it remains a risky venture. The expansion of social service functions engenders strong fears that schools will de-emphasize their traditional academic priorities. Critics argue that schools have enough trouble teaching complex concepts and skills without taking on the rest of children's services. Moreover, conservative critics believe that more school-linked services such as child care will encourage more women to work, with a subsequent loss of "high-quality" child rearing done by "homemakers." Still other critics think the schools should build "character" and promote positive behavior, while leaving health and other children's services to nonschool agencies (Finn, 1991).

The last recent push for integrated children's services was in the 1960s and early 1970s as an extension of President Lyndon B. Johnson's War on Poverty. Little remains from these efforts. But schools in that era were viewed by poverty warriors as part of the problem rather than part of the solution. The main strategy was to create new institutions, such as community action agencies or model city structures. But the reformers of that era learned that it is exceedingly difficult to create new institutions for poor people that endure over time. While many of these new agencies faded, schools remain the dominant institution for children ages five to eighteen. So the response in the 1990s has been less focused on circumventing the schools and more interested in capitalizing on schools' large organized constituencies (for example, teacher unions) and enduring organizational structure. Schools are everywhere; their ubiquity makes them local avenues for better delivery of children's services.

Another positive political impetus for school-linked services is the changed attitude of school leaders. After the advent of Chapter 1 (compensatory education) in the 1960s, schools took the view that they could provide social services and solve poverty. Compensatory education funds were used for dentistry, health care, and new clothes. School breakfasts proliferated, and pupil services expanded. But as the federal money leveled off and children's problems grew, school leaders' attitudes changed. The mood in the mid 1980s reflected the belief that schools were overwhelmed by negative changes in children's conditions and were not likely to receive the funds to construct needed social services under the school's sole authority.

School restructuring provides yet another impetus as school-linked services became one of the suggested restructuring components (see Table 9.3). In contrast to "restructuring," most 1980 reforms were characterized as "intensification" of the existing education roles, routines, and structure (Firestone, Fuhrman, & Kirst, 1991). The United States spent 30 percent more on schools (after inflation) in the 1980s, and gains were made, especially in completion of more science, mathematics, world studies, economics, and advanced placement courses. Teacher pay rose faster than inflation, and school policies "made the little buggers work harder," as one California legislator advocated (Firestone, Fuhrman, & Kirst, 1991). But by the

Table 9.3. The Main Pieces of Restructuring.

Curriculum and Instruction must change to:
- Actively engage students in learning
- Promote understanding and application of skills and knowledge
- Create curricular goals that embody challenging learning tasks
- Stimulate synthesis, inference, problem solving, and analysis

Authority and Decision Making must:
- Decentralize so important education decisions are made at school site
- Increase flexibility so there are decisions left to be made by schools
- Provide the authority and knowledge to make and carry out decisions

Roles and Responsibilities must change up and down the system to:
- Create new, more flexible roles for teachers and principals with built-in time for acquiring new knowledge and learning
- Encourage new roles for the community—parents, business, senior citizens
- Shift role of district and state administrators from rule making and monitoring to helping school faculties create stimulating learning environments

Accountability should:
- Focus on results, not procedures
- Use assessment instruments that measure valued goals well
- Put authority and accountability at same level (school)
- Create culture in which educators use information to assess how they are doing (and model this for students)

Beyond Education:
- Create links with social and health service agencies
- Ensure all students are ready for schools

Source: Compiled from David, 1990.

end of the 1980s there was a growing consensus that intensifying the existing schools would not be sufficient to overcome the obvious decline in many children's nonschool lives.

The school-linked services movement is presently on the fringes of the education restructuring movement. Most education restructuring focuses on decentralization from central offices to school sites, teacher participation, and curricular reform. School-linked services, however, need to be viewed as an essential rather than peripheral part of school restructuring, if they are to derive substantial political support from large education interest groups like teachers and administrators. Successful school restructuring must include all restructuring components rather than merely picking a few pieces that end up unrelated and not reinforcing each other. The biggest problem with school restructuring to date is that it has become seen as merely school-based management and decentralization. Fundamental overhaul of curriculum *and* linkages beyond the schools to social services are also necessary components; but these have received less attention in the experiments to date. It is unlikely that decentralization and school-based management will be sufficient to provide school-linked services without leadership from the school board and central administration. The education accountability system must also change to encompass outcomes from school-linked services as well as the traditional test scores.

This will not be easy because educators rarely come in contact with other children's services providers during teacher preparation or staff development. Schools of education deal primarily with classroom concerns and rarely even provide prospective teachers with the state or central school district office policy contexts. The professional meetings of educators rarely include personnel from the broader fields of children's services, so there is no way to meet health or protective services workers other than through formal referrals. Consequently, building alliances for school restructuring that includes school-linked services will take special arrangements and forums that bridge the diverse agencies and personnel involved in children's services. School administrators do not know much about health or other children's programs and must become familiar with these before school-linked services can operate at a school. A hopeful note, however, is the National School Boards Association's recent bill, S619, to establish federal link-up for learning demonstration grants "that provide coordinated services for at-risk youth at schools."

Another positive force for school-linked services is the recognition by major corporations of the necessity of restructuring to address influences beyond the schools. The Committee for Economic Development has published three major reports stressing the need for massive investments in preschool and other children's services (for example, see Committee for Economic Development, 1991). The demonstration schools in President Bush's Education 2000 plan will be supported largely by business donations and probably will include several sites with school-linked services. Moreover, President Bush's education plan explicitly recommends school-linked services, and the U.S. Secretary of Health and Human Services, Louis Sullivan, is in charge of developing this initiative.

There is little organized resistance to the concepts of school-linked services except for groups opposed to contraception assistance at secondary school health clinics and conservatives who may oppose day care. This suggests that the path of least political resistance would be to stress prevention at elementary schools. California's Governor Wilson recommended an elementary school–linked services initiative but ran into resistance from California education organizations that want full funding for education programs before new money is allocated for school-linked services.

The positive forces are probably strong enough to implement in the near future at least large-scale demonstrations of school-linked services. But school-linked services also must be viewed as an integral part of school restructuring and related to academic improvement as an important outcome. A sick child cannot learn, and a more challenging curriculum cannot be mastered by a child confronting chaos at home. Restructuring implies that school-linked services must be more than add-ons to the existing school routines and should not consist solely of isolated portable facilities in back of the school. Service providers other than teachers should be involved in discussions and plans for the academic progress of specific children. For example, case management of children's services must include teachers as part of the team and be focused in part on the impact of nonschool influences on daily classroom progress. In foster care prevention efforts, tutoring services and other intensive education interventions should be carried out as part of a coordinated family preservation effort, not as isolated activities.

Educators must be willing, moreover, to participate in linked services that are not near school grounds. In some localities, a family resource center might be a better location than on or near school grounds. There is no one best location for school-linked services given the diversity of U. S. communities. Some parents feel alienated from schools and would rather go to another facility, while in other localities schools are the best location.

Conclusion

The problems of children in the 1990s require an expansion of school finance to encompass children's finance. Most local school administrators know little about funding requirements and possibilities in fields like health, children's protective services, and juvenile justice. This new approach requires a drastic redefinition of what school finance should encompass. The era of the add-on school project for more children's services is giving way to a new vision of school-linked services that can be funded on a self-sustaining basis.

References

Center for the Study of Social Policy. (1991). *Refinancing in Kentucky: Expanding the base for family resource centers.* Washington, DC: Author.

Children's Defense Fund. (1990). *SOS America: A children's defense budget.* Washington, DC: Author

Committee for Economic Development. (1991). *The unfinished agenda: A new vision of child development and education.* New York: Author.

David, J. L. (1990). Restructuring in progress: Lessons from pioneering districts. In R. F. Elmore & Associates (Eds.), *Restructuring schools: The next generation of education reform* (pp. 209–250). San Francisco: Jossey-Bass.

Farrow, F. (1990, November). State financing strategies that promote more effective services for children. Paper prepared for the National Forum on Children.

Finn, C. E., Jr. (1991). *We must take charge.* New York: Free Press.

Firestone, W. A., Fuhrman, S., & Kirst, M. W. (1991). State education reform since 1983: Appraisal and the future. *Educational Policy, 5,* 233–250.

Gardner, S. (1989, Fall). Failure by fragmentation. *California Tomorrow*, pp. 17–25.

Halfon, N., & Klee, L. (1991). Health and development services for children with multiple needs. *Yale Law and Policy Review, 9*, 71–96.

Jehl, J. (1992, February). *New beginnings: Staffing, services, and funding sources*. San Diego Unified School District. Unpublished document.

Kirst, M. W. (Ed.). (1989). *Conditions of children in California*. Berkeley: University of California, Department of Education.

Kirst, M. W. (1991). Improving children's services: Overcoming barriers, creating new opportunities. *Phi Delta Kappan, 72*, 615–618.

San Diego Unified School District. (1991). *New Beginnings fact sheet*. San Diego, CA: Author.

Tyack, D. (1979). The high school as a social service agency: Historical perspectives. *Educational Evaluation and Policy Analysis, 1*, 45–57.

U. S. House of Representatives, Select Committee on Children, Youth, and Families. (1989). *Federal programs affecting children, and their families*. Washington, DC: U. S. Government Printing Office.

10

Toward the Twenty-First Century: A School-Based Finance

Allan R. Odden

The contours of school finance are changing. School finance in the twenty-first century may be quite different from what it has been in the past. In the 1970s and 1980s, the new school finance issues included alternative measures of fiscal capacity (Odden, 1977; Adams & Odden, 1981), cost-of-education indices (Chambers, 1981), municipal overburden (Sjogren, 1981), categorical program expansion (McGuire, 1982), and new general aid formulas such as guaranteed tax bases and power equalization (Callahan & Wilken, 1976). As the previous chapters have shown, new issues are likely to dominate the 1990s and beyond: altering the way teachers are paid (Chapter Two), budgeting dollars directly to the school (Chapter Four), creating fiscal incentives based on school performance (Chapter Five), financing public school choice across districts (Chapter Seven), developing a new federal role for reducing interstate education disparities (Chapter Eight), and financing noneducational social services at the school site (Chapter Nine).

There are several pressure points producing these new directions in school finance. First, education reform continued unabated throughout the 1980s and entered the 1990s with additional momentum. The nation's political and business leaders, and even most of the nation's education leaders, saw upgrading the nation's human capital as a key strategy for making the U.S. economy more competitive in world markets (Commission on the Skills of the American Workforce, 1990). Second, all organizations, both public and private (including schools), felt the pressure to improve system productivity (Johnston, 1987). Third, decentralized and more market-driven approaches were adopted by the private sector to accomplish enhanced productivity; these strategies also were applied to the public sector (Eisenhardt, 1989), including the public schools (Business Roundtable, 1991).

Fourth, and in many ways most important, the country established the first ever nationwide education goals. Today, the U.S. education system has the following goals to accomplish by the year 2000 (White House, 1990):

1. All children in America will start school ready to learn.
2. The high school graduation rate will increase to at least 90 percent.
3. American students will leave grades 4, 8, and 12 having demonstrated competency in challenging subject matter, including English, mathematics, science, history, and geography. Every school in America will ensure that all students learn to use their minds well, so they may be prepared for responsible citizenship, further learning, and productive employment in our modern economy.
4. U.S. students will rank first in the world in science and mathematics achievement.
5. Every adult in America will be literate and will possess the knowledge and skills necessary to compete in a global economy and to exercise the rights and responsibilities of citizenship.
6. Every school in America will be free of drugs and violence and will offer a disciplined environment conducive to learning.

As Chapter Eight pointed out, these goals were developed for all students. The vision is to teach all students how to engage in the learning process, to think, solve problems, communicate clearly, and work in collegial groups. As Porter, Archibald, and Tyree (1991) put it, we must teach hard content to all students. Accomplishing these goals will take intelligently directed effort.

While teaching hard content to all students is a resonant political ideal, it is meaningless unless it can be accomplished. What gives power to such an education goal for the 1990s is that it is supported by an emerging body of research that suggests it is a goal that can be attained. Based largely on emerging findings from research in cognitive psychology and good teaching, Elmore (1991, pp. 4–8) identified five precepts of best practice that should characterize classrooms and schools seeking to teach hard content to all students:

1. The object of teaching is to nurture understanding. Understanding is intentional learning or the active management of different types of knowledge and processes of cognition around concrete problems.
2. Understanding occurs in the context of specific bodies of knowledge.
3. Understanding requires the active construction of knowledge by learners.
4. Understanding requires the development of "basic" and "higher-order" knowledge simultaneously.
5. Learners differ substantially in the experience, the cognitive predispositions, and the competence they bring to specific bodies of knowledge.

Teaching students how to learn is very different from covering the curriculum and having students pass tests, even with high marks. Intentional learning means that students not only can solve problems but also can reflect upon the solutions they have derived. Students need to learn facts, but they must also be able to see implications from facts, develop solutions to new problems that facts may present, and link the solutions they develop to the broader constructs of the domain in which they are working (Resnick, 1989). While intentional learning might seem a lofty, unattainable goal, it has been shown that it is a type of learning that can be taught (Bereiter & Scardamalia, 1989) and that children taught with these goals in mind approach and construct problem solving in different and more powerful ways.

Such teaching and learning, moreover, are not generic but must be taught within different content domains, such as mathematics, science, history, geography, and English (Resnick, 1987). For example, "knowing" long division entails more than knowing how to divide one number by another; it entails knowing when division is needed to solve a particular problem, as well as knowing that division is the reverse of multiplication (Putnam, Lampert, & Peterson, 1990). Teachers who "aren't very good at math" would have a hard time teaching such mathematics. Being an expert thinker in history entails different knowledge than being an expert in science. In short, intentional learning is heavily content dependent. Therefore, teaching students intentional learning requires teachers who know well, at a deep level, the constructs associated with different subject matter areas.

Intentional learning also is referred to as "constructivist." Intentional learning is learning that goes beyond memorizing facts and knowledge and seeks to find the underlying relationships—the constructs—of a subject area. It is an act of discovering—constructing—the infrastructure of a discipline. Such learning entails building hypotheses and connections from facts, ideas, and prior strategies that a learner brings to the problem or task.

Teaching students, then, is not an act of presenting knowledge. Good teaching for these objectives of the national education goals requires that teachers understand the variety of constructs students may bring to the learning task and the types of common but intelligent "errors" they can make. Teachers need to understand how students learn to be constructivists in different content domains so they can help students build on prior strategies and errors for the purpose of extending their understandings. It means that constructivist learning occurs when the teachers confront the students with a dilemma and then help them work through it to a reasonable solution.

A corollary is that such processes do not separate basic from higher-order thinking skills. In the constructivist approach, knowledge and skills are needed to solve higher-order problems. The two go hand in hand (Resnick, 1987). Thinking, in other words, is not an advanced accomplishment. Thinking occurs the first moment a baby encounters a new object and tries to make sense of it or a toddler attempts to generalize the plural form of words by always adding an *s*. Thus, thinking is not only an act of constructivist learning but is the preeminent act of learning at all ages.

Finally, these precepts of teaching and learning, argues Elmore (1991), require that individual differences be recognized and used in constructing effective classroom learning activities. All students bring a different set of experiences, knowledge, conceptual understandings, and problem-solving strategies to new learning contexts. This variability is not unusual and should be expected. Exploiting these differences to advance the learning of all students is not only the right way to structure the classroom but also the most successful.

Palincsar and Brown (1984) have shown how reciprocal teaching of reading comprehension is a powerful strategy that produces learning for all students, including students in the bottom half of ability. Slavin (1990) has shown how various forms of cooperative learning produce similar learning advances for all students. Means and Knapp (1991) show how the cognitive approach to teaching can produce large gains in thinking and problem-solving achievement for economically disadvantaged students.

To help ensure that this type of teaching and learning occurs in the nation's schools and classrooms, the complementary state programs identified in Chapter One become critical: ambitious curriculum frameworks, new instructional materials, new forms of performance assessments, and sophisticated new approaches to staff development.

But all of these must be incorporated into schoolwide programs that work. School organizations must enable teachers to develop and deploy the knowledge and skills needed to engage students in constructivist learning as the key strategy for attaining the national education goals. Such schools are likely to be quite different from typical schools today. As Chapter Two described, such schools need to be:

- Student centered, that is, able to adapt their strategies and activities to make the particular students in a school successful in intentional learning activities.
- Focused on goals, taking the national goals as the primary student outcomes to accomplish.
- Staffed by highly competent professionals who know well the content they teach, how students learn it, and how successfully to guide student learning. This implies that curriculum frameworks and standards linked to key student achievement outcomes exist and that teacher training is strongly related to these content domains.
- Productivity oriented, that is, motivated to use resources effectively and efficiently to accomplish outcomes.
- Tightly coupled by a shared vision, understood purposes, and common values.
- Characterized by the following norms:
  Continuous improvement. These schools would be learning communities for both teachers and students. Teachers would be continuously improving what they know and can do, and students would be continuously improving their proficiencies in different content domains.
  Collegiality. Teachers would work together rather than in isolation, schoolwide initiatives would counter traditional teacher autonomy, and both teachers and site administrators would work interactively. The school would be characterized by joint planning, observing, improving, developing, creating, and assessing all school activities.
- Site managed. Teachers and site administrators would have the authority to make decisions concerning materials and instructional methods, staffing structures, organization of the school day, assignment of students, and allocation of site resources. High involvement (Lawler, 1986) would characterize the school's approach to management.
- Engaged in monitoring and assessing the teaching and learning processes and the outcomes of those processes.

The current system of state-to-district funding avoids the fact that accomplishing high levels of student achievement, such as those described in the nation's education goals, is quintessentially a school, not a district, function. *Schools* are the organizational unit where teaching and learning conditions are created to engage students in intentional learning. Adequate funding of such *schools* is clearly a key structural finance issue for the 1990s.

A School-Based Funding Structure

These conclusions imply that education financing in the twenty-first century should become primarily *school* rather than *district* based. While education funding historically has focused on state-to-district finance structures (Odden & Picus, 1992), the above arguments suggest that a more productive emphasis could be given to *school-based* financing. The issue of the level and kind of governance between the school and the state (or the federal government) is a separate policy issue. Such governance could include the current district structure, a broader regional or county structure, or no intermediate structure. But the pre-eminent finance issue is a school finance issue. Thus, education finance in the 1990s and in the twenty-first century might more productively consider how school sites should be financed.

A school-based finance structure suggests six possible new directions for education finance: (1) financing a high base program for all schools, (2) providing a school-based mechanism to spend above the base level, (3) implementing a school-based budgeting, management, information, and fiscal accounting system, (4) designing new forms of teacher compensation, (5) providing performance-based compensation bonuses, and (6) financing school-linked social services for children.

High-Level Foundation Programs for All Schools

The first requirement of a school-based funding structure is that the state provide each school a foundation per-pupil funding level supported with a combination of state and local funds. The foundation amount should be sufficient for schools to provide programs and services that would enable its students to meet the national student outcome goals. Each school would need to be guaranteed this level of general funding. It could be adjusted within states by intrastate cost-of-education indices (Chambers, 1981) and across states by interstate cost-of-education indices (Barro, 1992).

Conceptually, the best approach to determining the foundation funding level, as Chapter One discussed, is to identify and cost out specific education programs and services. Chapter Three began this process by identifying the costs of dramatic middle school restructuring. In the future, effective elementary and high school restructuring programs need to be identified and given a price tag (as do several programs) to ensure that *all* students in all schools perform at acceptable proficiency levels (see Madden, Slavin, Karweit, Dolan, & Wasik, 1991).

In addition to the foundation expenditure level, each school would need categorical aids to provide for the extra needs of low-income, limited-English-proficient, and handi-capped children (perhaps also for students in vocational education programs). One straightforward way to structure these additional funds is to weight each student by the amount of extra services needed and then allocate funds to schools on the basis of the number of weighted students. The weights would be the ratio of the extra costs relative to the foundation spending level.

An additional categorical program could be provided for students who needed extra time to meet the ambitious achievement objectives. As Finn (1991) observed, students' abilities vary. Thus, students need different amounts of time to meet annual performance goals. The school year, Finn proposed, could be divided into seven seven-week segments. Most students could learn the annual objectives in five of the segments, about the length of the current school year. Others would need six segments, and a smaller number would need seven segments. The extra segments would need to be financed separately over and above the base (possibly the need for extra segments could be included as a pupil weight).

As Chapter Eight showed, there are significant differences in both fiscal capacity and education spending level across states. Thus, the school finance of the future could well include a nationwide base spending level supported by a combination of local, state, and federal funds. This would entail a new federal role in interstate equalization, a policy whose time may have arrived with the advent of national education goals. Chapter Eight discussed various ways such a new federal role could be constructed and specifically suggested that the federal government provide 20 percent of the revenues for base per-pupil school spending.

A school-based funding structure also would require a school-based information and fiscal accounting structure. Florida already has such a fiscal accounting structure, and other states are moving toward creating more school-based information. But a school- rather than district-based funding structure strongly implies that the primary accounting base should be the school, rather than the district.

Spending Above the Foundation Level

If each school's spending were limited to the foundation level, it would mean that spending per pupil would be the same across the country (albeit with adjustments for prices and different pupil needs). But the level might not be high enough to satisfy the demands of many local school communities. Moreover, states that have attempted to limit district spending have experienced drops in relative education funding over time (Picus, 1991).

Chapter Seven outlined a way—using income tax revenues—that schools could be given the choice to spend above a common foundation level. Parents of students in a school could be given the option to increase spending by a majority vote, similar to what is now done on a district basis for the property tax. All parents could vote, and there would have to be ample notice. The vote would be for an income tax surcharge for all parents at the school.

If the parents approved the surcharge, the school would send an official form to the state listing all parents and their social security numbers. The state then would send a notice to all parents informing them of their income tax surcharge. When parents completed their state income tax form, there would be an additional line where they would indicate their surcharge and compute the additional amount for local school spending. The system would be monitored by computers, just as miscellaneous and interest income is now monitored through Form 1099 notices and taxpayer social security numbers.

This system could work through the federal income tax as well. Thus, another new federal role in school finance could be to provide parents the choice to spend above the nationwide per-pupil spending level.

To implement such a program, the state (or federal) government would construct a schedule that would indicate the additional dollars per pupil that would be provided for different levels of income tax surcharges. The per-pupil yield could be related to the statewide (or nationwide) average taxable income per pupil. Thus, a 1 percent additional income tax would produce an extra $500 per pupil if the statewide average income per pupil was $50,000. The state (or federal government) would send this amount to the school as additional resources.

Table 10.1 is an example of such a schedule. The surcharge could be capped at some level, for example, 2 percent. For parents with children at more than one school, the total surcharge could be capped at the maximum on the schedule. The schedule alone would determine how much the school would receive for an extra income tax effort, irrespective of how much the surcharge actually raised from the parents in a specific school.

Just as for current guaranteed tax base (GTB) or district power-equalizing systems, there are several constraints on this type of structure. The yield schedule would be subject to legislative or congressional appropriations. The schedule likely would have some type of surcharge cap built into it, just as is the case with most power-equalizing systems. Parents voting on a site surcharge proposal would face a price for their actions; if they approved a proposal, they would increase their income tax payments. Michigan is one of the few states with a full GTB program in effect, and it has not experienced runaway local tax

Table 10.1. Schedule of Per-Pupil Yield for a School Site
Income Tax Surcharge.

Income Tax Surcharge	Per-Pupil Yield
0.25%	$ 125
0.50	250
0.75	375
1.00	500
1.25	625
1.50	750
1.75	875
2.00	1,000

increases. The local price component acts, as an economist would predict, as a deterrent to irresponsible behavior.

Further, the poor would be protected from paying additional taxes to the degree that the poor do not pay state income taxes. All taxpayers in the state (or country) would help pay for this school finance increment. By using the state or national average income per pupil, the yield is much larger than would be raised just by the parents in any one school. School parents, just like district taxpayers in a traditional GTB program, would trigger the additional aid. But also (as in a traditional GTB program), no funds would flow unless local funds also increased; there would be a price for each site to trigger extra aid flows. To use school finance terminology, this plan has total recapture. If any school actually raised more than the scheduled yield, it would retain only the guaranteed yield. Finally, all these funds would be discretionary at the site level; they would come with no strings attached, just as extra general aid funds now flow to the district. Thus, fiscal freedom would be increased at each site.

Site-Based Budgeting

A school finance system almost by definition would require school-based budgeting. In most states today, districts receive local, state, and federal funds and use a variety of mechanisms to allocate resources to schools. Usually, schools receive teacher and administrator positions according to a central district formula. Further, operations and maintenance costs, substitute teacher costs, staff development, and a host of other support functions are financed directly from the district. Schools receive very few discretionary resources.

A school-based funding structure would be quite different from this type of organization. The school would be the primary recipient of local, state, and federal revenues. In other words, the revenues supporting the foundation expenditure level and all categorical revenues would be allocated directly to the school. The school then would have to budget the funds. The school would, thus, have the authority to determine the mix of professionals — teachers, administrators, adjunct teachers, and so on — at the school site and to hire, supervise, promote, and fire them. Further, the school would have fiscal and program responsibility for operations, maintenance, substitutes, books, materials, supplies, and staff development.

Such a plan raises the issue of the responsibilities that would be retained by the district or intermediate education unit. Running the accounting and check writing operation, financing and building schools, providing transportation, and monitoring school performance are potential functions that could be reserved for central offices. But much thought would need to be given to which functions would be delegated to schools and which retained by the central office (see Wohlstetter & Odden, in press). Further, functions carried out by the central office would need to be financed; a small portion of the overall education budget would need to be directed to remaining district central offices.

In short, the proposed structure would have real site-based management and real site-based budgeting. This structure is quite different from most site-based management programs created to date (Clune & White, 1988) and reflects current thinking on the devolution of powers to schools (Chapter Four) and the functions and authorities needed to make site-based management work (Wohlstetter & Odden, in press).

A school-based funding structure began operating in

Great Britain in 1988. Before 1988, Great Britain had a district-based funding structure. Under the 1988 education reforms, all schools directly receive 85 percent of the country's overall per-pupil funding level. Students also can choose to attend any public school. The total school budget is equal to the number of students attending the school multiplied by the per-pupil allocation amount. Schools have full authority over staff hiring and use of funds, subject only to an overall budget constraint. The country simultaneously implemented a national curriculum that all schools are expected to teach and new performance assessments for all students.

New Forms of Teacher Compensation

Teachers in the newly funded schools would need to have the knowledge and skills discussed above and in Chapter Two in order to help students meet the national achievement goals in mathematics, science, English, history, and geography. Thus, teacher compensation would need to be changed to reinforce the development and use of such knowledge and skills. Teachers would be paid *individually* on the basis of what they know and can do and *collectively* on what they produce in terms of student achievement.

Thus, teachers would no longer be paid on the basis of education and experience. After setting a beginning teacher salary target (on a statewide or regional labor market basis) that would allow all schools to recruit competitively for bright and able individuals, schools could then compensate teachers for the following knowlege and skills (as outlined in Chapter Two):

- *Content knowledge.* Elementary, middle, and high school teachers teach content. Thorough and deep knowledge of content is a prerequisite for being able to help students think and problem solve in the content domains.
- *Knowledge of how students learn.* While different from being able to *use* such knowledge to teach students effectively, it is a separate and identifiable arena of knowledge.
- *Knowledge of pedagogy.* This includes knowledge of instruc-

tional and classroom management strategies effective with different types of students and, for elementary teachers, with different content areas. Again, while this is different from being able to use such knowledge to teach students effectively, it is a separate and identifiable knowledge domain.

- *Effective use of pedagogical skills.* This entails assimilation of the above three sets of knowledge into action that is effective in producing student learning. While there has been disagreement in the past about how to assess different stages of proficiency in use of these skills, there is rapidly advancing knowledge that would make this feasible in the near future.
- *Board certification.* This could be from the National Board for Professional Teaching Standards, the National Association of Social Studies Teachers, or any other professional group that seeks to identify outstanding experienced teachers.
- *Performance assessments.* This skill is needed to develop portfolios of student performance on a variety of tasks as the country moves to performance-based student assessments.
- *Schoolwide leadership skills.* These skills are needed to participate effectively in schoolwide education improvement activities, in mentoring new and experienced teachers, in providing coaching and staff development assistance to teachers, and generally in a wide range of activities outside one's individual classroom.

While other skill domains are possible, the idea is for schools to identify the array of knowledge and skills they would like teachers to possess, communicate those expectations to teachers, provide a series of mechanisms, for example, professional development and peer assistance, to support such development, and price each knowledge and skill domain so teachers know what each element would produce in terms of a higher salary. No quota would be placed on the amount of knowledge and skills that would qualify for extra pay.

Further, as Chapter Two argued, such a compensation system reinforces teachers working together to build, expand, and solidify professional practice, knowledge, and skills. A key objective of collegial activities in effective schools is development of teaching expertise (Little, 1982; McLaughlin & Yee, 1988; Rosenholtz, 1989). Thus, the proposed compensation structure would be a further stimulus to build the kind of school organization and culture discussed above. The current education- and experience-based salary schedule would not undercut the type of school organization needed to accomplish the nation's education goals, while merit and incentive pay would (see Chapter Two). However, the proposed structure would actively help support the kind of school organization and culture needed to engage all students successfully in the intentional learning process.

Performance-Based Compensation

In addition to being compensated for knowledge and skills, teachers also could be paid collectively on the basis of student performance, that is, what they produce. Chapter Two discusses the various reasons why *individual*-based incentive and merit pay plans do not work in education or the private sector. Thus, traditional merit pay is not recommended. Indeed, a merit pay plan likely would impede school attainment of the nation's ambitious education goals by working against a cooperative and collegial style.

The private sector has successfully designed production unit, division, and plant productivity bonus pay schemes (Blinder, 1990; Lawler, 1990). These programs provide all individuals in the unit with a bonus when outcome goals are attained or improvements in outcome goals are reached. In education, the analogy would be to provide school-based performance incentives.

A system could be devised to provide annual bonuses to staffs in schools that produce improvements in student achievement. While there are several design issues associated with school-based incentive programs (see Chapter Five), the key issue is that this component of teacher compensation is the analogue to profit sharing in the private sector, which has been shown across several types of private-sector organizations to improve productivity. Further, research has shown that teachers can respond positively to economic incentives (Jacobson, 1988).

Albert Shanker (1990), who heads a major teacher union, suggested that President Bush's 1990 merit school proposal be turned into a school-based performance program that could provide bonuses up to $30,000. He believed such an incentive would foster renewed teacher effort to increase student achievement. Further, several states have implemented incentive programs, and the oldest one, in South Carolina, receives high marks from both policy makers and teachers.

A school-based performance incentive would send signals to the public that part of teacher pay would be linked to student performance. That signal likely would strike a receptive chord. Properly designed, moreover, such a program would also reinforce the type of cooperative, collegial, and intense work in schools needed to bring all students to high levels of performance in different content areas. Further, a school-based performance incentive could be financed either by the federal government or by state governments.

Financing School-Linked Social Services

A final dimension of the new school finance is to broaden the policy umbrella from "school" to "children's policy" and view the school as a location where noneducation social services can be provided. This will entail mastering not only the myriad of education categorical programs but the even larger number of children's programs in the U.S. departments of Health and Human Services, and Labor. It would also include diverting the multiple revenue streams now supporting such social services to single local institutions, such as schools, in order to provide one-stop shopping for these services, increasingly needed by a rising percentage of students.

In Chapter Nine, Kirst profiled what this might mean for schools. Schools would stay open from 6 A.M. to 6 P.M. to provide education during the normal school hours and support services such as counseling, parenting assistance, day care, recreation, and adult education. Made eligible for Medicare by the Health and Human Services Department, schools also would have health clinics or nurse practitioners to provide an array of medical services, with the bills for such services processed by the accounting department of a local hospital. Federal Title IV E could help schools provide protective services for abused children. Federal maternal and child health grant funds could be used for mental health counseling. State categorical grants could provide for planning and administration of the overall program using federal and state drug abuse prevention funds. United Way dollars then could fill voids missed by federal and state categorical funds, including, for example, emergency money for clothes and rent. City funds could be tapped for before- and after-school day care and recreation. Community colleges could provide training to enable parents to get better jobs.

Orchestrating the financing of these broader services at a school clearly expands school finance beyond education. It involves not only diverting a variety of noneducation service revenue streams toward schools or locations near schools but also designing a more comprehensive and coherent service program that uses the funds more effectively. This approach also suggests switching funds from downstream intervention (after problems have occurred) to upstream prevention programs and developing collaboration to counter the service fragmentation that now characterizes the maze of children's noneducation programs and services (Kirst, 1991).

To accomplish such a comprehensive and cohesive school program would require intense collaboration on the part of teachers, social workers, health professionals, law enforcement personnel, and parents. Such collaboration could be reinforced by new state and federal fiscal policies that Kirst (Chapter Nine) labels hooks, glue, and joint ventures. Hooks would formally link participation in one program with participation in another; for example, a foster child in high school would automatically become eligible for a local job-training program. Glue money would allow one agency, such as the school, to subcontract with other agencies for services. Glue money also would allow each child to be assigned a case manager to broker these other agency services such as health, social service, and job training. Finally, joint ventures would entail several agencies' creating a partnership to jointly operate a cohesive program, such as using the large increase in drug prevention money to launch a health program rather than just add a drug prevention categorical program.

Kirst (Chapter Nine) suggests that federal and state funding sources could be modified to encourage these local site comprehensive approaches. The largest potential revenue sources for school-linked services are five federal programs.

The student population is increasingly characterized by poverty, broken families, lack of access to good health care, immigrant status, and ethnic diversity. The old fragmented approach to children's services is ineffective. To improve the chances of accomplishing the nation's education goals, "education policy" must be broadened to "children's policy" to capture the 91 percent of children's lives that are spent outside of formal education (White House, 1991). As a result, school finance must be broadened beyond education finance to include the finance dimensions of noneducation social services that might be provided at or near the local school.

Conclusions

It will take several years for states and the federal government to design, fund, and implement the proposed school-based finance structure described above. The task is further complicated if it includes financing school-linked social services as well. The overall strategy derives from the imperative to teach hard content to all students and thus to develop high levels of student proficiency in mathematics, science, English, history, and geography. The strategy assumes that the school is the primary education organization to accomplish that task since schools are the service delivery units in the education system.

The strategy proposes several new federal roles in school finance that derive from the national nature of education outcome goals and the current fiscal, program, and achievement disparities that exist across the states (Chapter Eight). Three major changes are proposed for the federal government:

- A federal role reducing interstate education spending disparities by helping to provide a uniform foundation
  expenditure-per-pupil level across all schools in the country,
  with 20 percent of the funds deriving from federal sources
- A federal role, linked to the federal income tax, providing
  fiscal choice at the school to spend above the foundation
  level
- A federal role providing school-based performance awards
  for faculties in schools that meet or exceed student performance improvement objectives

The proposed new school finance structure is compatible
with nearly all forms of public school choice, including charter
schools. As Chapter Seven argued, a common school-level foundation expenditure per pupil is needed to support interdistrict
public school choice programs, as is an income tax–linked
option to spend above the base. Further, the proposed funding
program could just as easily provide funds to newly formed
charter schools as to schools that now exist within a school
district structure.

In short, moving education finance from district to
school finance focuses education funding on the organizational
units—schools—responsible for producing the bold student
performance levels embodied in the country's education goals.
The new finance structure would meld with public school choice
programs that are rapidly expanding across the country. It is a
structure that fits with school-linked social services, a policy that
also is rapidly gaining momentum. It is a structure that, while
dramatic on the surface, simply takes many elements of the
current district-based finance structure and shifts them to the
school. Thus, it is a structure that could be quite rapidly designed by making a few technical policy changes. But it is a
structure that would require new political understandings as
support. Finally, if the school is the production unit in the
system, the proposed structure could dramatically improve the
productivity of the education system, a long-sought-after goal.

References

Adams, E. K., & Odden, A. R. (1981). Alternative wealth measures. In K. F. Jordan & N. H. Cambron-McCabe (Eds.), *Perspectives in state school support programs* (pp. 143–165). New York: Ballinger.

Barro, S. M. (1992). *Cost-of-educational differences across the states.* Washington, DC: SMB Educational Research.

Bereiter, C., & Scardamalia, M. (1989). Intentional learning as a goal of instruction. In L. Resnick (Ed.), *Knowing, learning and instruction* (pp. 362–392). Hillsdale, NJ: Erlbaum.

Blinder, A. (1990). *Paying for productivity.* Washington, DC: Brookings Institution.

Business Roundtable. (1991). *Essential components of a successful education system.* Washington, DC: Author.

Callahan, J., & Wilken, W. (1976). *School finance reform: A legislator's handbook.* Denver, CO: National Conference of State Legislatures.

Chambers, J. G. (1981). Cost and price level adjustments to state aid for education: A theoretical and empirical view. In K. F. Jordan & N. Cambron-McCabe (Eds.), *Perspectives in state school support programs* (pp. 39–85). New York: Ballinger.

Clune, W. H., & White, P. A. (1988). *School based management: Institutional variation, implementation, and issues for further research* (Rep. No. RR-008). New Brunswick, NJ: Rutgers University, Consortium for Policy Research in Education.

Commission on the Skills of the American Workforce. (1990). *America's choice: High skills or low wages.* Rochester, NY: National Center on Education and the Economy.

Eisenhardt, K. (1989). Agency theory: An assessment and review. *Academy of Management Review, 14,* 57–74.

Elmore, R. (1991, April). *Teaching, learning and organization: School restructuring and the recurring dilemmas of reform.* Paper presented at the annual meeting of the American Educational Research Association, Chicago.

Finn, C. E., Jr. (1991). *We must take charge.* New York: Free Press.

Jacobson, S. (1988). The effects of pay incentives on teacher absenteeism. *Journal of Human Resources, 24,* 280–286.

Johnston, W. (1987). *Workforce 2000*. Indianapolis, IN: Hudson Institute.

Kirst, M. W. (1991). Improving children's services: Overcoming barriers, creating new opportunities. *Phi Delta Kappan, 72,* 615–618.

Lawler, E. E., III. (1986). *High-involvement management: Participative strategies for improving organizational performance.* San Francisco: Jossey-Bass.

Lawler, E. E., III. (1990). *Strategic pay: Aligning organizational strategies and pay systems.* San Francisco: Jossey-Bass.

Little, J. W. (1982). Norms of collegiality and experimentation: Workplace conditions of school success. *American Educational Research Journal, 19,* 325–340.

Madden, N. A., Slavin, R., Karweit, N., Dolan, L., & Wasik, B. (1991, April). *Multi-year effects of a schoolwide elementary restructuring program.* Paper presented at the annual meeting of the American Educational Research Association, Chicago.

McGuire, C. K. (1982). *State and federal programs for special student populations.* Denver, CO: Education Commission of the States.

McLaughlin, M. W., & Yee, S. M. (1988). School as a place to have a career. In A. Lieberman (Ed.), *Building a professional culture in schools* (pp. 23–44). New York: Teachers College Press.

Means, B., & Knapp, M. S. (1991). Models for teaching advanced skills to educationally disadvantaged students. In B. Means & M. S. Knapp (Eds.), *Teaching advanced skills to educationally disadvantaged students* (pp. 1–20). Washington, DC: U.S. Department of Education, Office of Planning, Budget and Evaluation.

National Board for Professional Teaching Standards. (1989). *Towards high and rigorous standards for the teaching profession.* Detroit, MI: Author.

Odden, A. (1977). Alternative measures of school district wealth. *Journal of Education Finance, 2,* 356–379.

Odden, A. R., & Picus, L. O. (1992). *School finance: A policy perspective.* New York: McGraw-Hill.

Palincsar, A. M., & Brown, A. (1984). Reciprocal teaching of comprehension-fostering and comprehension-monitoring activities. *Cognition and Instruction, 1,* 117–175.

Picus, L. O. (1991). *Cadillacs or Chevrolets: The effects of state control on school finance in California*. Los Angeles: University of Southern California, Center for Research in Education Finance.

Porter, A. C., Archibald, D. A., & Tyree, A. K., Jr. (1991). Reforming the curriculum: Will empowerment policies replace control? In S. Fuhrman & B. Malen (Eds.), *The politics of curriculum and testing* (pp. 11–36). Philadelphia: Falmer.

Putnam, R., Lampert, M., & Peterson, P. (1990). Alternative perspectives on knowing mathematics in elementary schools. In C. Cazden (Ed.), *Review of educational research* (Vol. 16, pp. 57–150). Washington, DC: American Educational Research Association.

Resnick, L. (1987). *Education and learning to think*. Washington, DC: National Academy Press.

Resnick, L. (Ed.). (1989). *Knowing, learning and instruction*. Hillsdale, NJ: Erlbaum.

Rosenholtz, S. J. (1989). *Teachers' workplace: The social organization of schools*. White Plains, NY: Longman.

Shanker, A. (1990). The end of the traditional model of schooling—and a proposal for using incentives to restructure our public schools. *Phi Delta Kappan, 71*, 344–357.

Sjogren, J. (1981). Municipal overburden and state aid for education. In K. F. Jordan & N. Cambron-McCabe (Eds.), *Perspectives in state school support programs* (pp. 87–111). New York: Ballinger.

Slavin, R. (1990). *Cooperative learning: Theory, research and practice*. Englewood Cliffs, NJ: Prentice-Hall.

White House, The. (1990). *National goals for education*. Washington, DC: Author.

White House, The. (1991). *America 2000*. Washington, DC: Author.

Wohlstetter, P., & Odden, A. R. (in press). Rethinking site-based management policy and research. *Educational Administration Quarterly*.

Name Index

Subject Index ===